A Political Companion to Saul Bellow

A Political Companion to
Saul Bellow

Edited by
Gloria L. Cronin
and
Lee Trepanier

UNIVERSITY PRESS OF KENTUCKY

Copyright © 2013 by The University Press of Kentucky
Paperback edition 2014

Scholarly publisher for the Commonwealth,
serving Bellarmine University, Berea College, Centre College of Kentucky, Eastern Kentucky University, The Filson Historical Society, Georgetown College, Kentucky Historical Society, Kentucky State University, Morehead State University, Murray State University, Northern Kentucky University, Transylvania University, University of Kentucky, University of Louisville, and Western Kentucky University.
All rights reserved.

Editorial and Sales Offices: The University Press of Kentucky
663 South Limestone Street, Lexington, Kentucky 40508-4008
www.kentuckypress.com

The Library of Congress has cataloged the hardcover edition as follows:

A political companion to Saul Bellow / edited by Gloria L. Cronin and Lee Trepanier.
    pages cm.
  Includes bibliographical references and index.
  ISBN 978-0-8131-4185-5 (hardcover : alk. paper) — ISBN 978-0-8131-4186-2 (epub) — ISBN 978-0-8131-4187-9
  1. Bellow, Saul—Political and social views. 2. Politics and literature—United States—History—20th century. I. Cronin, Gloria L., 1947- editor of compilation. II. Trepanier, Lee, 1972- editor of compilation.
  PS3503.E4488Z8185 2013
  813'.52—dc23   2013003838

ISBN 978-0-8131-4741-3 (pbk. : alk. paper)

This book is printed on acid-free paper meeting the requirements of the American National Standard for Permanence in Paper for Printed Library Materials.

Manufactured in the United States of America.

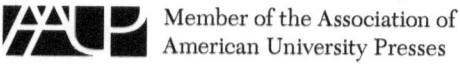 Member of the Association of
American University Presses

Contents

Series Foreword   vii

Introduction: Saul Bellow's Political Thought   1
   Lee Trepanier and Gloria L. Cronin

1. Trotskyism in the Early Work of Saul Bellow   9
   Judie Newman

2. Bellow as Jew and Jewish Writer   29
   Ben Siegel

3. Saul Bellow and the Absent Woman Syndrome: Traces of India in "Leaving the Yellow House"   57
   Michael Austin

4. The Politics of Art: The Colonial Library Meets the Carnivalesque in *Henderson the Rain King*   67
   Daniel K. Muhlestein

5. The Jewish Atlantic—The Deployment of Blackness in Saul Bellow   101
   Carol R. Smith

6. "Washed Up on the Shores of Truth": Saul Bellow's Post-Holocaust America   129
   Victoria Aarons

7. *Mr. Sammler's Planet:* Saul Bellow's 1968 Speech at San Francisco State University   153
   Andrew Gordon

8. Biography, Elegy, and the Politics of Modernity in Saul Bellow's
   Ravelstein   167
   Willis Salomon

9. Our Father's Politics: Gregory, Adam, and Daniel Bellow   185
   Gloria L. Cronin

Saul Bellow's Politics: A Selected Annotated Bibliography,
   1947–Present   233
   Gloria L. Cronin

List of Contributors   277
Index   279

Series Foreword

Those who undertake a study of American political thought must attend to the great theorists, philosophers, and essayists. Such a study is incomplete, however, if it neglects American literature, one of the greatest repositories of the nation's political thought and teachings.

America's literature is distinctive because it is, above all, intended for a democratic citizenry. In contrast to eras when an author would aim to inform or influence a select aristocratic audience, in democratic times, public influence and education must resonate with a more expansive, less leisured, and diverse audience to be effective. The great works of America's literary tradition are the natural locus of democratic political teaching. Invoking the interest and attention of citizens through the pleasures afforded by the literary form, many of America's great thinkers sought to forge a democratic public philosophy with subtle and often challenging teachings that unfolded in narrative, plot, and character development. Perhaps more than any other nation's literary tradition, American literature is ineluctably political—shaped by democracy as much as it has in turn shaped democracy.

The Political Companions to Great American Authors series highlights the teachings of the great authors in America's literary and belletristic tradition. An astute political interpretation of America's literary tradition requires careful, patient, and attentive readers who approach the text with a view to understanding its underlying messages about citizenship and democracy. Essayists in this series approach the classic texts not with a "hermeneutics of suspicion" but with the curiosity of fellow citizens who believe that the great authors have something of value to teach their readers. The series brings together essays from varied approaches and viewpoints for the common purpose of elucidating the political teachings of the nation's greatest authors for those seeking a better understanding of American democracy.

Patrick J. Deneen
Series Editor

INTRODUCTION

Saul Bellow's Political Thought

Lee Trepanier and Gloria L. Cronin

This volume looks at the political thought and milieu of one of the great American writers—perhaps the greatest—of the second half of the twentieth century: Saul Bellow. Not only does Bellow confront some of the major political themes of his and our time—religious identity, race relations, and multiculturalism—but the evolution of his own political thinking from Trotskyism to neoconservatism reflects some of the significant changes in mainstream American political thought and politics itself. In this sense, Bellow's own political thought in his novels, short stories, and essays captures the general political shift in mainstream America from liberalism to conservatism. A closer look at Bellow's works therefore offers a closer look at America's own political evolution.

It is also important to note that Bellow's political thought was fundamentally rooted in philosophical and religious concerns about alienation, spirituality, and the nature of modern civilization. For Bellow, the disorienting nature of modern civilization with its materialism and misleading knowledge was to be recognized and sometimes resisted by his heroes, who are often alienated and suffering from spiritual emptiness. Overwhelmed by the sheer abundance that modern civilization offers in material and sexual gratification, these Bellovian heroes struggle to find spiritual meaning either in themselves, in religious and intellectual traditions, or in embracing a flawed but potentially beautiful world. The quest to cultivate individuality and discover meaning in a world that continues to become more homogeneous and that continually drives out private life was one, if not the primary, philosophical occupation in Bellow's writings.

In Bellow's world, European-trained and tradition-bound intellectuals are paired alongside wise-guy thugs and business con men, creating a comic style that combines the high and the low: penetrating philosophical insights are juxtaposed with street slang and bawdy jokes. The mixture of these classes of people in Bellow's world creates a fertile, imaginative space where we recognize not only the shallowness and distraction of the street and finance but also the dangers of intellectual solipsism and spiritual isolation. Like Charlie Citrine in *Humboldt's Gift,* the world may keep "us from the large truth"; but, also like Harry Trellman in *The Actual,* our intellect and ideas can cut us off from humanity.

Although he bristled at being called a "Jewish writer," Bellow heroes are often Jewish, which allows him to play their tragic sense of history against American optimism. In some works, like *The Adventures of Augie March* and *Henderson the Rain King,* Bellow accents the American ethos of exploration, restlessness, and enthusiasm, while in other novels, such as *The Victim, Mr. Sammler's Planet,* and *Herzog,* Judaism plays a defining role in the protagonists' identities of resignation and a return to a religious tradition. In all of his novels, however, Bellow not only criticizes aspects of American life, but also shows a genuine appreciation of it, expressing an endless fascination with the uniqueness and vibrancy of this country.

Saul Bellow was born on June 10, 1915, in Lachine, Montreal, to parents who had emigrated from St. Petersburg in 1913. He was raised, however, in Humboldt Park, Chicago, after his family moved there in 1924. As a first-generation American Jew, Saul attended Hebrew school, in addition to the Chicago public schools. When he was eight, he was diagnosed with tuberculosis and had to spend several months in isolation at a hospital ward. During this time he created an imaginary world for himself and encountered Jesus and the New Testament, but chose not to tell his family about it for fear of their scorn. Later, when he was seventeen, his mother died. These two events—his mother's death and his bout of tuberculosis—left him permanently scarred with a fear of death.

After graduating from high school in 1933, Bellow entered the University of Chicago and then transferred to Northwestern in 1935 to study anthropology under Melville J. Herskovits. He graduated with a B.A. with honors in anthropology and sociology from Northwestern in 1937 and traveled to New York with plans to study at New York University. Instead, he returned to Chicago that Christmas and married his first wife, Anita Goshkin, where they lived in Ravenswood. During this period, Bellow began working on *Dangling Man* as well as working at a variety of jobs, including at the Chicago branch of the Works Progress Administration Writers' Project. Although outnumbered by Stalinist-leaning writers, Bellow embraced Trotskyite communism as his brand of politics.

In 1940, Bellow was called up for military service and entered the Maritime Camp at Sheepshead Bay; and in 1941 he became a naturalized U.S. citizen. In 1942, Bellow's short stories "Two Morning Monologues" and "The Mexican General" appeared; and in 1944, *Dangling Man* was published, and his first son, Gregory, was born. He taught at the University of Minnesota during 1946–1948, with *The Victim* being published in 1947. Bellow was awarded a Guggenheim Fellowship in 1948, which he used to live and work in Paris during 1948–1950. In 1950, he returned to New York City to teach part-time and published several short stories, such as "Looking for Mr. Green," "By the Rock Wall," and "Address by Gooley McDowell to the Hasbeen's Club of Chicago."

In 1952, Bellow received a creative-writing fellowship at Princeton University, and the following year his break-out novel, *The Adventures of Augie March*, was published. Bellow published *Seize the Day* and married his second wife, Alexandra Tschacbasov, in 1956. They had a son, Adam. Their marriage ended in divorce in 1960, with *Henderson the Rain King* appearing the year before. During this period, Bellow embarked on a lecture tour in Europe to recuperate from the breakup of his second marriage.

By 1961, Bellow had married Susan Glassman, with his third son, Daniel, being born from this marriage. In 1962, he joined the Committee on Social Thought at the University of Chicago and published *Herzog* in 1964. His play *The Last Analysis* opened on Broadway but quickly failed. In 1968, Bellow published his first short-story collection, *Mosby's Memoirs and Other Stories,* and divorced Susan Glassman that same year. He was elected a Fellow of the American Academy of Arts and Sciences in 1969.

During the 1970s, Bellow published several short stories as well as the novels *Mr. Sammler's Planet* in 1970 and *Humboldt's Gift,* for which he won the Pulitzer Prize, in 1975, and his nonfiction account *To Jerusalem and Back* in 1976. He also married his fourth wife, Alexandra Tulcea in 1975, a marriage that would end in divorce in 1985. In 1970, Bellow walked out of a lecture at San Francisco State College after having been booed and catcalled by student radicals before an unprotesting faculty. He received the Nobel Prize in Literature in 1976.

Bellow continued to publish novels for the next two decades: *The Dean's December* in 1982; *More Die of Heartbreak* in 1987; *A Theft* and *The Bellarosa Connection* in 1989; *The Actual* in 1997; and *Ravelstein* in 2000. He also published a collection of short stories, *Him with His Foot in His Mouth* in 1984; *Something to Remember Me By: Three Tales* in 1991; and *Collected Stories* in 2001. He also continued teaching at a variety of institutions, such as Yale University, Bard College, and Boston University. Bellow married his fifth wife, Janis Freedman, in 1989 and had a daughter, Naomi. On April 5, 2005, Saul Bellow died in Brookline, Massachusetts.

Besides the Nobel and Pulitzer Prizes, Bellow has also been awarded the National Medal of Art in 1988 and the National Book Award three times (1954, 1965, 1971). With Philip Roth and Eudora Welty, Bellow is one of three living writers to have their works published by the Library of Congress (in 2003). His place in American letters is well secured, and it will take several years to unravel his impact not only in literature but in politics, philosophy, religion, and American studies. Our hope is that this volume will begin this task.

This volume is targeted at a diverse audience of scholars interested in literature, philosophy, intellectual history, religious studies, and the social sciences. Although there are a few articles that focus on a particular aspect of Bellow's political thought, until now no work has explored the range of his political thinking and the social and political milieu in which he was situated. This volume will fill this void in the literature about Saul Bellow, with the understanding that not every work of his will be analyzed here. Given the number of novels, short stories, essays, and works of nonfiction that Bellow produced, we have restricted ourselves to what we think are key developments in Bellow's personal life and political thought. We hope that this volume, with contributions by some of the foremost scholars on Bellow, will engage scholars from a variety of specialties and perspectives. It should serve as a valuable resource to scholars and students of Saul Bellow as well as members of the general public with an interest in his works and politics.

In the first chapter, "Trotskyism in the Early Works of Saul Bellow," Judie Newman looks at the early writings of Bellow, including *Dangling Man* and his short stories "Two Morning Monologues," "Mr. Katz and Mr. Cohen," and "The Mexican General." What we discover is that during this period Bellow's own political thinking evolves from Trotskyism to social democracy. In his later years, however, Bellow reflects in *Mosby's Memoirs* upon the naïveté of his political youth. Yet he also recognizes that these formative experiences will never leave him and, as a consequence, he will always be engaged with a political dialogue with the Left, even when he may disagree with them.

In the second chapter, "Bellow as Jew and Jewish Writer," the late Ben Siegel traces the history of Bellow's early politics of Jewish identification, disaffiliation, and subsequent reaffiliation. Siegel shows how Bellow's feelings gradually changed after the Holocaust and then again during the 1960s and 1970s. Siegel concludes with a discussion about Bellow's revelations about his Jewish emotional code, his use of biblical allusions, and his uncomfortable feelings about becoming the "gold standard" for Jewish American writing.

The third chapter, "Saul Bellow and the Absent Woman Syndrome: Traces of India in 'Leaving the Yellow House,'" explores Bellow's misogynist reputation. Contrary to the popular perception, Michael Austin argues that Bellow did portray strong female characters. By comparing the two characters, Hattie and India, Austin reveals that Bellow is able to break down the traditionally defined roles of masculine and feminine and is more open to the complexities inherent in human relationships and roles than his critics claim.

In "The Politics of Art: The Colonial Library Meets the Carnivalesque in *Henderson the Rain King*," Daniel K. Muhlestein explores the role that colonial politics, specifically race, play in Bellow's novel. Although the novel at first glance appears to reinforce the racist ideologies of colonial politics, it actually subverts these perspectives through the carnivalesque and grotesque elements in the novel. Adopting the theory of Bakhtin in his analysis of the novel, Muhlestein contends that these comic elements undermine the ideological discourse of colonial politics, thereby revealing the limitations of such views.

In the fifth chapter, "The Jewish Atlantic—The Deployment of Blackness in Saul Bellow," Carol R. Smith continues Bellow's understandings of race with an examination of *Henderson the Rain King*, *Humboldt's Gift*, and *Mr. Sammler's Planet*. In these works, Smith argues, Bellow conceives of America in the liberal humanist tradition of the Enlightenment and as the place of refuge from lands of oppression. However, the presence of African Americans underscores the racial understanding of this liberal humanist tradition as white assimilation. The implication is that Bellow's commitment to this liberal humanist tradition creates complication, as he himself recognized, with the continual presence of African Americans in this country.

Victoria Aarons, in "'Washed up on the Shores of Truth': Saul Bellow's Post-Holocaust America," examines the presence of the Holocaust in Bellow's works *The Victim* and *Mr. Sammler's Planet*. For Bellow, the Holocaust exposes not only the moral bankruptcy of modern civilization, but also its intellectual failure to imagine a world where ideas and culture can be regenerative. In other words, the Holocaust reveals a failure of reason and demonstrable proof that humans are capable of unlimited forms of pathological justification. In both novels, New York City becomes the living graveyard of a war-torn Europe that is teetering on despair.

In the seventh chapter, "*Mr. Sammler's Planet:* Saul Bellow's 1968 Speech at San Francisco State University," Andrew Gordon discusses the relationship between the fictional event in the novel and the actual event at San Francisco State. By the late 1960s, Bellow was seen as the defender of a cultural conservatism against the New Left of student protest and multicultural politics. Gordon ultimately concludes that the New Left, personified here as Floyd Salas, was not nearly as destructive or threatening to Western civilization as Bellow made him out to be.

In chapter 8, "Biography, Elegy, and the Politics of Modernity in Saul Bellow's *Ravelstein,*" Willis Salomon illustrates how the actual friendship between Allan Bloom and Saul Bellow is shown in the novel to be an intellectual response to the cultural Left's political correctness. Whereas Ravelstein represents the philosophical and intellectual tradition of the Western tradition, Chick embodies the literary and aesthetic values of civilization. The novel's elegiac mode is a type of appeal to see how one can contribute to Western tradition and see that tradition can continue.

Chapter 9 comprises a series of interviews with Bellow's sons, Gregory, Adam, and Daniel Bellow. In these fascinating discussions, Gloria L. Cronin examines how Bellow's political thought evolved from his early years at the *Partisan Review* to his later neoconservatism.

The final chapter is a bibliography composed by Gloria L. Cronin that reviews the major secondary criticism of Saul Bellow's works with a focus on his politics and political thought. Here we see Bellow's evolution from Trotskyite communism to neoconservatism, with several articles dealing with his views on class, race, and gender as well as Israel, American Jews, and the Holocaust. Including books, dissertations, articles, and reviews, this is an excellent resource for scholars who want to further explore Bellow's political thinking.

Ultimately what we will discover is that the genius of Saul Bellow is such that neither his work nor his biography can be reduced to a purely political investigation; rather, as Andrew Gordon writes in this volume, "the proper subject matter of the writer [Bellow] was not politics but the soul." Bellow's political thought is not that of a political scientist or philosopher but that of an artist who is wary of abstractions in favor of the concrete and the complexity of life. These chapters show us a Bellow who is sensible, skeptical of public life, and hopeful that the values of civilization will continue. Although he may at times be naïve, sexist, and racist, Saul Bellow rejects the tragic conception of life for one of love, decency, and contemplation.

Again, we hope that this volume will introduce a broader conversation about Saul Bellow's political thought in both the academy and among the public. We do not claim that this is the definitive account of Bellow's political thought; rather, we think it is the beginning of our exploration of it. We look forward to future books, articles, and essays on this topic. But for now, let us seize the day.

Trotskyism in the Early Work of Saul Bellow

Judie Newman

Bellow's enthusiasm for Trotskyism tends to be summarily dismissed as a youthful peccadillo, or as just one among many of the weltering ideas which populate his fiction. As Edward Shils commented, "If there's a bad idea out there—Trotskyism, Reichism, Steinerism—leave it to our friend Saul to swallow it."[1] Arguably, however, the later Bellow's reputation as a neoconservative has obscured the importance to his life and writings of his early enthusiasm for Trotskyism. The 2010 publication of a selection of his letters opens with Bellow aged seventeen writing to Yetta Barshevsky, a fellow high school student who introduced him to Trotskyism. In the letter, the callow Bellow, disappointed in love, writes, "I sever relations with you," conceding only that "We may still be casual friends."[2] In fact, they stayed friends for more than sixty years. When she died, Bellow wrote her eulogy, describing how she had introduced him to world politics when they were in high school, and had given him Trotsky's pamphlet on the German question.[3] Bellow was still thinking about Trotsky in the 1990s in his correspondence with Albert Glotzer (his lifelong friend and at one point Trotsky's secretary).[4] Bellow's involvement in radical left-wing politics, at Tuley High School and at university, produced his first publications (political pieces) in left-wing journals (the *Beacon* and *Soapbox*) and his first published short story, an antifascist fable. Although critics have tended to see Bellow's Trotskyism as a product of his involvement with the *Partisan Review* group during that journal's Trotskyist phase, he appears to have been recruited to the journal because of his established political reputation rather than for his as yet unproven literary talent. Writing to F. W. Dupee in 1941, the editor Philip Rahv described Bellow as one of the "apprentice writers" he had met in Chicago.[5] In fact, *Partisan Review* was the least radical of the journals to which the young Bellow contributed. Between the 1930s and the 1950s, Bellow's literary output centered on the political specificities of the time, most notably in "The Mexican General" (1942), based on Bellow's visit to Trotsky in Mexico, where he arrived within hours of the assassination.

In some respects, Bellow's enthusiasm for Trotsky is unsurprising. Writing in 1993, Bellow pointed out that when the Russian Revolution took place in 1917, he was two years old and his parents, who had emigrated from Saint Petersburg to Montreal in 1913, followed subsequent events in Russia very keenly: "At the dinner table the Tsar, the war, the front, Lenin, Trotsky were mentioned as often as parents, sisters and brothers in the old country."[6] Grandfather Bellow had taken refuge in the Winter Palace during the revolution; his mother's relatives were famous Mensheviks. While the older generation assumed that the Bolsheviks would soon be suppressed, their children were keen to join the revolution, including the son of Bellow's Hebrew teacher: "He went off to build a new order under Lenin and Trotsky. And he disappeared."[7] Despite embracing Americanization, Bellow's friends believed that "they were also somehow Russian" and read Tolstoy and Dostoyevsky, going on to Lenin's *State and Revolution* and the pamphlets of Trotsky.[8] The Tuley High School debating society discussed *The Communist Manifesto*. Bellow read it and described himself as "swept away by the power of the analysis."[9] When a Commission of Inquiry was set up in Mexico in 1937 to consider the charges made against Trotsky in the Moscow Show Trials (in which he was alleged to be a fascist collaborator, and condemned to death in his absence), Bellow and his Trotskyist friends "followed the proceedings bitterly, passionately, for we were of course the Outs; the Stalinists were the Ins."[10] Even much later in his life, Bellow still admired Trotsky, both for his politics and his culture: "How could I forget that Trotsky had created the Red Army, that he had read French novels at the front while defeating Denikin? That great crowds had been swayed by his coruscating speeches?"[11]

Bellow's political education began in earnest at "The Forum," a church hall on California Avenue which hosted debates between socialists, communists, and anarchists. He read Marx and Engels, "blasting away at *Value, Price and Profit* while the police raided a brothel across the street."[12] When the Young Communist League attempted to recruit him in the late 1930s, they were far, far too late. "I had already read Trotsky's pamphlet on the German question and was convinced that Stalin's errors had brought Hitler to power."[13] Trotsky wrote two major pamphlets on the German question. The first, in 1930, to which Bellow is referring, argued that the ideological error of the Comintern (Stalin) consisted in always seeing the main enemy as social democracy, and therefore not standing up to Hitler. Trotsky called instead for a united struggle against fascism, to include democratic forces as well as socialists, not an enticing prospect for the purists of the Communist Party. In the second pamphlet, written in 1932, Trotsky foresaw the radicalization of the American working class once the country began to emerge from its economic crisis.[14] Reflecting his Trotskyist beliefs, Bellow's early short stories, much more political than his novels, are marked by a profound ambivalence to war, distrust of democratic reforms, and a belief that capitalism had failed.

For Bellow, 1933 marked graduation from Tuley and entry into the University of Chicago, where he and Isaac Rosenfeld organized "Cell Number Five" of the Trotskyist Youth Group. As Alan Wald records, the Socialist Club of the University of Chicago published *Soapbox,* a sixteen-page magazine with a quotation on its masthead from William Randolph Hearst: "Red Radicalism has planted a soapbox on every campus of America."[15] Under the leadership of Nathan Gould, *Soapbox* made no secret of its political allegiances. It hailed Trotsky's fifty-seventh birthday enthusiastically and attracted endorsements from Max Shachtman, James T. Farrell, Sidney Hook, and Meyer Shapiro, among others. Bellow published political commentary, including "This Is the Way We Go to School" in December 1936, under the pseudonym John Paul.[16] Bellow had moved to Northwestern University in Evanston in 1935, and may have used a pseudonym to deflect undue attention from his instructors.[17] The piece attacked a local resident of Evanston who had published a "handbook" for patriots, giving an exposé of Communist activity in the United States. Bellow was scathing about bourgeois Evanston and Northwestern, which he described as "intellectually flat-chested," and supplied details of the poor working conditions and pay of the grounds and building staff.[18] In 1934, the general strikes had produced a new mood of activism in America, and Bellow rode the rails with his friend Herb Passin to see for himself, cheering on the sit-in strikers at the Studebaker plant from a boxcar. "Of course, I sympathized with the strikers."[19] When his old friend Sydney J. Harris founded a journal, the *Beacon*, which featured articles about local political disputes and union activities, he appointed Bellow as associate editor. For the young Bellow, however, Harris was not nearly radical enough, and he was incensed when Harris allowed the Stalinist Young Communist League to advertise in the journal. In 1936, "Saul Gordon Bellow" had reviewed J. T. Farrell's *A World I Never Made* in the *Beacon*, applauding its left-wing politics. Writing to Farrell in 1937, he complained: "Editorially I can't push the magazine to the left because Harris is a shrewd opportunistic bastard who won't permit it. However, if we load the magazine with Bolshevik writers of national reputation, we can have Harris hanging on a ledge before long."[20] In this, however, he was sadly mistaken; it was Bellow who would leave the *Beacon*.

Bellow also published pieces for the radical student newspaper the *Daily Northwestern*. "Pets on the North Shore" (1936) again targeted the Evanston bourgeoisie via their pampered pooches. More importantly, Bellow's first published story, "The Hell It Can't," appeared there in 1936. The story takes its title from the response of a character in Sinclair Lewis's novel *It Can't Happen Here* (1935) to the suggestion that America could never turn fascist.[21] In the novel, "Buzz" Windrip, the populist leader of a "patriotic" movement in America, creates his own militia (the Minute Men, or "MM," modeled on Hitler's "SS"), seizes power, and sets up a fascist dictatorship with martial law and concentration camps. The hero writes for a radical paper and survives to see Windrip's power waning. Lewis's novel was more optimistic than Bellow's story, in which Henry Howland is seized in the night by a group of paramilitary "patriots" and taken away for a brutal whipping which is still in progress as the story ends. Set in Chicago (the hero recalls friendly neighborhood exchanges about the Cubs), the story draws its horror from the absolute familiarity of the surroundings, emphasizing that militarism and fascism could be right at home in America. As the story opens, the enemy is already within the door. Henry hears a bell ringing, a hinge creaking, boots on the stairs, and the door of his room flying open. The action then consists entirely of the walk along the familiar street, past everyday landmarks, with Henry longing for a familiar face to appear, to witness his fate, "Now they were about to end him."[22] The story ends "he was five blocks from home" (8). The street teems with military activity, including young soldiers fresh from "some high school camp," who ignore Henry's plight, their faces "young, hard and unforgiving." "They were getting them young now, and well-trained" (5). The walls are plastered with propaganda posters, "Fight. Don't Be An Enemy At Home" (5) runs the caption to the face of a soldier with a bayonet, in front of a girl holding bandages. In the background, men sing war songs in saloons, chorusing "it won't be long till we're there" (5), with "there" meaning London, Lisbon, or Rome. Whereas in Lewis's novel, Windrip decides to invade Mexico and introduces the draft, Bellow's emphasis is on the European theater of war. Henry recalls newsreels of Austrian troops on the run, and French troops leaving a fortress. Henry's crime is to have opposed American involvement in European war. Despite its early date, the story resonates powerfully with *Dangling Man* (1944) and *The Victim* (1947), each in their different ways engaging with Bellow's doubts about the war, the one reflecting his opposition to it, the other, in its theme of anti-Semitic persecution, his postwar remorse. Confronted with the Holocaust, Bellow viewed his earlier position with horror.[23] "Not only did I feel that my Jewish Marxist friends were wrong in theory, but I was horrified by the positions they—we—had taken."[24] In *Dangling Man*, the deradicalized Joseph eventually succumbs to the social regimentation of war, though his final statement was described by Bellow as ironic:[25]

> Hurray for regular hours!
> And for the supervision of the spirit!
> Long live regimentation![26]

Bellow's distaste for war was typical of the Left in the period. In an interview in 1999, Bellow described his visit to Mexico, where he had an appointment to meet Trotsky, with whom he wanted especially to discuss the problem of Finland and the issue of the war.[27] Trotsky had refused to dissociate himself from Stalin's invasion of Finland, in 1939, in the belief that it would advance the cause of socialism by nationalizing land and by setting up cooperatives and workers' councils. As Bellow notes, he had his first doubts about Trotsky over Finland, but dismissed them: "The Trotsky line was that a workers' state, no matter how degenerate, could not wage an imperialist war."[28]

As a result, Bellow stood by the party line, "the main enemy is at home, it's an imperialist war."[29] Later his doubts grew. While the Socialist Workers Party stood by the USSR, a minority led by James Burnham and Max

Shachtman described the USSR as no longer a workers' state, but a new form of bureaucratic collectivism, and eventually in 1940 split to form the Workers' Party, taking 40 percent of the membership with them, including, eventually, Bellow. Writing to Oscar Tarcov in 1940, he describes his alienation from the factional fight, deploring Trotsky's "attempt to knife Burnham and cast him out of the movement," the hysteria of the old-timers, and the stupidity of the polemics.[30] He was unwilling, however, at first to leave, "just when it is becoming dangerous."[31] More importantly, he saw the split as a disaster. "It's a goddam shame that at the time that the war is on us the only revolutionary party in the country falls to pieces."[32] Trotsky's own advice, when asked in 1940 what an American Trotskyist should do if drafted, was "let him be drafted. . . . [H]e must go with his generation and participate in its life."[33] Eventually (after delays as a result of his Canadian citizenship and a hernia operation), Bellow joined the merchant marine in the last months of the war. Tellingly, in the early manuscript of *The Adventures of Augie March*, Augie is not the eager recruit to the war of the published novel, but chooses the merchant marine because it offers greater independence and an easier discharge.[34]

Hindsight always offers twenty-twenty vision, but it is important to underline that even after the outbreak of war, the Left in the 1940s did not prioritize the need to fight fascism but rather the creation of an international brotherhood of the working class that would make war obsolete. The Workers' Party started its own journal, *Labor Action*, in 1940. Even as late as May 20, 1940, it ran the headline "Let Bankers Fight on the Maginot Line; Labor's Fight Is at Home on the Picket Line," subtitled "Against the Allies and the Axis." On its front page on August 5, it argued that the Nazis feared too swift a British collapse lest the disintegration of the empire lead to world revolution ("The air raids are more for show than serious attempts to kick at the enemy"). One article was headed "40 Hour Week Will Be the First War Victim," which, as Edward Alexander remarks, conveniently ignored the casualties at Pearl Harbor.[35] *Partisan Review* was altogether more measured. On November 15, 1939, its editors advertised in *New Republic* that they had "consistently exposed the imperialist nature of this war, after as well as before it began."[36] They argued that although the Allies were preferable to the Nazis, their differences would be eliminated by an all-out war, with its erosion of individual liberties. The overthrow of the Chamberlain-Churchill and Roosevelt administrations was likely to be the only way to stave off the intellectual repression and regimentation required by war. A 1939 statement signed by *Partisan Review*'s editors read: "This war must give birth to military dictatorship and to forms of intellectual repression far more violent than those evoked by the last war."[37]

The war eventually divided them, however. *Partisan Review* published Dwight Macdonald and Clement Greenberg's antiwar essay "10 Propositions on the War," proclaiming that "All support of whatever kind must be withheld from Churchill and Roosevelt."[38] Later, however, the editors themselves attacked Macdonald, and he left to form his own antiwar periodical.[39] The introduction of the Voorhis Act in 1940 also complicated matters for writers and publishers. *Labor Action* described it (August 26, 1940) as a huge threat to civil liberties since it required an organization to hand over every scrap of information about itself and its membership if it was directly or indirectly affiliated with a political party in a foreign country or an international political organization, thus implicating any labor organization with international affiliations. Concerned that *Partisan Review* could be suppressed if it seemed to be publishing antiwar propaganda, Rahv and Phillips became increasingly reluctant to condemn the war, even more so when a financial crisis in 1943 almost closed the journal, which was rescued only by the financial support of Mrs. Norton, the wife of a high-ranking army officer, who asked them not to embarrass her husband by political statements as long as the war lasted.[40]

If the Trotskyist position on war finds expression in Bellow's first story and in *Dangling Man,* the Trotskyist view of the Depression was also influential. For Bellow, "the beginning of the Great Depression was also the beginning of my mental life."[41] The Depression saw a widespread conviction that capitalism had failed and that only the most radical social change could restore social and economic order. In 1937, the second great slump of the Depression looked even more promising for the growth of labor movements, but in fact 1938 was a disaster for them, as the working-class movement split between the CIO and AFL. Quite apart from the additional split in 1940 of the Trotskyist movement, it became almost impossible for American intellectuals to sustain their Marxism in the absence of any effective connection to the working class.[42] Bellow's "Two Morning Monologues" (1941) centers on the failure of the system, and the illusion that prosperity can be restored by orthodox methods. As Bellow noted, "the depression was the first time capitalism was under direct attack for its failures."[43]

Reminiscing about the period in "In the Days of Mr. Roosevelt," Bellow remembered his algebra teacher singing "Happy Days Are Here Again." (She was not being paid; City Hall had gone bust.) Bellow, however, did not share her enthusiasm for rescue by Roosevelt. As a socialist, he believed that Roosevelt's reforms were merely saving the country for capitalism. Radical orthodoxy in the 1930s held that parliamentary European reformism had failed and that "the real choice was between the hateful dictatorship of the Right and the temporary and therefore enlightened dictatorship of the Left."[44] Wryly, the later Bellow noted how the masses actually fell in behind Roosevelt, a thoroughly patrician figure. "They did not call for a proletarian President."[45]

"Two Morning Monologues" (1941) contrasts different reactions to the imminent demise of capitalism. In the first, "9 A.M. Without Work," the educated Mandelbaum complains that his workman father cannot see that the system has failed, and therefore remains wedded to the American dream. His father has invested money in Mandelbaum's education, and in good capitalist fashion he expects a return. "Pride and Investment. I take those words to supply the whole meaning of his attitude."[46] To Mandelbaum's consternation, he advertises his son's capacities in the paper, as if he were selling a product. Mandelbaum spends long hours killing time, reading the papers, and "following the fight between the bookies and the courts" (233). The latter phrase links the first monologue to the second, "11.30 A.M. the Gambler." In the Depression, there had been a crackdown on illegal gambling, and 1940 saw the Chicago Crime Commission's fight against Frank "the Enforcer" Nitti, and his control of bookies' establishments, a by-product of his efforts to control the Bartenders' Union.

If capitalism had failed, organized labor did not appear to be offering a solution. Unions found it difficult to resist "the Outfit" in Chicago, where labor racketeering (the illicit use of unions by criminal groups) was a specialty. Importantly, the gambler never lays eyes on the horses on which the bets are placed. He dreams about one day seeing them run, far away from "the book in the tobacco shop, beyond the room where the smooth billiards run" (234). He is part of an illegal operation and has no connection with the labouring masses, "the sucker scraping the griddle" (234) and the girls he hears pushing laundry carts with their twelve-hour days, "eight on the books and four around the block" (235). The gambler's comment that "System is nothing" (234) extends beyond the story from the naïve beliefs of other gamblers that there is a magical "system" to winning, to the political system. The capitalist system and the unions are rackets.

This point was reinforced in a 1942 story set in mid-October 1922, a period of full prosperity. "Mr. Katz, Mr. Cohen, and Cosmology" appeared (credited to "S. G. Bellow") in the first issue of *Retort,* an anarchist-pacifist literary journal edited by Holley R. Cantine from a cabin in Bearsville, near Woodstock, New York. Cantine also published an anthology compiled by war resisters.[47] Again Bellow employed the device of contrasting characters, and again the story centers on two men spending a day without work, though in this case only because it is Sunday. Mr. Katz is a clothing cutter and Mr. Cohen, a tailor. Katz and Cohen are both immigrants, Katz from Warsaw via Amsterdam, Cohen a fugitive from Russia under the tsar. As he tells Katz: "I was in Kishinev in the days of Stolypin. I served in the Kavkaz."[48] Stolypin, minister of the interior and then prime minister (1906–1911), was notorious for his ruthlessly repressive measures against revolutionaries; Kishinev was the site of a pogrom which shocked the world; the Caucasus region was a hive of revolutionary activity, where Stolypin used the army to put down disturbances.[49] As their leisurely Sunday indicates, in contrast to their pasts, Katz and Cohen are now enjoying peace and prosperity, unworried by political conflict (significantly the setting is Canada, not America).

Yet the story does not endorse any nostalgic vision of the 1920s. Mr. Katz, self-educated and keenly interested in cosmology, takes a walk with Mr. Cohen, a flat-earther with no intellectual curiosity whatsoever. Intellectual and social gifts appear to be at odds. Katz is a frightening figure to his landlady's children whereas Cohen benevolently funds their movie attendance. Katz's lectures on the universe are repeatedly interrupted by Mr. Cohen's sociable encounters, "Mr. Katz standing aside, alone" (17). On the Esplanade, "everyone Mr. Cohen knows in the city seems to be promenading" (17). In response to Katz's lengthy account of the eons of time before life existed, Cohen comments merely that he is more than sixty years old and that a year is now not a lot of time for him. "Sneeze and wipe your nose and it's a year already" (19). It strikes Mr. Katz that he has never thought personally about time and that he is only some thirty "sneezes" behind his companion. "What have my thirty-three years meant?" he asks himself, saddened (19). The wind has risen, dusk is falling, and the day has turned more autumnal. The pair separate, Cohen to visit friends, Katz to return alone to his rooming house, still wondering "why he never thought of Time in a more personal sense" (19). Contemplating the stars from his window, setting his alarm for 6:00 a.m. and yet another week of work: "He sees his life as pieces of cloth fed under the falling and again falling needle of a machine" (20). A distant train, the sound of his clock, a whistle in the street, all appear to form "one apparatus," one system: "all are stitching shut long seams, drawing in—to close it forever—all of past life" (20). The story closes with the image of human subjection to mechanical labor, as if work were stitching Mr. Katz's own shroud.

Like "Two Morning Monologues" and "Mr. Katz and Mr. Cohen," "The Mexican General" also focuses on two opposed characters, the idealist intellectual (Trotsky) and a petty opportunist, the General, a Mexican police chief who stage-manages the exhibition of Trotsky's body to the press to milk publicity for his own political career in the forthcoming election in Jalisco. He poses in photos in Trotsky's study, with the ice pick, with the body of Trotsky, with his widow; his character is partly based on General José Manuel Nuñez, the chief of police in Mexico City, who was pictured posing in similar photographs in the press.[50]

Again, the action of the story covers one day, following the General and his three "nieces" (paid women) on a tourist excursion around Patzcuaro, while Citrón describes the aftermath of Trotsky's death, two weeks ago, to his fellow bodyguard, Paco. Trotsky had visited Patzcuaro in 1938 where he, André Breton, and Diego Rivera drew up the "Manifesto for an Independent Revolutionary Art." Patzcuaro was a haunt of bohemians and artists, part of the world of the avant-garde. But the Patzcuaro of the story has no affiliations with avant-garde art or revolutionary fervor. Rather it is designed to suggest that revolution did not transform Mexican culture. The contrast between Trotsky and Felipe is part of a generalized disillusionment. Mexico may embody a successful revolutionary past, but the General, who is following in his father's footsteps in seeking political office, is not the man his father was (181) and serves to illustrate the decadence of the revolutionary spirit, in a state which, like the USSR, now has opportunist heirs looking out only for their own interests.

In Patzcuaro, the group notes with amusement the old-fashioned cinema. The film showing is *Rosa De Xochimilco*.[51] This is not a stray detail. This is one of a small group of Mexican films in the late 1930s which focus on Indians and invoke ideas of a primitive paradise. Characters tend to be stereotypical Indians, marked by dignity, silence, and inscrutability.[52] In the story, the General is cast in the Indian role in his impassivity and concern for his own dignity, and is described as "austere" (183), "expressionless" (185), and "like a film star" (181). "Maybe it's the Indian part of him," jokes Paco (184). *Rosa de Xochimilco* (1939) is primarily notable for the views of Xochimilco, the pre-Hispanic settlement where floating gardens of flowers and vegetables are surrounded by canals, as in the days of the Aztecs.

The film promulgates a timeless, museumized image of prerevolutionary Mexico. Patzcuaro, famed for its indigenous peoples and their "butterfly" fishing nets, sells the same image to tourists. These films also tended to celebrate local religious or popular ceremonies, such as the choice of the most beautiful local woman.[53] Bellow's story makes much of the rivalry between the three nieces (with comments on their differing charms from the bodyguards) and effectively follows a similar scenario, closing as the General summons one of the three to his bed, leaving Citrón and Paco guessing which is the chosen one. The film carries an ironic charge using the museumized image to undercut any revolutionary content.

In *The Adventures of Augie March,* Augie makes a vigorous defense of directness. Augie plans to make the record freestyle: "first to knock, first admitted; sometimes an innocent knock, sometimes a not so innocent."[54] In his view there is no fineness or accuracy of suppression; "if you hold down one thing, you hold down the adjoining," and no way of camouflaging the nature of the knock "by acoustical work on the door or gloving the knuckles." In contrast, Bellow's story is ruled by indirection and suppression, structured around a series of doors and thresholds, its action split into passages of prose which are carefully separated from each other by typographic spaces.[55] Citrón recounts how the General had managed the press as Trotsky lay on his deathbed, letting them into his room in twos and threes.

What the story suppresses is the fact that one of those admitted, posing as a reporter, was Saul Bellow. Bellow had set off to visit Trotsky with his friend Herb Passin, and arrived in Mexico City shortly after Trotsky had died: "We had an appointment with Trotsky and we came to the door of the house: an unusual amount of excitement."[56] Bellow and Passin "said we were newspapermen" and were directed to the hospital. The shock of the event resonates through his account with its repeated emphasis on blood: "We asked to see Trotsky and they opened the door and said, he's in there, so we went in and there was Trotsky. He had just died. . . . He was covered in blood and bloody bandages and his white beard was full of blood."[57] Bellow stayed for Trotsky's funeral, and as the story demonstrates was clearly aware of the way Trotsky's body was treated, exhibited in a public autopsy to which the police admitted crowds of "the curious" (193), while Trotsky was turned around like a slab of beef, his brain extracted and weighed. As Citrón says, "The curio hunters would have got his heart if we had let them" (193). He makes this comment as the party are themselves buying tourist curios, in one of many parallels between the frame tale and the inset tale. Citrón acknowledges that his own role in the aftermath of the assassination was quite minor. He is one of: "'the others' who crowd in at the doors and are never thought the issue of the struggle but who are nevertheless those whom leaders lead, oppressors oppress, and saviours save" (188).

"The Mexican General" is a threshold story, between Bellow's earlier enthusiasm for Trotsky and a more realistic assessment, a form of self-criticism in the best Marxist style on the part of Bellow, a horrified spectator at the deathbed of his hero. The inset story of Trotsky's assassination emerges only slowly. The opening mimes the difficulty of entering into the story proper, with a convergence between story theme and narrative environment: it opens with a door which will not open. Maria cannot get her hotel room door to open, and there is a violent struggle on the threshold. The doors are like "the doors of a church" (178), and the walls covered with images of Quiroga, a figure whom the ignorant visitors assume to be a king or a saint. Imagistically, therefore, sex and violence combine to gain entry to a sacred space, in a subtextual image of desecration. Vasco de Quiroga (ca. 1470–1565) was a social reformer, influenced by More's *Utopia*, who built schools and hospitals, encouraged trades and crafts, and protected indigenous peoples.[58]

The story therefore opens with an image of progressive political utopianism, which is closed off at the end, as the door shuts on the woman. The second scene occurs in the General's room, when the clerk "rapped lightly at the door" (179), and in the third scene, the General knocks at the door of his "nieces," who leave him irritated on the threshold. Despite the passive resistance of Maria, who tends to hold things up, the General insists on being admitted: "I'll wait inside; I don't want to loiter in the passage" (182), just as he will gain sexual admittance at the close. The fourth scene moves the group to the dining room, where the bodyguards' meal is cut short: "The girls were already at the door." When they set off on a tour of the sights, the General sets the pace, with the bodyguards in the rear. Thereafter the stages of Citrón's story follow the stages of the tour. Describing Trotsky's wife, he says, "The old woman had gone to the hospital and that was our next stop. They had reached the top of the street" (189).

The group enters a church, pausing on the threshold to cross themselves, and the story pauses. Then Citrón continues:

> "Where was I? . . . That digression threw me off. Had we come to the hospital?"
> "You were just arriving." (189)

At the hospital, the General comes out of Trotsky's room with a portentous air. "He shut the door carefully and waited till he had everyone around him. And then he announced, 'He is dead'" (191).[59] At this point, the group leaves the church. "The tour is over" (191), as is the account of Trotsky's death. Back at the hotel, the two guards rest in their room (they may be called upon later to take the party to see *Rosa de Xochimilco*) and hear the three taps from the General on the wall of the women's room. "They listened to the swift steps at the General's door" (194). The door opens and closes, and the guards are left grinning as the story ends in darkness. A woman has entered, but which one? All we know (and they know) is that a door has opened and closed.

What is striking in this structure is that effectively it is the General who controls the pace of the story. It is almost as if Bellow ceded control of the text, which is opened and closed by the General's control of access. To enter the story, we have to push through that first door; when the door closes, the story ends. Citrón's narrative can only proceed at the General's pace. When he calls on the guards, the inset story hangs fire, giving the impatient reader a feeling that nothing much is happening. The embedded narrative is the real action, but it is subject to the control of the frame tale (the door to the story) and runs at the pace of the General. Throughout, Trotsky is never named, and is merely the "russo," the "Viejo."

Though it is tempting to see here a prudent awareness of the Voorhis Act (America was now at war), nobody in the *Partisan Review* readership would have had the slightest doubt of the identity of the "Old Man," Trotsky's usual sobriquet. Rather, the indirection underlines the extent to which the story cannot go directly at its own pace; its progress is repeatedly halted. In the background, soldiers are drilling in the mud; they "stumbled heavily and out of rhythm" (185), just as Eulalia stumbles on the road in her fashionable shoes. Access to the narrative space is controlled, just as the masses who pushed in at the doors were eventually controlled by the General, just as he regulates access to rooms (and sexual access to their occupants) in the present of the story. Bellow makes the reader share his own frustration. As readers we are like the masses, under control, with no longer any easy access to progress or utopian possibilities.

As a result, Trotsky remains in some ways unsullied. The story is infused with irony but not lost to idealism. In focusing on the General, Bellow may have taken his cue from the opposition developed in other memoirs of Trotsky. Dwight Macdonald contrasted the principled Trotsky and the opportunist Churchill in his memoir.[60] James T. Farrell remarked on the absence in any of his letters of a single cynical statement about the methods necessary to achieve power, unlike "genuine Machiavellians" like Napoleon.[61] Whatever anyone thought of Trotsky, he was no opportunist. As Citrón says, everything about him was based "on principle, principle. I remember him expounding the principle when they chopped up his room with bullets" (188). Trotsky's reputation will live on, as Quiroga's does. But the point is also made that he can no longer set the pace, and draw his followers behind him. Nor is it possible now to envisage peaceful change or to hold to pacifist principles. Nonetheless, Bellow did not give up lightly on his lost hero. In *The Adventures of Augie March* (1953), Augie glimpses Trotsky and has a sense of "navigation by the great stars, of the highest considerations, of being fit to speak the most important human words and universal terms" (435). When Augie leaves Mexico, Trotsky is still alive, as if Bellow had somehow resuscitated him in all his glory.

Bellow's politics now evolved away from Trotskyism and *Partisan Review* toward the more socially democratic position of Max Shachtman, rejecting party and national politics in favor of the creation of an internationalist third force on the democratic Left.[62] It is a change which is clearly envisaged in the evolution of *The Adventures of Augie March*, which Bellow thought of originally as a political novel, with Augie a much more studious and serious character than his later, larky incarnation. In the published version, the political theme is almost nonexistent and the original activist Augie March becomes the *ingénu* hero of a boisterously comic novel.[63]

In contrast, in the earlier version, Augie is involved with a group called the "Committee for a Reconstituted Europe" (CRE) run by Frazer and

Robey, both much more serious political figures than their later versions. The CRE is designed to combat the idea of the world as regimented and homogenized, a universal anthill. It aims to preserve the individuality of ancient cultures—Basque, Catalan, Piedmontese, Welsh, Bohemian—so that the dominant states can be met with effective passive resistance, and a new European federation formed (the plan also involves land distribution and socialist practices in industry). Augie becomes their man in Spain, swayed by Robey's theory of gigantism, the idea that great states become tyrants.

Similar "Third Camp" positions were common from the late 1930s onward, as the rise of a bipolar international order left the independent European Left demoralised.[64] The CRE bears some resemblance to Dwight Macdonald's 1948 plan to create an organization called "Europe-America Groups," to create a new force on the democratic left. (Supporters included Bellow's friends Isaac Rosenfeld, Philip Rahv, William Phillips, and Delmore Schwartz.) Even during the war, Max Shachtman and the Workers' Party supported the idea that the best hope for democracy and lasting peace would be movements independent of the Allied governments. Shachtman's was an internationalist vision of the warring empires' common defeat by popular resistance movements independent of British, Russian, or American governments. Shachtman identified the Yugoslavian partisans as the most promising example.[65]

As did another of Bellow's protagonists. Bellow's last fictional word on his political past is "Mosby's Memoirs," written on his return to Mexico in 1968. Bellow now looked back on his political views as naïve: "Our own movement . . . was often foolish, even comically absurd. During the Spanish civil war, the issue of material aid for the Spanish Republic was furiously debated by comrades who didn't have a dime to contribute."[66] In "Mosby's Memoirs," Bellow ascribes his own political errors satirically to Lustgarten, and allows him to expiate them. Importantly, the Jewish Lustgarten suffers from the same political naïveté as the younger Bellow, the same recondite examinations of the same issues: "Whether the American working class should give *material* aid to the Loyalist government of Spain. . . . There was, of course, no material aid to give. But *had* there been any, *should* it have been given."[67] Lustgarten also displays an agonized ability to split hairs over the issue of Finland: "Technically, Stalinism could not be Imperialism by definition. What then should a revolutionary party say to the Finns?" (156).

Jewish Lustgarten remains in America throughout the war "just sitting around" (163), but arrives in Europe immediately after its end and gives Trotskyism one more chance. In the internationalist belief in the theory of permanent revolution ("you don't build socialism in one country" [165]), he sets off for Yugoslavia, for what he assumes is a "V.I.P. deal" (165) as a foreign observer, declaring, "I really believe Tito may redeem Marxism by actually transforming the dictatorship of the proletariat" (165). He returns emaciated, sun-blackened, and embittered from what has turned out to be a forced labor brigade. As a member of a chain gang in Dalmatia, Lustgarten has been thoroughly punished for his political errors. But the Right, in the shape of his chronicler, Mosby, comes off worse.[68] For all his clever political-historical pronouncements, Mosby has no connection to society at all. Unmarried, friendless, childless, Mosby has suppressed all human ties—unlike Lustgarten, a keen father and uxorious husband. Mosby and Lustgarten are alter egos, doubles, the one conservative and the other socialist, allowing Bellow to satirize both sides of the political spectrum, but in the end the socialist still comes off best in the comparison. As Bellow said in 1993: "What you invest your energy and enthusiasm in when you are young you can never bring yourself to give up altogether."[69]

Notes

1. Joseph Epstein, "The Long, Unhappy Life of Saul Bellow," *New Criterion* 29, no. 4 (December 2010): 1.
2. Saul Bellow, *Letters*, ed. Benjamin Taylor (New York: Viking, 2010), 4.
3. Ibid., 528.
4. Ibid., 470–72.
5. Hugh Wilford, *The New York Intellectuals: From Vanguard to Institution* (Manchester: Manchester University Press, 1995), 55.
6. Saul Bellow, "Marx at My Table," *Guardian*, April 10, 1993, 23.
7. Ibid.
8. Ibid.
9. Saul Bellow, *It All Adds Up: From the Dim Past to the Uncertain Future: A Non-Fiction Collection* (London: Secker and Warburg, 1994), 301.
10. Bellow, "Marx at My Table."
11. Ibid.
12. Ibid.
13. Ibid.
14. See Albert Glotzer, *Trotsky: Memoir and Critique* (Buffalo, N.Y.: Prometheus, 1989).

15. Alan Wald, *The New York Intellectuals: The Rise and Decline of the Anti-Stalinist Left from the 1930s to the 1980s* (Chapel Hill: University of North Carolina Press, 1987), 246.

16. Richard Peter O'Brien, "The Radical Politics of American Fiction: Saul Bellow and *Partisan Review*, 1941–1953," Ph.D. diss., Leeds Metropolitan University, 2010. O'Brien's is much the most comprehensive discussion of the topic. He also notes John Paul, "Northwestern Is a Prison," *Beacon* 1, no. 1 (April 1937): 8–9.

17. It is also common for Trotskyists to use pseudonyms. See those listed by Peter Drucker, *Max Shachtman and His Left: A Socialist's Odyssey through the "American Century"* (Atlantic Highlands, N.J.: Humanities, 1994), xv.

18. John Paul, "This Is the Way We Go to School," *Soapbox* 2, no. 2 (December 1936): 7.

19. Bellow, *It All Adds Up*, 24.

20. Bellow, *Letters*, 5.

21. Sinclair Lewis, *It Can't Happen Here* (London: Jonathan Cape, 1935), 26.

22. Saul Bellow, "The Hell It Can't," *Daily Northwestern*, February 19, 1936, 8, hereafter cited parenthetically.

23. See Judie Newman, "Bellow's Ransom Tale: The Holocaust, *The Victim*, and *The Double*," *Saul Bellow Journal* 14, no. 1 (Winter 1996): 3–18.

24. Bellow, *It All Adds Up*, 310.

25. Bellow, *Letters*, 36.

26. Saul Bellow, *Dangling Man* (London: Penguin, 1963), 159.

27. Saul Bellow, "Before I Go: A Conversation with Norman Manea," *Salmagundi* 155–56 (Summer–Fall 2007): 152. According to Gregory Bellow (e-mail to the author, April 11, 2011), the meeting was arranged by Albert Glotzer.

28. Bellow, *It All Adds Up*, 307.

29. Ibid., 306.

30. Bellow, *Letters*, 15.

31. Ibid.

32. Ibid.

33. Nicolas Mosely, *The Assassination of Trotsky* (London: Michael Joseph, 1972), 14.

34. Daniel Fuchs, *Saul Bellow: Vision and Revision* (Durham, N.C.: Duke University Press, 1984), 65.

35. Edward Alexander, "Irving Howe and the Holocaust: Dilemmas of a Radical Jewish Intellectual," *American Jewish History* 88, no. 1 (2000): 96.

36. S. A. Longstaff, "*Partisan Review* and the Second World War," *Salmagundi* 43 (Winter 1979): 111.

37. Ibid., 112.

38. Ibid., 118–19.

39. William Phillips and Philip Rahv, "10 Propositions and 8 Errors," *Partisan Review* 8, no. 6 (November–December 1941): 449–508.

40. Longstaff, *"Partisan Review* and the Second World War," 123.

41. Saul Bellow, "In the Days of Mr. Roosevelt," *Esquire*, December 1983, 533.

42. See Christopher Phelps, *Young Sidney Hook: Marxist and Pragmatist* (Ann Arbor: University of Michigan Press, 2005), chap. 4; and Mike Davis, *Prisoners of the American Dream: Politics and Economy in the History of the U.S. Working Class* (New York: Verso, 1986), 67–69.

43. Bellow, *It All Adds Up*, 297.

44. Bellow, "In the Days," 536.

45. Ibid., 532.

46. Saul Bellow, "Two Morning Monologues," *Partisan Review* 8, no. 3 (1941): 230, hereafter cited parenthetically.

47. *Retort: An Anarchist Review*, vols. 1–5 (Bearsville, N.Y., 1942–51, repr., Santa Barbara: Greenwood, 1968).

48. S. G. Bellow, "Mr. Katz, Mr. Cohen, and Cosmology," *Retort: A Quarterly of Social Philosophy and the Arts* 1 (1942): 18, hereafter cited parenthetically.

49. Abraham Ascher, *P. A. Stolypin: The Search for Stability in Late Imperial Russia* (Stanford: Stanford University Press, 2001).

50. Photographs of him appear in "Bloody Murder in Mexico Ends Great Revolutionary Career of Trotsky," *Life*, September 2, 1940; and in Alain Dugrand, *Trotsky in Mexico* (Manchester: Carcanet, 1992), 17–21.

51. Saul Bellow, "The Mexican General," *Partisan Review* 9, no. 3 (May–June 1942): 186, hereafter cited parenthetically.

52. I am greatly indebted to Minister Ignacio Duran Loera, John King, and Andrea Noble for their assistance in tracing details of these films.

53. See Jorge Ayala Blanco, *La aventura del cine Mexicano* (Mexico City: Ediciones Era, 1968); Anne T. Doremus, *Culture, Politics and National Identity in Mexican Literature and Film, 1929–1952* (New York: Peter Lang, 2001); Emilio García Riera, *Historia Documental del Cine Mexicano*, vol. 2. (Mexico City: Universidad de Guadalajara, 1992).

54. Saul Bellow, *The Adventures of Augie March* (London: Penguin, 1966), 7.

55. The typographical spaces are maintained in the reprinted version: Saul Bellow, "The Mexican General," in *Atlantic Anthology*, ed. Nicholas Moore and Douglas Newton (London: Fortune, 1945), 22–34.

56. Manea, "Before I Go," 151.

57. Ibid., 152.

58. Thomas Walsh, "Heroism in Bellow's 'The Mexican General,'" *Saul Bellow Journal* 1, no. 2 (Spring–Summer 1982): 31–33.

59. Bellow derives this scene from a different police chief, L. A. Salazar, chief

of the Mexican secret police, who made the announcement in just these terms (see Judie Newman, "Saul Bellow and Trotsky," *Saul Bellow Journal* 1, no. 1 [1981]: 26–31).

60. Dwight Macdonald, "Trotsky Is Dead: An Attempt at an Appreciation," *Partisan Review* 7, no. 5 (September–October 1940): 339–53.

61. James T. Farrell, "The Cultural Front: Leon Trotsky," *Partisan Review* 7, no. 5 (September–October 1940): 389.

62. O'Brien, "The Radical Politics of American Fiction," 195.

63. Fuchs, *Saul Bellow: Vision and Revision*, 43–49.

64. Wilford, *The New York Intellectuals*.

65. Drucker, *Max Shachtman and His Left*, 147.

66. Bellow, *It All Adds Up*, 100–101.

67. Saul Bellow, *Mosby's Memoirs and Other Stories* (London: Penguin, 1971), 155, hereafter cited parenthetically.

68. See Judie Newman, "Zapotec Man and the Torajan Granny: *Mosby's Memoirs* and the Sacrifice of the Heart," in *Small Planets: Saul Bellow as Short Fiction Writer*, ed. Gerhard Bach and Gloria Cronin, 113–26 (East Lansing: Michigan State University Press, 2000).

69. Bellow, "Marx at My Table."

2

Bellow as Jew and Jewish Writer

Ben Siegel

In the years following the publication of *Herzog*, with the 1960s drawing to a close, Saul Bellow could well take stock of his new position as a major American literary figure. When launching his writing career, Solomon Bellow had become Saul Bellow. Now, a quarter century after publishing his first stories and novels, he could lay claim to being an international man of letters. But recognition and success had not come easily. During his early professional years—the 1940s and 1950s, as well as the decades immediately preceding them—America's most celebrated writers were resoundingly non-Jewish. John Dos Passos, F. Scott Fitzgerald, Ernest Hemingway, William Faulkner, and Thomas Wolfe represented the prevailing literary standards. American letters then revealed a genteel but pronounced anti-Semitism—an attitude especially discernible in Hemingway and Wolfe. Naturally sensitive and suspicious, Bellow would harbor a lifelong resentment of the slights he felt he received not only as a student and young college instructor but also as a writer. As James Atlas has pointed out, Bellow had valid cause for his feelings of exclusion. "Bellow's congenital suspiciousness," noted Atlas: "found a convenient object in what he took to be the resistance of the WASP literary establishment to his fiction. In later life, when his reputation was secure, he continued to dwell upon the contempt he had been forced to endure from English departments at Northwestern, Minnesota, and Princeton, and from the modernists championed in the pages of *Partisan Review*, whose ignorance of his work he turned into a deliberate slight."[1] Bellow could cite and quote anti-Jewish lines and figures in the writings of not only older contemporaries like T. S. Eliot and Ezra Pound, but also in that of earlier figures like Henry James and Goethe.

As already noted, Bellow was not one to forgive or forget. In a talk he gave rather late in life, he again revisited the hostile literary climate that had not only slowed his own early career but had also infected the thinking of many Jewish writers and critics. "Descendants of those same people whose cackling and shrieking set Henry James's teeth on edge when he visited them on the East Side," he noted, many of them Jewish critics now, "accuse themselves secretly of presumption when they write about Emerson, Walt Whitman, or Matthew Arnold." Bellow rejected such self-denigration. "My own view," he declared: "is that since Henry James or Henry Adams didn't hesitate to express their own dislike of Jews, there's no reason why Jews, while respecting these masters, should not be free to write as they please about them. To let them, the hostile American WASPS, determine once and for all what the American psyche is, not to challenge their views, would be disloyal and cowardly."[2]

Postwar Jewish Writing and Bellow's Fiction

In the years following World War II, anti-Semitism in America had become somewhat muted but was still discernible. "Direct experience of this exclusion was harder to document in the fifties than it had been in the thirties," said Atlas. The Holocaust had made anti-Semitism unacceptable—which didn't mean it no longer existed. Bellow pointed to Allen Tate, a self-proclaimed "Agrarian" from Tennessee who made no secret of his disdain for the predominantly Jewish *Partisan Review* crowd. "He thought we were an immigrant eruption into the literary life of the post-Confederate period," as Bellow wryly put it.[3] It bothered him that Edmund Wilson never reviewed any of his books after *Dangling Man*—further evidence of "the whole WASP effort to suppress the Jewish novel." Bellow was convinced, according to Atlas, that "even Jewish critics collaborated in this act of literary suppression." "They have their own axes to grind," Bellow insisted in old age, still rehearsing the injustices, both real and imaginary, that had impeded his early career.[4] Bellow may have occasionally exaggerated the degree to which bigotry had affected his career; still, his "sensitivity to ethnic slights," Atlas conceded, "wasn't without basis: There *was* a strain of anti-Semitism in American literature and its spokesmen. Among critical keepers of the gate, Jews who wrote novels in those days were regarded with the same suspicion that, a generation later, black writers would face (often at the hands of Jewish critics)."[5] Edmund Wilson, at least in Bellow's view, was one such gatekeeper. He "was no less guilty of casual anti-Semitism than his contemporaries Fitzgerald and Hemingway." For Wilson, noted Atlas, as for them: *"Jew* was a term of physical identification as descriptive as *tall* or *thin*. In light of the fact that T. S. Eliot was the literary standard-bearer of the day, Bellow's vigilance on this score could be excused. As his friend Delmore Schwartz liked to say, even paranoids have real enemies."[6]

In addition to external barriers and pressures, Jewish life in postwar America was itself in transition. The Yiddish-speaking immigrant generation and its life had almost disappeared. Gone with that life were the familiar Jewish social and literary themes so easily available in earlier decades, themes that had enabled Jewish novelists to bridge "the chasm" dividing their generation's American goals and standards from their parents' European cultures and values. Still, neither the earlier Yiddish-speaking novelists nor the first-generation American writers who started publishing in the 1920s and 1930s, Pearl Bell has argued, had "left any substantial trace as memory or influence on the young writers who followed."[7] Except for the writings of Henry Roth and Daniel Fuchs, two novelists "who have remained cult figures despite periodic revivals, most of the Jewish fiction published in the first third of the century rapidly came to seem ideological or lachrymose, and badly dated."[8] Therefore, following World War II, serious readers should not have been surprised to find that Jewish fiction in America often seemed a "literature of escape." Young Jews were recording in novel and story, stage play and essay, their efforts to escape not only the Jewish life of their parents but also Judaism itself. Religious leaders and other communal spokesmen began expressing their concern, a concern persisting to the present, that assimilation, primarily intermarriage, was endangering the existence of the Jewish community as a discrete, identifiable cultural entity. Jews were entering the American mainstream in increasing numbers—at least in economic, professional, and cultural terms. Norman Podhoretz even provided his contemporaries with a handbook to success by means of literary journalism. In *Making It,* he glorified in personal terms the country's four-decade-old "dirty little secret": the driving hunger of immigrants and their children for acceptance and success. He did so by tracing his own cultural journey from Brownsville to Manhattan. "One of the longest journeys in the world," Podhoretz boasted, "is the journey from

Brooklyn to Manhattan—or at least from certain neighborhoods in Brooklyn to certain parts of Manhattan."⁹

Norman Podhoretz was hardly alone. Many Jews had made it in America. Some were now not only experiencing a change in mood and attitude but were also reassessing their ethnic and religious identities. Causes for this change were numerous, among them the Holocaust and the founding of the State of Israel. In addition, most Jews and many other Americans were also now living amid the harsh realities—whether central or peripheral to their individual lives—of the civil rights movement, the assassinations of John and Robert Kennedy and Martin Luther King, the Vietnam War and its protestors, the sexual revolution, the feminist movement, and the Cold War. These events would soon be followed by the demise of Soviet communism, the AIDS epidemic, terrorism abroad and at home, and one American military expedition after another.[10]

Bellow and the Immigrant Tradition

During these tumultuous years, Bellow was in the forefront of those helping to give a new significance to American Jewish writing. His every narrative centered on a sensitive, thinking social adventurer keenly aware of the personal cost of modern existence. Other writers (Jewish and non-Jewish) then emerging found in his work a means of confronting the day's social and human dilemmas. No other novelist depicted as effectively the postwar confusions. Bellow transformed America's urban complexities into a sort of principle, "a mixture of health and sickness," that exemplified the modern condition. Here his Jewishness proved significant. "Would it be excessive to say," asked Irving Howe, "that this principle draws some of its energies from the Jewish tradition, the immigrant past?"[11]

Bellow's debt to this immigrant tradition was clear and repeatedly acknowledged, but it was not always understood. With all his gifts and special qualities, Bellow owed—as did most American Jewish writers—a considerable debt both to Russian and Yiddish literatures. This blessing was hardly unmixed. Multiple national or cultural identities are in themselves, as Mark Shechner pointed out, neither "ennobling [n]or charming." Generally caused by "flight and disruption," such cosmopolitanism results in "anguish and disorientation." Changing countries and continents may mean, Shechner noted, that "families are broken up, loved ones are lost, and a place in the world is left behind. It is neither a normal nor a happy state of affairs." For the Jewish immigrant generation, even the New World's freedoms exacted a heavy cost in "misery and alienation."[12] The writers among the early Jewish immigrants then had the singular task, as Pearl Bell observed, of bridging their "worlds of the *shtetl* and of urban modernity." They struggled "to do justice to both the immigrant life they were born to and the assimilationist and cosmopolitan culture in which they had to make their way."[13]

But the goals—social and literary—of their children were different. The literary members of the next generation saw a primary need to reconstruct their culture to fit their own goals and dreams. "After all, these first-generation Americans were growing up in two worlds," noted Mark Shechner, "the Old World preserved in the home and New World confronting them in the street." They developed a sensitivity to their own contradictions and paradoxes and an "ironic awareness" of their own special emotional and intellectual possibilities.[14] Led by Bellow and Bernard Malamud, and then by Herbert Gold and Philip Roth, Norman Mailer and Leslie Fiedler, among others, this generation established postwar Jewish fiction and nonfiction as a "formidable presence" in American culture. These writers "were the first to make it on their own terms," said Pearl Bell. They were "at once alien and American, and they had no doubt about their rightful place in the literary mainstream."[15] However, despite their determination and confidence, they saw themselves as "cultural hybrids." Some were defeated by their inability "to achieve wholeness," but others derived from their bicultural situation "strength, an advantage . . . a point of view."[16] One careful earlier observer of Jewish intellectual achievements, especially of eminence in Western scientific studies, was Thorstein Veblen. "It is by loss of allegiance, or at the best by force of a divided allegiance to the people of his origin," that the Jew, Veblen insisted, "finds himself in the vanguard of modern inquiry."[17] Veblen's broad comments, as Shechner points out, apply with equal validity to this first native generation of Jewish intellectuals "who were, at their most creative, masters of discrepancy and accomplished tightrope walkers."[18]

Bellow and Malamud, Mailer and Roth were hardly alone. For example, Michael Seide, Irvin Faust, Jerome Weidman, and then Herbert Gold and Stanley Elkin, among others, were producing "a similar breed of fiction." All could be said to have fused in their writing, Pearl Bell observed, "the racy inflections of Yiddish idiom and diction with the nervous rhythms of urban life."[19] However, Bellow and Malamud added yet another character element. They did so through their key characters, who proved to be "the archetypal embodiments of a newly complex Jewish personality full of intellectual ambition, ironic self-confidence, and erotic sophistication." These novelists of the Bellow–Malamud generation can be viewed as a group. For despite their many differences as writers, as individuals, and as Jews, they "were the first to regard success as their American birthright."[20]

But with their dreams came responsibilities—in Delmore Schwartz's memorable axiom. Postwar Jewish writing in America did exude moral and social concerns, but its commitment to responsibility was an old idea. Jews and their writings had been characterized since earliest times by a "craving to be used," to be of service to themselves and others. This need had been true of the Jewish personality, said Judd Teller, since the first encounter of Jew and Greek. Without denying himself experience or pleasure, the Jew had sought "for some transcendental meaning . . . for 'a piece of the action' in a greater universal scheme."[21] Jewish writing (Hebrew, Hellenic, Judaeo-Arabic, or Yiddish) had been marked by this search for ultimate meaning and purpose, for order amid chaos, for the rule of law. Admittedly, this "sense of purpose" was hardly restricted to Jewish writers, and some Jews in every generation lacked this concern. Teller cited as contemporary "hedonists" Edward Dahlberg, Paul Goodman, Norman Mailer, and Allen Ginsberg. Teller's general point appears valid, but his every example could be argued. Indeed, Teller himself conceded this. "Norman Mailer, the closest to a pure hedonist among the Jewish writers," he stated, was not free of this compulsive "groping for purpose." That was most evident "in *The American Dream,* a clear piece of parabolic writing."[22] But to most Jewish writers, these themes had proved central—in particular the desire to be useful to others. "Who can make use of him?" Moses Herzog says of himself. "He craves use. Where is he needed? Show him the way to make his sacrifice to truth, to order, peace."[23]

Of course Jewish literature revealed other characteristics as well, some of which (primarily by way of Yiddish writings) were derived from the Russian. Modern Jewish novelists' most obvious borrowings here, Teller noted, had been their strong use of internal dialogue and deep concern with "the ineffectual man, the non-achiever in the marketplace."[24] Writers in other times treated the nonachiever differently. In the Depression's proletarian fiction, the woeful individual was lamented as a social and economic victim.

But postwar Jewish novelists replaced lamentation with near-celebration. Bellow's dangling Joseph, Asa Leventhal, Tommy Wilhelm, and Moses Herzog embody various aspects of this figure. Each distills much of his thought and energy into internal dialogue. Joseph and Herzog are especially given to this traditional Jewish form. Such inner discourse, Teller explained, "has been the manner of Talmudic study in East Europe, the scholar reciting aloud to himself, in singsong, the arguments of first one, then another disputant, and alternatingly performing in each of these roles."[25]

This emphasis then on the material nonachiever had deep roots in Jewish literature. Hebrew and Yiddish fiction writers (often influenced by their Russian predecessors) had repeatedly traced the aimless meanderings of an ineffectual provincial Jewish intelligentsia. Generally, these characters were adrift "in a disintegrating *shtetl* with its gossip, hopelessness, and obsolescent customs."[26] Bellow's intellectual antiheroes resemble strongly their marginal counterparts in both Russian and Jewish literary traditions. But even without direct interaction between those two literatures, Teller observed, Jewish writers were fated to "produce an identical type," as the spirit of emancipation found in so many Russian shtetlach "was typical of the entire country.[27] This did not mean that those American Jewish novelists familiar with European Jewish writing always presented similar figures. Bernard Malamud, influenced strongly by the Hasidic folktales of Isaac Leib Peretz, leaned more to the unworldly or naive common man as protagonist than did most of his American colleagues.

But in focusing on the nonachiever, Bellow and Malamud and their Jewish contemporaries rejected the familiar American hero as successful entrepreneur. Most earlier American Jewish writers had accepted and—at his best—admired this protean figure derived from the mythic rugged frontier individualist. Even Clifford Odets, the unflinching "champion of the ineffectual man," blamed "the system" rather than the individual for the latter's material failures.[28] However, for Bellow and most other postwar Jewish writers, the hard-driving American entrepreneurs were the true failures. Odets saw such men as both exploiters of capitalism and its moral victims. Bellow saw them as having created their own moral plight. He and his Jewish contemporaries repeatedly downgraded "material achievement as a gauge for success." In doing so, they may have been defending, Teller suggested, "their 'unsuccessful' fathers or grandfathers" and repudiating the American success myths. For these myths too often implied "that material failure is somehow subversive" and may have resulted from "congenital inferiority" or some form of "pathological condition."[29]

Bellow's emphasis on the nonachiever was hardly the only reason his fiction proved so significant to American Jewish writing. His early novels and stories told—as the best Jewish stories always do—of this world's confusions as opposed to God's certainties. Bellow's Jews struggled in a world run by strangers, with the Jew reduced to the status, said Alfred Kazin, of "newcomer, parvenu, displaced person."[30] Thus in Bellow's fiction, the individual Jew's "self-ordering" becomes his personal and the story's central issue. Maybe the individual's "business of life, the real business," muses a beleaguered Tommy Wilhelm in *Seize the Day,* is "to carry his peculiar burden, to feel shame and impotence, to taste these quelled tears." Tommy even wonders if perhaps "the making of mistakes expressed the very purpose of his life and the essence of his being here."[31] In the Eisenhower–McCarthy era (the novel's publication and narrative period), many Americans (Jews and non-Jews) could identify with such emotional confusion. They could do so because Bellow presented his Jewish meanderers as representative postwar Americans who did not embrace the nation's alluring middle-class values. At the same time, he presented them with a wry irony that managed to be both subtle and comic.

Gentile Resentments

Due in part to Bellow's critical success, Jewish novelists and short-story writers, as well as poets and essayists, dominated the American literary scene by the late 1950s. This proved true on all cultural levels. Bellow's emergence "as the first Jewish-American novelist to stand at the center of American literature," Leslie Fiedler observed at the time, "is flanked by a host of matching successes on other levels of culture and subculture. What Saul Bellow is for highbrow literature, Salinger is for upper middlebrow, Irwin Shaw for middle middlebrow and Herman Wouk for lower middlebrow." One result of this Jewish literary centrality, said Fiedler, was that on all of the nation's cultural "levels, the Jew is in the process of being mythicized into the representative American."[32]

Of course, not all literary quarters accepted this Jewish success with equanimity. Indeed, some non-Jewish writers—Truman Capote, Katherine Ann Porter, and Gore Vidal, among others—expressed displeasure at this sudden emergence of a "Jewish Literary Establishment." Capote, for instance, used a *Playboy* interview to lament "the rise of . . . the Jewish Mafia in American letters." Smelling a cultural cabal, he felt obligated to expose it. "This is a clique of New York–oriented writers and critics who control much of the literary scene through the influence of the quarterlies and intellectual magazines. All these publications are Jewish-dominated," Capote insisted: "and this particular coterie employs them to make or break writers by advancing or withholding attention. I don't think there's any conscious, sinister conspiracy on their part—just a determination to see that members of their particular clique rise to the top. Bernard Malamud and Saul Bellow and Philip Roth and Isaac Bashevis Singer and Norman Mailer are all fine writers, but they are not the *only* writers in the country, as the Jewish literary Mafia would have us believe."[33] Capote then added: "I could give you a list of excellent writers, such as John Knowles and Vance Bourjaily and James Purdy and Donald Windham and Reynolds Price and James Leo Herlihy and Calder Willingham and John Hawkes and William Goyen; the odds are that you haven't heard of most of them, for the simple reason that the Jewish Mafia has systematically frozen them out of the literary scene."[34] Capote's list seems quaintly foolish today, as all his allegedly neglected writers soon enjoyed both critical and popular success.

Employing an only slightly more "genteel" approach, Katherine Anne Porter and Gore Vidal focused on the "corruption" of American prose in Jewish fiction. After Bellow had received the 1953 National Book Award for *The Adventures of Augie March,* Porter, clearly stung by his success, warned the nation that granting Bellow such recognition posed a danger to the American language. By his use of "foreign"—that is, Yiddish—words, inflections, syntax, he was literally "bastardizing" the English language. She offered herself as contrast. "I am an old North American," stated Porter, who habitually lied about her family background. "My people came to Virginia in 1648, so we have had time to become acclimatized," she argued. As Porter read the nation's literary history, it was: "Truly, the South and the West and other faraway places [that] have made and are making American literature. We are in the direct, legitimate line; we are people based in English as our mother tongue, and we do not abuse it or misuse it, and when we speak a word, we know what it means."[35] But these Jews, "these others have fallen into a curious kind of argot, more or less originating in New York." Their idiom, in contrast to that of true Americans, is "a deadly mixture of academic, guttersnipe, gangster, fake-Yiddish, and dull old wornout dirty words." What their writings then reveal is "an appalling bankruptcy in language, as if they hate English and are trying to destroy it along with all other living things they touch."[36]

Such attacks were hardly new. Several decades earlier, H. L. Mencken, who had made no secret of his pro-German sentiments not only during World War I, but also in the Hitler years, had set the tone for such comments. Referring to some contemporary Jewish writers, he had sniffed that "they think in Yiddish and write in English."[37] But by the mid-1960s, Bellow, Bernard Malamud, Philip Roth, and Herbert Gold, among others, were establishing at least the temporary dominance of the Jewish novel, and such spiteful comments had little effect. Alan Lelchuk soon put matters in clear perspective. "Although strains of anti-Semitism have always existed in the literary community," he noted, "Porter's genteel attack found few believers." This may have been "because it was already clear to most, including Edmund Wilson and Philip Rahv, that not only was Bellow a gifted talent, but also an outstanding new stylist."[38]

Still, literary envy of the more prominent Jewish novelists persisted, with attacks appearing on occasion even in a Jewish publication. For instance, five years after Porter's snide comments, Gore Vidal, with customary chutzpah, attacked, in *Commentary* no less, those he considered "literary gangsters," most of whom were clearly Jewish. He even echoed Porter's sentiments by complaining of the damage done by such pushy intruders to contemporary American writing. "With each generation American prose grows worse," he declared, "reflecting confused thinking, poor education, and the incomplete assimilation of immigrant English into the old language."[39] That such "nativist" complaints had been voiced in earlier decades by luminaries like Henry Adams and Henry James, Frank Norris and Theodore Dreiser, Ernest Hemingway, Thomas Wolfe, and Scott Fitzgerald, E. E. Cummings, Willa Cather, and Henry Miller hardly made them more palatable in the postwar years. Even as late as 1977, Joan Didion, in her familiar cutesy fashion, did not consider it distasteful to begin a review of John Cheever's *Falconer* by observing: "Some of us are not Jews. . . . Some of us are even Episcopalians."[40]

Clearly, then, for these and other "native" writers who muttered darkly about the literary preeminence of Jewish novelists (and of Jewish critics, playwrights, and poets), this sad turn of postwar events revealed most pointedly to them, Judd Teller observed, "the Jewish cultist conspiracy to alter America's mores and literary and stage idiom."⁴¹ Such jibes struck Bellow keenly just when he should have been at his most euphoric and basking in critical and public acclaim for *The Adventures of Augie March*. "I began to discover," he later recalled, "that while I thought I was simply laying an offering on the altar like a faithful petitioner, other people thought I was trying to take over the church. It came at a strange point when I think the WASP establishment was losing confidence in itself, and it felt it was being challenged by Jews, blacks and ethnics."⁴² Some of its members began to claim "there was a Jewish mafia, and other people, who should have had more sense, spoke of—well, they didn't use the word conspiracy, but they saw it as an unwelcome eruption." In defense, Bellow then started to refer to Malamud, Roth, and himself "as Hart, Shaffner & Marx." He recognized "there was a pathetic absurdity under it all." The truth was more mundane: "All we wanted was to add ourselves to the thriving enterprise we loved; no one wanted to take over. That's a motive worthy of the Mafia, and I don't think Hart, Shaffner & Marx were Mafiosi."⁴³

But his irony did not alleviate then or later his hurt or his need to explain his position. "I think of myself as an American of Jewish heritage," he stated. "When most people call someone a 'Jewish writer,' it's a way of setting you aside. They don't talk about the powers of the 'Jewish writers' who wrote the Old Testament."⁴⁴ Instead, they insist that "to write novels you need to know something about manners, which is something you have to be raised in the South to know. I felt many writers [in the 1950s and early 1960s] treated their Jewish colleagues with unpardonable shabbiness, and anti-Semitism after the Holocaust is absolutely unforgivable"⁴⁵ Later, Bellow adopted a softer tone. He then claimed not to have been disturbed by such comments and insisted that such WASP resentments belonged to the past: "Today I don't think that there is any prejudice against Jewish writers among the writers belonging to the Protestant majority. Some did experience a certain discomfort about our displaying the ability to write in English. But then the blacks came along and swept us off the stage. Their turn's coming—maybe the women will replace them as the vogue. Nothing lasts long in fashions. We are so overwhelmed by so many facts hurled at us all the time that I wonder who'll remember any writing, and for how long."⁴⁶

Admittedly, postwar Jewish novelists were less concerned than their predecessors had been with gentile opinions of the Jew and were more focused on their own "interior world."⁴⁷ Earlier Jewish writers—other than those committed to Marxism or Zionism—would have been reluctant to judge, much less criticize, Anglo-American culture. But the "new" or postwar Jewish writers did not share the qualms of their forerunners, having gained confidence in their validity as Americans and in their right to introduce Jewishness into American literature. Certainly Bellow did not hesitate to have Moses Herzog target his wife's psychologist, "calm, Protestant Nordic Edvig," for much of what was morally wrong with American culture. "I've read your stuff about the psychological realism of Calvin. I hope you don't mind my saying that it reveals a lousy, cringing, grudging conception of human nature. This is how I see your Protestant Freudianism."[48] Herzog has also little patience with Christian criticism of Jews. "Do you think that any Christian in the twentieth century has the right to speak of Jewish Pharisees?" he demands of Edvig. "From a Jewish standpoint, you know, this hasn't been one of your best periods." For that matter, he adds, "I don't agree with Nietzsche that Jesus made the whole world sick, infected it with his slave morality. But Nietzsche himself had a Christian view of history." He saw "the present moment always as some crisis, some fall from classical greatness, some corruption or evil to be saved from. I call that Christian."[49]

These comments (like his earlier ones) suggested that Bellow was not as sanguine about gentile attitudes toward Jewish writers as his later reassurances would suggest. He revealed his resentments in *Humboldt's Gift*. Recalling the impact of Von Humboldt Fleisher's first volume of ballads, Charlie Citrine observes that "You would have thought that [as] the son of neurotic immigrants . . . that his syntax would be unacceptable to fastidious goy critics on guard for the Protestant Establishment and the Genteel Tradition."[50] Bellow may have been revealing his concern about his own career in the early postwar years. His struggles to find his proper literary voice reflected in many ways, he admitted, the difficulties of two Jewish generations—as exemplified by his family or their friends or himself—to determine their proper "place" in American society. "You must appreciate," he stated, "that the American experience is unique; in my opinion it is a tremendous event in world history."[51] It had been for newcomers also a baffling and bruising one. "Making it" in this country, he pointed out, had generally been painful for every immigrant group, and the Jews were no exception. Many newcomers, in their desire to become Americans, set the wrong goals and accepted the wrong stereotypes and standards. In the generation preceding his own, and even later, many immigrants tried to adapt their lifestyles to what were essentially "journalistic, publicity creations, and products of caricature." No one had yet described, he insisted, "the queer hunger of immigrants and their immediate descendants for true Americanism." Their need for acceptance "may sound like fun, but I find it hard to think of anyone who underwent the process with joy." He recalled an immigrant cousin, Arkady, who declared his new American name to be Lake Erie. Luckily, poetry soon gave way to practicality, and Cousin Arkady became "Archie."[52]

More Midwesterner Than Jew

Bellow's own generation hardly had an easier time. Many immigrant contemporaries, in their quest to be good Yankees, he explained, "copied even the unhappiness of the Protestant majority." They embraced "its miseries," even to "battling against Mom." Soon they too were reluctant, after work, to board their suburban train. Drinking downtown, or in the club car, they too were "handed down drunk to the wife and her waiting station-wagon like good Americans. These people martyred themselves in the enactment of roles that proved them genuine." They were determined to prove they could be "just as madly wretched in marriage as Abe Lincoln and Mary Todd." He did not exclude himself from "that mixture of imagination and stupidity with which people met the American Experience, that murky, heavy, burdensome, chaotic thing."[53] His way of coping with the cultural confusion was by having "intellectual romances" with varied ideologies like Marxism and Reichian psychology.[54] Later he realized that his major error, a common one, lay in seeking sanctuary in the country's various "corners of culture." He wished to enjoy "high thoughts" and to perfect himself in an art's "symbolic discipline." He overdid it. "One didn't need," he confessed, "as much sanctuary as all that."[55] Still, he felt his concerns were justified, as he had found good reason to fear he "would be put down as a foreigner, an interloper. It was made clear to me when I studied literature in the university that as a Jew and the son of Russian Jews I would probably never have the right feeling for Anglo-Saxon tradition, for English words. I realized even in college that the people who told me this were not necessarily disinterested friends. But they had an effect on me, nevertheless. This was something from which I had to free myself. I fought free because I had to."[56]

In his fiction Bellow made clear that such comments left deep scars. He also conveyed there, especially in *Humboldt's Gift*, his dislike of those Jews who choose to play the genteel gentile. Thus Charlie Citrine is (like Moses Herzog before him) openly disdainful of those Jewish academics (those "Ivy League kikes") who deny their gutter origins. Mark Harris, in his *Saul Bellow, Drumlin Woodchuck*, recorded his dismay at hearing Bellow use in conversation the phrase "a Harvard kike."[57] However, in his *Paris Review* interview, Bellow summed up bluntly his rejection of the academic bigotry and snobbery he felt had long emanated from the Ivy League East. Indeed, he considered himself "lucky to have grown up in the Middle West, where such influences are less strong. If I'd grown up in the East and attended an Ivy League university, I might have been damaged more badly. Puritan and Protestant America carried less weight in Illinois than in Massachusetts. But I don't bother much with such things now."[58]

Yet he had to have been bemused if not angered to read a *New York Times Book Review* article by Alan Lelchuk entitled "The Death of the Jewish Novel," a recounting of two incidents involving him and "the varieties of ethnic displeasure he has caused."[59] Lelchuk recalled that on a trip to Israel in the 1970s he visited Gershom Scholem, "the great scholar of Jewish mysticism and one of the tribal chiefs of secular Judaism." The conversation turning to American literature, Bellow's name was mentioned. At that point, Lelchuk stated: "Scholem, normally cool and relaxed, immediately grew livid, stood up and, striding back and forth, began to downgrade Bellow as a writer and to berate him personally. At the bottom of Scholem's ire, it turned out, was Bellow's remark after he had received the Nobel Prize, that he was 'An American writer first, and a Jew second.'" What Scholem wanted to know, as Lelchuk remembered the event, was, "How could an intelligent man who was Jewish say such a thing . . . instead of acknowledging his Jewish identity first and foremost?" To this great scholar, Bellow's statement "was either stupid or cowardly, the product of an assimilationist culture and/or personality, and Scholem would never forgive Bellow for it. For Scholem had not come to primitive Palestine in the early 1930s—abandoning his civilized Germany to be mocked by family and assimilationist friends—only to hear a Jewish Nobel Prize winner deemphasize his Jewish heritage. Reading this account, Bellow had to have been struck by the irony of being attacked for downgrading his Jewishness—the very act that had caused him to lash out at academic "kikes."

The second incident recalled by Lelchuk occurred at the 1974 commencement ceremonies at Brandeis University, where he was then teaching. Bellow and Lionel Trilling were among those receiving honorary degrees, and the former was the commencement speaker. Bellow's "talk, that hot Sunday," Lelchuk noted,

> was unusual in that it bypassed a public topic in order to track his own life as a young writer. He recounted his early days in Montreal, where he studied in a Hebrew school, and then in Chicago, where he composed on a table in the kitchen while his aunt made Russian borscht and argued in Yiddish with family members. With affection and humor, Bellow spoke of his student days at the University of Chicago, too, and his growing mixture of college sophistication and homespun wisdoms. Characteristically, along the way, Bellow offered rich autobiographical glimpses into the making of a novelist.[60]

Lelchuk remembered clearly his pleasure at Bellow's unexpected approach. "For me, a young writer about to have yet another commencement address inflicted on him," he stated, "it was a wonderful surprise." Bellow had regaled his audience with "an honest and detailed talk, free of the usual piety and palaver that clutter those speeches." Lionel Trilling did not agree. Later, when speaking with Trilling, Lelchuk asked him if he had liked Bellow's presentation. "His face tightening, Trilling retorted, 'Not at all.'" When Lelchuk wondered why not, Trilling replied: "'It was inappropriate. Highly inappropriate.' Trilling announced it like a judge repeating the jury's verdict, 'Guilty.' Clearly, for Trilling, Bellow had committed a gross act of violence, a violation of the strict code of academic behavior. Poor Bellow—in his way he was being an errant patient, a wayward Jew, not quite in touch with reality. You just didn't talk about your personal life, especially not a Jewish ghetto life, at a university ceremony."[61] Lelchuk's account of that incident brought a quick rebuttal from Diane Trilling. Lionel Trilling had been dead for about a decade when Lelchuck published his piece in 1984, but Mrs. Trilling was very much alive. In a letter to the *New York Times Book Review*, she pointed out that by Lelchuk's date of 1978 her husband had been dead for three years, and that the Brandeis commencement to which Lelchuk referred had been held in 1974. "My husband very much admired Bellow's work," she wrote, adding: "his laudatory review of 'Augie March' served indeed as the introduction to the Modern Library edition of that book.... [M]y husband was a man of most moderate temper. His face did not readily tighten and he did not make staccato pronouncements.... He was in fact the least judgmental of people."[62]

Ironically enough, as a beginning novelist, Saul Bellow had been keenly sensitive about his Jewishness and had reacted defensively to societal pressures. In those early years, he preferred to think of himself "as a Midwesterner and not a Jew." As already noted, he did not go to his neighborhood public library "to read the Talmud but the novels and poems of Sherwood Anderson, Theodore Dreiser, Edgar Lee Masters, and Rachel Lindsay."[63] Starting out, his specific means of defense, as he would explain repeatedly, was to write like the traditional American or, better yet, English novelist. He wrote his first two novels, *Dangling Man* and *The Victim*, in that escapist mood. "I think that when I wrote those early books I was timid," he later confessed. "I still felt the incredible effrontery of announcing myself to the world (in part I mean the WASP world) as a writer and an artist. I had to touch a great many bases, demonstrate my abilities, pay my respects to formal requirements. In short, I was afraid to let myself go." Self-conscious about being Jewish, he wanted his first two novels to be "well made." He wrote *Dangling Man* "quickly," he stated, but he "took great pains with it." He labored with *The Victim* "to make it letter perfect... [having] accepted a Flaubertian standard." This was "not a bad standard," he conceded in retrospect, but for him it proved "repressive" due to his life and his

> upbringing in Chicago as the son of immigrants. I could not, with such an instrument as I developed in the first two books, express a variety of things I knew intimately. Those books, though useful, did not give me a form in which I felt comfortable. A writer should be able to express himself easily, naturally, copiously in a form which frees his mind, his energies. Why should he hobble himself with formalities? With a borrowed sensibility? With the desire to be "correct"? Why should I force myself to write like an Englishman or a contributor to *The New Yorker*? I soon saw that it was simply not in me to be a mandarin.[64]

Bellow may have remembered vividly his early need to throw off an acquired cultural gentility and to express freely his own Jewish sensibility. But he need not have feared any loss of ethnic identity. Those who knew him in those years would recall him in essentially Jewish terms. "The man had been an anthropologist, a traveler, a musician, an editor of the University of Chicago's 'great books,'" observed Alfred Kazin.[65] He also "was a teacher, a lover, a liberated Jewish male and the most watchful of Jewish sons." Indeed, Bellow "had found a way through the thickets of the big-city ghetto, the big-city university, the Depression, the merchant marine during the war; he had been a left radical, a welfare investigator; he was soon to become the sternest of Jewish moralists." On another occasion, Kazin remembered other impressions: "Listening to Bellow, I became intellectually happy—an effect he was soon to have on a great many other writers of our generation. We were coming through." There seemed to Kazin "nothing deliberate about Bellow's sense of destiny. He was proud in a laconic way, like an old Jew who feels himself closer to God than anybody else."[66] True, Bellow "could be unbearable in his unresting image of himself, but he was never smug and could be as openly vulnerable as anyone I ever met. . . . Saul was clearly a man chosen by talent, like those Jewish virtuosos—Heifetz, Rubinstein, Milstein, Horowitz—who had been shaped into slim and elegant men of the world by talent alone." Even the young novelist's "conscious good looks were those of a coming celebrity." But Bellow's major strength, Kazin thought, was his "talent for the literature of direct experience. . . . It was refreshing to be with a man who disposed of so many pedantic distinctions. It seemed to have something to do with his love of Yiddish and Jewish jokes, his affection for big-city low life, his sense of himself as a creative Jew. Saul was the first Jewish writer I met who seemed as clever about life as a businessman. He was in touch."[67]

Bellow had brought his Jewish sensibilities into more direct play when he began *The Adventures of Augie March*. He then experienced a significant change in attitude and style. Here and in subsequent novels, "despite his natural caution," Bellow traced, as Kazin put it, "the sexual impatience of the rising Jewish middle class."[68] Perhaps Bellow, like Norman Mailer and Paul Goodman—Kazin suggested—"had been delivered by the Reichian analysis to be bold, defiant of convention and body armature." Or perhaps, as Bellow himself insisted, he was simply determined to throw off the inhibitions of literary Protestantism. He did so, but he would later feel he overdid it. "I took off many of these restraints. I think I took off too many, and went too far, but I was feeling the excitement of discovery. I had just increased my freedom, and like any emancipated plebian I abused it at once."[69]

The Jewish-Writer Tag

Keenly aware and even proud of being Jewish, Bellow still considered his—or anyone else—being Jewish a quirk of fate, an "accidental exoticism."[70] He therefore found all ethnic categorizing, especially the label of "American Jewish writer," to be odd, discomforting, and imprecise: "It is accurate only insofar as it is true that I am an American and a Jew and a writer. But I don't clearly see the value of running all three of these items together. Over the years I have been faintly amused at the curious linkage of Bellow, Malamud, and Roth. . . . Somehow it always reminds me of Hart, Shaffner & Marx."[71] In short, he needed no one to remind him he was an American, a Jew, and a writer. All such labels were irrelevant, Bellow argued, as was the fact that "I'm also a hockey fan, a fact which nobody ever mentions."[72] He saw no "division" in viewing himself as both American and Jew. What did bother him—despite his own free use of the term—was being viewed as a "Jewish writer" rather than a writer who was Jewish. "I am a Jew, and I have written some books. I have tried to fit my soul into the Jewish-writer category, but it does not feel comfortably accommodated there." Yet he was often tagged a Jewish writer, he complained, "in much the same way one might be called a Samoan astronomer or an Eskimo cellist or a Zulu Gainsborough expert."[73]

Clearly, Bellow had given the subject careful thought. Asked the source of "the whole phenomenon of the American Jewish writer," he responded quickly. It came about "in a peculiarly American way," he explained: "When of a sudden certain Jewish writers were being hailed in America, the Jews felt themselves making progress. Being as P.R. conscious as anyone else—it's a sign of their being Americanized—they were immensely pleased. And why not? Jews had made it in America in business and in politics—and now they were making it in culture. How very pleasing indeed."[74] The previous year, in a give-and-take session with a panel of Israeli writers in Tel Aviv, Bellow had made known his feelings on the same subject. "I will say one further thing about the Jewish writer in America," he had told a large audience, "and that is that the Jewish community in America was delighted when the Jewish writers appeared on the scene because they felt it would be good for the Jews in America. This put us in a rather awkward position of doing public relations, unwillingly, for the American Jews, and we were also expected to refrain from any sharp criticism of persons who were Jews."[75]

Bellow found this situation to be "extremely disagreeable," as it appeared to him "to be an imposition on truth to have to make things come out nicely as Israel Zangwill did, and give the people a pleasing impression." Not surprisingly, some Jewish writers reacted negatively to such expectations. Consequently, he added, they

> bent over backwards just because there was this pressure put on them and they decided that they would be, on the contrary, or out of contrariness, quite nasty in their realistic portrayal of Jews. This is an accusation that has been brought against Philip Roth, who has gone much farther in this direction than I ever dreamed of going. But he went farther in that direction because he felt the provocation. Or the challenge, I think, whereas I always refuse to be provoked or challenged and simply went my stubborn, mulish narrow way without accepting either the task of making good public relations for the Jews or reacting against this demand.[76]

Such public expectations or cultural pressures were for Bellow then part of the down side of being tagged a "Jewish writer." What is the intent of those applying the label? For "apart from the comfort all this appears to have given certain American Jews," he reasoned: "I wonder if there isn't an implied put-down in the label American Jewish Writer. One doesn't, after all, any longer speak of American Irish Writers or American Italian Writers or, for that matter, American Wasp Writers. What's more, the label seems to me without a shred of literary accuracy, for the writers who have had it pasted on their backs seem to me to vary tremendously in their styles, in their subject matter and certainly in their quality."[77] He also disdains the Jewish-writer tag for having "a flavor of the ghetto about it" and for being "intellectually vulgar, unnecessarily parochializing and utterly without value"—especially since, "from a personal point of view, it avoids me both as a writer and as a Jew."[78]

It is worth noting again that Bellow had no problem applying the Jewish-writer "label" to others when it suited his purpose. But he was at this point primarily concerned to reject all attempts to define *him* in ethnic or even national terms: "Like the exile writers of Paris 50 years ago I do not think of myself as representing any national culture. I am simply a modern writer."[79] Thus he bristled at the claim made in a *Time* magazine essay that he was "the godfather of a Jewish literary revolution" and at critics who insisted he led a "school" of eastern Jewish writing.[80] "What point is there in getting into these wrong-headed pygmy battles?" he asked. "I don't live in the East, I reside in Chicago. And I find the whole Jewish writer bit tedious."[81] Indeed, that ethnic tag was for him nothing more than a "sheer invention" created and perpetuated "by the media, by critics and by 'scholars.'"[82] He could conclude only "that when American Jews began to write in English, people were so astonished that they could do so that they quickly gave them a tag. Malamud, Roth and I are all tied together in this way, and it's rather unfortunate."[83]

Bellow tried hard to play down his anger at being squeezed into a literary trio, but he could not refrain from repeating his now-familiar joke. Indeed, the frequency with which he alluded to this "linkage" suggested he was more angry than amused. The three of them, he observed wryly,

> have made it in the field of culture as Bernard Baruch made it on a park bench, as Polly Adler made it in prostitution, and Two Gun Cohen, the personal bodyguard of Sun Yat-Sen, made it in China. My joke is not broad enough to cover the contempt I feel for the opportunists, wise guys, and career types who impose such labels and trade upon them. In a century so disastrous to Jews, one hesitates to criticize those who believe that they are making the world safer by publicizing Jewish achievements. I myself doubt that this publicity is effective.[84]

Recrossing the same ground on another occasion, Bellow explained that he rejected ethnic labels partly because he did not "like the people who make the classifications."[85] He did not believe "they have much mind," and he did not care to have them put him into a category." For although he was "very keen" to learn his true category, he had not, he stated, "found anyone yet who's able to tell me what it is." Some critics had informed him that he was "a Jewish writer. Well, that's an odd sort of social description. They make me feel that, together with writers like Roth and Malamud, I'm a literary equivalent to the Jewish clothing industry." But he wished to make it clear that when he wrote he did not feel "any sense of ethnic responsibility. That is not my primary obligation. My primary obligation is to my trade and not to any particular ethnic group." He had "no objection," he declared, to those "writers who have so strong a sense of justice, so strong an ethical or moral sense, that they feel themselves compelled to write in this way." In fact, he admired them a great deal. For he "suppose[d] that if Tolstoy hadn't hated war he wouldn't have written *War and Peace*. If a man feels that way, he writes that way. Why not?" But for any writer "to generate falsely that kind of feeling, or to prime it from nothing, to get it going because he thinks *it's* the thing he should get going—that I'm very much opposed to."

Some critics insisted that Bellow laid himself open to ethnic labeling by writing mostly about Jews. "It is naive of him to use Yiddish idiom, Jewish themes, perspectives, characters, and subject matter," observed L. H. Goldman, "and expect not to be considered a 'Jewish' writer."[86] But Jews were the people he knew best, Bellow explained, and "I like to know what I'm talking about."[87] Some readers insisted that even his non-Jewish characters were disguised Jews. "Henderson is not a Jew," Bellow protested,

> but he has been accused by some of being a sort of convert. But that's false, that's simply not the case. One has one's character—a given—and that's it. He had better be faithful to the given and *if* other people don't like it that's unfortunate. I have never consciously written as a Jew. I have just written as Saul Bellow. I have never attempted to make myself Jewish. I've never tried to appeal to a community, I never thought of writing for Jews exclusively. I never wanted to. I think of myself as a person of Jewish origin—American and Jewish—who has had a certain experience of life, which *is* in part Jewish.[88]

How much of his experience is Jewish? He rejected the question: "Proportions are not for me to decide. I don't know what they are: how much *is* Jewish, how much *is* Russian, how much *is* male, how much is twentieth century, how much is Midwestern. That's for others to determine with their measuring sticks. I have no sticks myself."[89]

What he did have was an aversion for those who held "that any literature should be so special that it can't be understood by non-communicants."[90] A literature's "human quality," he countered, "should appeal to anyone. If it doesn't, it's a mistake. Something is wrong. It's too parochial. No good literature is parochial." But then recognizing that he may have pushed this thought too far, Bellow retracted it in part. "All good literature," he conceded, does have "some color of this sort because there is no such thing as a generalized human being. He's an Irishman, or an Italian, or an Indian, or a Japanese, whatever it is that he is, he is. We in America have a feeling that perhaps it would be a nice thing, if we had a generalized human being who didn't have these characteristics, but only, let's say, desirable American characteristics, shared by all. There is really no such thing. It's a total impossibility and it would be an undesirable thing, if anyone could achieve it."[91]

Bellow's rejection of "parochial" labels did not go unchallenged. Novelist-essayist Cynthia Ozick, later to become a friend of Bellow's, offered the sharpest rebuttal. A vigilant Jewish traditionalist, Ozick focused on a *New York Times* interview in which Bellow, according to the interviewer Alden Whitman, identified himself with "'large-public' writers—those who voice social concerns and write for a general readership."[92] Bellow included here Americans like Carl Sandburg, Sherwood Anderson, Theodore Dreiser, and Upton Sinclair, as well as Europeans like Charles Dickens, Bernard Shaw, Émile Zola, and H. G. Wells. "Their novels," he observed, "were addressed to a mass audience, and they thought of themselves as spokesmen for a national conscience. They addressed grand issues of social justice and political concern." Their readers regarded them "as oracles." Conversely, Bellow disassociated himself from "small-public" academic favorites like T. S. Eliot, Ezra Pound, James Joyce, and Marcel Proust.

Embarrassed by the outcry his comments evoked, Bellow tried in later interviews to recant in part by explaining their source and background. In one conversation, he emphasized that these "small-public" writers had "worked within the late-nineteenth-century romantic tradition of opposing and defying the bourgeoisie" and that their private sensibilities have since appealed strongly to academic critics.[93] With most affluent Americans absorbed in business, technology, and the mass media, Bellow argued, thoughtful writers here cannot expect to win easily their countrymen's attention. So most serious writers consider their primary audience to be their fellow writers and the professional critics. In short, they write for their "guild" rather than the ordinary reader. His own literary orientation, he stated in another interview, was different. "Chicago kids, fifty years ago, were devouring the masterpieces of modernism—what Wyndham Lewis in his autobiography, *Rude Assignment,* called 'small-public art.'"[94] Lewis was distinguishing "between great-public and small-public artists," Bellow explained. He was establishing the fact that in the mid-nineteenth century such novelists of "great power" as Balzac, Dickens, Tolstoy, and Dostoyevsky addressed and were understood by the great public. "Ordinary literacy was all that was required of a reader."[95]

However, in the late nineteenth and early twentieth centuries, said Bellow, "a more sophisticated public" and a more complex and difficult writer appeared. In a later *New York Times* interview with Joseph Epstein, Bellow insisted that he had only admiration and respect for people like Rilke, Joyce, Proust, and Mallarme.[96] Indeed, he now claimed his remarks on these writers in the earlier Whitman interview were misquoted and hence misinterpreted. But in that earlier interview, at least as published, Bellow did insist that his own work fell into the first category. In fact, what appeared to trouble him most there was that academics and other critics perceived him neither as a large-public nor small-public writer but primarily as an "ethnic" or Jewish one. To emphasize his own broad vision and literary scope, he cited his then-latest work, *Humboldt's Gift.* "The whole novel," he stated, "is intended to hold up a mirror to our urban society and to show its noise, its uncertitudes, its sense of crisis and despair, its standardization of pleasures. And the city is a universal for almost everyone in America." Yet despite his sharing of the "grand issues" of Dickens, Wells, and Zola, he was grouped ethnically with Malamud and Roth. "The Protestant majority thought it had lost its grip," Bellow argued, "so the ghetto walls went up around us." As a result, those writers who were Jews and blacks had been confronted by "a ghetto description of themselves." It added up, he concluded, to "giving a dog a bad name in order to hang him."[97]

Cynthia Ozick, as noted, was quick to respond. She understood Bellow's dislike of being placed in tandem with others. "No writer likes to be thought of as running in a pack," she conceded; "every writer prizes his unique gifts, and Bellow above all knows his own power, especially as to scope and ambition."[98] Still, she could not help but wonder whether Auden, Spender, and MacNeice, when treated as a trio in the 1930s, complained "of ethnic ghettoization"? Did Ransom and Tate protest being termed the "Southern Agrarians"? For that matter, did Yeats and his colleagues lament their designation as founders of an "Irish Renascence"? Clearly, these writers had given little thought to ethnic labels. Why was Bellow so concerned? What if the Protestant majority did view a group of writers "as linked by a common heritage"? Did that prove malice or ghettoization? What Bellow may fear, Ozick speculated, "is the taint of the parochial." If so, his fear was "unworthy of his stature." He should recognize that "all genius is parochial. Shakespeare wrote out of a tiny island, Yeats out of a still tinier one. Tolstoy had all the spaciousness of Russia, yet imagined the world mainly out of the French-speaking fraction of the Russian nobility. And Bellow himself had Augie famously begin, 'I am an American, Chicago born,' giving us a parochial Chicago with all the allure and reverberation of the more ancient capitals of literature."[99]

Ozick's anger was understandable. But what had sensitized Bellow to the Jewish-writer label was the occasional critic's suggestion that readers had to be familiar with Judaism to grasp the "special Jewish slant" of his fiction. "I think that's nonsense," Bellow had flared in an essay. "It really is. One of the charms of life in the twentieth century is that a variety of human beings pass before you, people who were formerly unknown or could only be dealt with mythologically. You know we don't do it mythologically nowadays, not that way. We don't create Jews as Marlowe created them in *The Jew of Malta* or as Shakespeare did when he created . . . [Shylock]. There is something mythic about these characters."[100] Writers and readers now "are somewhere in between" myth and literal fact . . . we have some kind of knowledge, some kind of science . . . some kind of recognition of the humanity of exotic peoples."[101]

Bellow was suggesting that even this limited knowledge meant writers no longer needed to romanticize their "exotics," as did Gauguin, Melville, or D. H. Lawrence. Their characters could be more realistic. Such realism was not always a gain, Bellow admitted, but it did make all characters—even the most "Jewish"—more accessible.[102] This accessibility, in turn, rendered the Jewish-writer tag "false and wrong." Still, he did not blame the Jews for applying it. They were forced to strengthen their public position whenever possible: "Since the holocaust they have become exceptionally sensitive to the image the world has of them and I think that they expect Jewish writers to do good work for them and propagandize for them. In that respect I was a great disappointment to them. Since then, Philip Roth has made me more acceptable by writing *Portnoy's Complaint.* Naturally, they prefer Malamud and me to the sexual wildmen who have recently appeared in fiction."[103]

Notes

1. James Atlas, *Bellow: A Biography* (New York: Random House, 2000), 204.
2. Ibid.
3. Ibid.
4. Ibid.
5. Ibid.
6. Ibid.
7. Pearl K. Bell, "New Jewish Voices," *Commentary*, June 1981, 62.
8. Ibid.
9. Norman Podhoretz, *Making It* (New York: Random House, 1967), 3.
10. Ben Siegel, "Introduction: Erasing and Embracing the Past: America and

Its Jewish Writers—Men and Women," in *Daughters of Valor: Contemporary Jewish American Women Writers*, ed. Jay L. Halio and Siegel (Newark and London: University of Delaware Press/Associated University Presses, 1997), 36–37.

11. Irving Howe, *World of Our Fathers* (New York: Harcourt Brace Jovanovich, 1976), 594.

12. Mark Shechner, "Saul Bellow and Ghetto Cosmopolitanism," *Modern Jewish Studies Annual II* (1978): 37.

13. Bell, "New Jewish Voices," 62.

14. Shechner, "Saul Bellow and Ghetto Cosmopolitanism," 37.

15. Bell, "New Jewish Voices," 62.

16. Shechner, "Saul Bellow and Ghetto Cosmopolitanism," 37.

17. Thorstein Veblen, "The Intellectual Pre-Eminence of Jews in Modern Europe," *Political Science Quarterly* 34 (1919): 38.

18. Shechner, "Saul Bellow and Ghetto Cosmopolitanism," 37.

19. Bell, "New Jewish Voices," 62.

20. Ibid.

21. Judd L. Teller, "From Yiddish to Neo-Brahmin," in *Strangers and Natives: The Evolution of the American Jew from 1921 to the Present* (New York: Delacorte, 1968), 265.

22. Ibid., 266.

23. Saul Bellow, *Herzog* (New York: Viking, 1964), 308.

24. Teller, "From Yiddish to Neo-Brahmin," 266.

25. Ibid.

26. Ibid.

27. Ibid.

28. Ibid.

29. Ibid.

30. Alfred Kazin, "The Earthly City of the Jews," in *Bright Book of Life: American Novelists and Storytellers from Hemingway to Mailer* (Boston: Little, Brown, 1973), 133.

31. Saul Bellow, *Seize the Day* (New York: Viking, 1956), 56.

32. Leslie A. Fiedler, "Saul Bellow," in *To the Gentiles* (New York: Stein and Day, 1972), 103–10.

33. Eric Norden, "Playboy Interview: Truman Capote," in *Truman Capote: Conversations*, ed. M. Thomas Inge (Jackson: University Press of Mississippi, 1987), 158. This interview originally appeared in *Playboy*, March 15, 1968: 51–53, 56, 58–62, 160–62, 164–70.

34. Ibid.

35. Katherine Anne Porter, "A Country and Some People I Love," interview by Hank Lopez, *Harper's*, September 1965, 58, 68, reprinted in *Katherine Ann*

Porter Conversations, ed. Joan Givner (Jackson: University Press of Mississippi, 1987), 120, 134.

36. Ibid.

37. Edgar Kemler, *The Irreverent Mr. Mencken* (Boston: Little, Brown, 1950), 128.

38. Alan Lelchuk, "The Death of the Jewish Novel," *New York Times Book Review*, November 25, 1984, 38.

39. Gore Vidal, "Literary Gangsters," *Commentary*, March 1970, 62.

40. Joan Didion, "Falconer: Review of *Falconer* by John Cheever," *New York Times Book Review*, March 6, 1977. See also Arnold Foster and Benjamin R. Epstein's *The New Anti-Semitism* (New York: McGraw-Hill, 1974); and Alvin H. Rosenfeld's discussion of contemporary literary anti-Semitism in "What to Do about Literary Anti-Semitism," *Midstream* (December 1978): 44–50.

41. Teller, "From Yiddish to Neo-Brahmin," 268.

42. Michiko Kakutani, "A Talk with Saul Bellow: On His Work and Himself," *New York Times Book Review*, December 13, 1981, 28–29.

43. Ibid.

44. Ibid.

45. Ibid.

46. Philip Gillon, "Bellow's Credo," *Jerusalem Post Weekly*, December 24, 1974, 13.

47. Teller, "From Yiddish to Neo-Brahmin," 268.

48. Bellow, *Herzog*, 57–58.

49. Ibid., 54.

50. Saul Bellow, *Humboldt's Gift* (New York: Viking, 1975), 10.

51. Gillon, "Bellow's Credo," 13.

52. Saul Bellow, "Starting Out in Chicago," *American Scholar* 44 (Winter 1974–1975): 76–77.

53. Ibid., 77.

54. Walter C. Clemons and Jack Kroll, "America's Master Novelist," *Newsweek*, September 1, 1975, 39.

55. Bellow, "Starting Out in Chicago," 77.

56. Gordon Lloyd Harper, "Saul Bellow," in *Writers at Work: The Paris Review Interviews*, ed. George Plimpton (New York: Viking, 1968), 183.

57. Mark Harris, *Saul Bellow: Drumlin Woodchuck* (Athens: University of Georgia Press, 1980), 113–15.

58. Harper, "Saul Bellow," 183.

59. Lelchuk, "The Death of the Jewish Novel," 38.

60. Ibid.

61. Ibid.

62. Diana Trilling, "Letters: The Jewish Writer," *New York Times Book Review*, December 23, 1984, 21.
63. Bellow, "Starting Out in Chicago," 44, 73.
64. Harper, "Saul Bellow," 182–83.
65. Alfred Kazin, "The Earthly City of the Jews," in *Bright Book of Life: American Novelists and Storytellers from Hemingway to Mailer* (Boston: Little, Brown, 1973), 132.
66. Ibid.
67. Alfred Kazin, *New York Jew* (New York: Knopf, 1978), 42.
68. Ibid., 255.
69. Harper, "Saul Bellow," 182.
70. Patrick O'Sheel, "Laughter from the Styx," *Humanities* 7, no. 2 (1977): 4.
71. Joseph Epstein, "Saul Bellow of Chicago," *New York Times Book Review*, May 9, 1971, 12.
72. Sanford Pinsker, "Saul Bellow in the Classroom," *College English* 34, no. 7 (1973): 982.
73. Bellow, "Starting Out in Chicago," 72.
74. Epstein, "Saul Bellow of Chicago," 12.
75. Ruth Miller, *Saul Bellow: A Biography of the Imagination* (New York: St. Martin's, 1991), 43.
76. Ibid.
77. Epstein, "Saul Bellow of Chicago," 12.
78. Gillon, "Bellow's Credo," 13; see also "A Laureate for Saul Bellow," *Time*, November 1, 1976, 91.
79. O'Sheel, "Laughter from the Styx," 4.
80. "A Laureate for Saul Bellow," 91.
81. Digby Diehl, "Saul Bellow Waiting for Dreams to Begin," *Los Angeles Times Calendar*, March 21, 1971, 45.
82. Pinsker, "Saul Bellow in the Classroom," 982.
83. Gillon, "Bellow's Credo," 13.
84. Bellow, "Starting Out in Chicago," 72–73.
85. Jim Douglas Henry, "Mystic Trade—The American Novelist," *Listener*, May 22, 1969, 706.
86. L. H. Goldman, *Saul Bellow's Moral Vision: A Critical Study of the Jewish Experience* (New York: Irvington, 1983), 236.
87. Chirantan Kulshrestha, "A Conversation with Saul Bellow," *Chicago Review* 23, no. 4, and 24, no. 1 (1972): 13.
88. Ibid.
89. Ibid.
90. Ibid.

91. Ibid.

92. Alden Whitman, "For Bellow, Novel Is a Mirror of Society," *New York Times*, September 25, 1975, 44.

93. Walter C. Clemons and Chris J. Harper, "Bellow the Word King," *Newsweek*, November 1, 1976, 89.

94. Wyndham Lewis, *Rude Assignment: A Narrative of My Career Up-to-Date* (London and New York: Hutchinson, 1950).

95. Matthew C. Roudané, "An Interview with Saul Bellow," *Contemporary Literature* 25, no. 3 (1984): 275.

96. See Joseph Epstein, "A Talk with Saul Bellow," in *Conversations with Saul Bellow,* ed. Gloria L. Cronin and Ben Siegel (Jackson: University Press of Mississippi, 1994), 135. This interview appeared originally in the *New York Times Book Review*, December 5, 1976, 3, 92–93.

97. Whitman, "For Bellow, Novel Is a Mirror of Society," 44.

98. Cynthia Ozick, "Hanging the Ghetto Dog," *New York Times Book Review*, March 21, 1978, 47.

99. Ibid.

100. Kulshrestha, "A Conversation with Saul Bellow," 14.

101. Ibid.

102. Ibid.

103. Ibid.

3

Saul Bellow and the Absent Woman Syndrome: Traces of India in "Leaving the Yellow House"

Michael Austin

With increasing frequency, scholars are approaching Saul Bellow's texts with an eye on his female protagonists. While the vast majority of these critics focus on the inadequacy of Bellow's portrayal of women and the out-and-out misogyny evidenced in his male-female relationships, a few have tried to salvage something of the author's reputation by locating strong female characters in scattered Bellow texts and attempting to read these characters as rare examples of Bellow's ability to portray female characters with both sympathy and intelligence. With the publication of *A Theft* in 1989, Bellow critics were presented with a bona fide female Bellow heroine, someone who could serve as a focal point for debate over Bellow's inability to create positive female protagonists. Though *A Theft* represents Bellow's first novel-length treatment of a female heroine, it is not his first attempt to tell a woman's story. Bellow's 1958 short story "Leaving the Yellow House," written three decades before the publication of *A Theft*, presents the story of Hattie Waggoner, an aging desert dweller whose only tangible possession, her Yellow House, becomes the focal point of what some have called a typically Bellovian quest for meaning and identity.

The scholarly debate over "Leaving the Yellow House" has tended to focus on whether or not Hattie Waggoner should be considered a female forerunner of such prominent male protagonists as Tommy Wilhelm and Moses Herzog. Noriko M. Lippit, in affirming the proposition, insists that Hattie constitutes a partial rebuttal to Charles Newman's charge that "there is not a single woman in all of Saul Bellow's work whose active search for identity is viewed compassionately."[1] "While I agree, in the final analysis, with Mr. Newman's remark," Lippit writes, "I believe that Bellow's 'Leaving the Yellow House' (1958) provides an exception; Hattie . . . is a female searcher."[2] In a later article, Constance Rooke insists that Hattie's quest for identity cannot be viewed as on par with that of other Bellow heroes because the author stops drastically short of granting Hattie "the full status of 'sympathetic intellectual' that he grants to male protagonists: Hattie Waggoner is not a typical Bellow protagonist. While Bellow can grant Hattie certain of the characteristics which he has parceled out from his own riches for the male protagonists, and can accord her the sympathy which is due to her participation in such qualities, he is obliged because she is a woman to withhold the Bellowesque sine qua non of a genuine intellectual life. He cannot in a single leap make of her a woman, a sympathetic character, and an intellectual."[3]

Both Lippit and Rooke ask the same important question: Does "Leaving the Yellow House" present a substantial portrait of a female character searching for meaning and identity—one that would allow us to acknowledge Hattie Waggoner as the one female star in Bellow's constellation of quest heroes? On an even more basic level, though, both scholars ask us to consider how we should read Bellow's fiction within a critical environment that values gender equality and rejects the long tradition of sexism in literature. Can Bellow's reputation as a misogynist be rehabilitated by examining a story like "Leaving the Yellow House," or does this story confirm, from yet another perspective, Bellow's reluctance or inability to portray women in a subject position?

While these are precisely the questions that concern me in this article, I propose to approach them from a slightly different perspective. Instead of looking only at Hattie Waggoner and her "active search for identity," I would like to consider Hattie in relation to the character I consider to be a second protagonist in the story—India (no last name given), the mysterious woman who brought Hattie into her house as a maidservant and subsequently left her the Yellow House in her will. Approaching "Leaving the Yellow House" from India's perspective presents certain challenges: she has been dead for years when the story begins, she is mentioned only a few times in the text, and what mention we do have of her comes entirely through Hattie's confused and unreliable memory. Nevertheless, given what we do know about India, I would argue that she exerts a tremendous influence over the way we should read the story, both because she successfully accomplished what Hattie seems unable to do—decide to whom to leave the Yellow House—and because she helps define, through opposition, the character traits that make Hattie unable to come to resolve this important matter. India's influence, and her importance to my analysis of gender relations in this story, stems directly from the way that she uses power in her relationship with Hattie. India is a very powerful woman, and while powerful woman are not necessarily a rarity in Bellow's fiction, India seems to be able to access types of power that have generally been considered "masculine"—and this fact alone makes her worthy of substantial analysis by anyone concerned with the status of women on Mr. Bellow's planet.

As I have already suggested, India exists in this story not as a full-fledged, present-tense character, but as a specter—the long-dead benefactor who managed simultaneously to both save and ruin Hattie's life by leaving her the Yellow House. In the deconstructionist's vernacular, India might be described as a "trace," or that part of a binary opposition that has been erased but that continues to define both the remaining term in the equation and the system as a whole. In typically dense prose, Jacques Derrida defines the trace as follows: "The trace, where the relationship with the other is marked, articulates its possibility in the entire field of the entity, which metaphysics has defined as the being-present starting from the occulted movement of the trace. The trace must be thought before the entity. But the movement of the trace is necessarily occulted, it produces itself as self-occultation. When the other announces itself as such, it presents itself in the dissimulation of itself 'as such,' has always already begun and no structure of the entity escapes this."[4]

As a trace, India functions in constant, unseen opposition to Hattie, the ostensible protagonist of the story, and represents a fixed nature against which the definition of "Hattie" can take place. The initial India–Hattie opposition serves as a focal point for all of the binary terms that go into the making of Hattie. India was rich, cultured, and well traveled; Hattie is poor, uneducated, and tied to one place. When they lived together, India was the property owner, the provider, and the master, while Hattie was the tenant, the beggar, and, ultimately, the slave. Each of these binary oppositions stems from the one overarching dichotomy that feminist critics see as the organizing opposition of our culture: the masculine versus the feminine. These two terms, which should not be confused with the biological terms *male* and *female,* each represent a store of culture constructions and stereotypes about power and gender-identity. India, who occupies the "male" space in each system, correspondingly exercises a masculine form of power on Hattie; Hattie, on the other hand, relegated to the "female" space, has access to a much more limited type of power—one that stems from passivity rather than action.

The gendered nature of the India–Hattie dichotomy becomes especially clear in view of what Bellow deigns to tell us about their past relationship. Though the text contains very little about the time Hattie spent with India—it is, after all, the story of Hattie's life years after India's death—what does come through suggests that it was an emotionally abusive relationship of the sort generally associated with a dominating male figure: "Literature. Education. Breeding. But Hattie's interest in ideas was very small, whereas India had been all over the world. India was used to brilliant society. India wanted her to discuss Eastern religion, Bergson, and Proust, and Hattie had no head for this, and so India blamed her drinking on Hattie. 'I can't talk to you,' she would say. 'You don't understand religion or culture.'"[5]

If India's criticisms of Hattie are stereotypically "male," Hattie's responses are equally "female." She submits patiently to India's tirades and never raises her voice to her benefactor. "I am a Christian person," Hattie would respond. "I never bear a grudge."[6] Of course, when Hattie was still living with India, she could never have afforded to bear a grudge even if she had wanted to. India owned the Yellow House, and Hattie depended on the older woman completely for shelter and support.

Ultimately, India manipulated Hattie by creating an economic dependency. She seemed to compel both servitude and sycophancy by subtly promising the house to Hattie and tacitly threatening to take this gift away at any time. By manipulating Hattie in this way, India converted her one potential asset—the Yellow House—into a hard currency that enabled her to hire a servant, a nursemaid, and a court jester without ever having to spend any real money. The unstated threat of eviction kept Hattie's frontier spirit in check and ensured that India would have the physical and emotional needs of her final days met. We might realistically assume—though Bellow never says so directly—that India used Hattie's eventual inheritance of the Yellow House as a bargaining chip in whatever tacit negotiations for services occurred between the two. Hattie, who has never worked a day in her life and seems unable to perform even the smallest tasks in the world outside of the Yellow House, seemed to have no choice but to submit to India's regime.

What all of this amounts to is that India manipulated her wealth quite skillfully in her dying days. This might be, I admit, a somewhat cynical take on the relationship between the two women, but it points unquestionably to the point I wish to establish here: that India manifests an impressive ability to negotiate the traditionally male field of economic hegemony, an ability that makes her a singular character in the Bellow universe. While Bellow has created a number of extremely strong female characters, India is perhaps the only one who exercises power in such a typically male fashion. Other Bellow heroines—such as Valeria (the dying Romanian matriarch in *The Dean's December*) and Sorella Fonstein (the indomitable wife in *The Bellarosa Connection*)—epitomize the perfection of traditionally female modes of power. They derive their ability to influence others precisely from the fact that they are good wives, good mothers, or powerful matriarchs. India, on the other hand, exhibits none of these qualities of a "good woman." Except for the unsubstantiated accusation of an affair with Wicks, India is never mentioned in connection with a man, be it a father, a husband, a son, or a lover. She does not depend on her relationship to a man for her power, but instead manipulates Hattie the same way that men have controlled women for centuries: by making herself the provider of a sustenance that can be taken away at any time.

Though reflections about India occupy only a few paragraphs in the story, she constantly peeks through the pages of the text as the buried half of the oppositions that define Hattie. When the story actually opens, Hattie finds herself in the same situation that India once faced: she is lonely, aging, and emotionally needy. Unlike India, however, Hattie cannot seem to find a solution. From the opening paragraph, we are alerted to the fact that Hattie is in need of somebody to take care of her as she took care of India: "The neighbors . . . told one another that old Hattie could no longer make it alone. The desert life, even with a forced air furnace in the house and butane gas brought from the town in a truck, was still too difficult for her. . . . Hattie was not exactly a drunkard, but she hit the bottle pretty hard, and now she was in trouble and there was a limit to the help she could expect from even the best of neighbors."[7] As the story progresses, we are increasingly made aware that Hattie has neither the financial nor the emotional resources necessary to live on her own and that she would have perished years ago had India not left her the Yellow House. When an automobile accident forces Hattie to acknowledge these needs, she sets out to find a way to do what India did: convert the Yellow House into some form of negotiable currency.

Like India, Hattie has clear title to the Yellow House, and even though she has little prospect of finding a buyer for it, she does have a number of options that would allow her to meet her temporal needs adequately. Throughout the story, Hattie receives and rejects two offers that would allow her to convert the potential asset of her house into tangible assets such as emotional and financial support. The first of these comes when Amy Walters offers, through Jerry Rolfe (who, knowing Hattie, refuses even to mention the matter to her), to make the same contract explicitly that Hattie made with India implicitly: to live with her and take care of her in exchange for the right to inherit the Yellow House. The second offer comes from her neighbor, Pace, who offers to give Hattie five hundred dollars up front and fifty dollars a month perpetually in exchange for the same privilege. While both Amy and Pace are clearly interested only in taking advantage of Hattie's needs, both of their offers represent the same type of bargain that India once made with Hattie: she would gain something that she needs now without having to part with anything until after she has died and doesn't need anything at all.

More than anything else about the house, however, Hattie seems to cherish the fact that the Yellow House is hers to bequeath or dispose of as she sees fit. Unlike India, she does not intend to exchange her birthright for economic sustenance. But even though she rejects economic gain as a criterion for leaving the Yellow House to somebody, she seems unable to come up with an alternative, and so she chooses to do nothing at all. In her long interior monologue on the subject, she brings up and rejects a number of possible bases for making a decision, including family loyalty, pride, love, and friendship:

> And first of all she wanted to do right by her family. None of them had ever dreamed that she, Hattie, would ever have something to bequeath. Until a few years ago it had certainly looked as if she would die a pauper. So now she could keep her head up with the proudest of them. And, as this actually occurred to her, she actually lifted up her face with its broad nose and victorious eyes.... She returned to the old point of her struggle. She had decided many times and many times changed her mind. *Who would get the most out of the Yellow House?* It was a tearing thing to go through.[8]

The problem here is that, while Hattie revels in her ability to leave the house to somebody, she is unable to articulate a suitable criterion for deciding to whom to leave it. Unlike India, who knew exactly what she wanted in exchange for the Yellow House, Hattie, playing with essentially the same cards, can come to only one decision: to get drunk and take up the decision later. India acted decisively and manipulated her economic assets, and she did so with some degree of skill. Hattie, on the other hand, even when presented with a fairly large set of options for disposing of the house and meeting her own needs, becomes impotent, crippled by her own indecision, and ultimately self-destructive.

To understand why Hattie cannot make these decisions, we must once again invoke the notion of India as part of the series of binary oppositions that define Hattie. As I have already argued, India and Hattie occupy spaces that our society has traditionally coded as "masculine" or "feminine." As a corollary to this statement, I would further propose that Hattie represents a feminine cultural space that can be considered "domestic," while India represents the masculine space that we would usually call "foreign." Even India's name—the name of an exotic foreign country—stresses her identification with the nondomestic sphere. The domestic–foreign dichotomy, when applied to a more localized gender economy, becomes the dichotomy between home and work, with the former generally considered the woman's sphere and the latter the domain of the man. This crucial opposition explains the differences in the way the two women treat "leaving the yellow house." India is able to see bequeathing the house as a business proposition—one that works particularly well for her in that it enables her to practically enslave Hattie. Hattie, on the other hand, operating from a culturally coded feminine/domestic viewpoint, sees the house as a home; it is part of the domesticity that defines her. Hattie's ultimate nondecision about the house reveals the extent to which her own identity is wrapped up in her home: "Even though by my own fault I have put myself in this position. And I am not ready to give up on this. No, not yet. And so I'll tell you what, I leave this property, land, house, garden, and water rights, to Hattie Simmons Waggoner. Me! I realize this is bad and wrong. Not possible! Yet it is the only thing I really wish to do, so may God have mercy on my soul."[9]

I now return to my initial question: Does "Leaving the Yellow House" present an atypically sympathetic picture of a woman in Bellow's fiction? Yes and no. Certainly Hattie Waggoner resembles many of Bellow's men: she is confused, helpless, and desperately searching for both personal identity and metaphysical meaning. I would assert, however, that the portrait Bellow draws of Hattie does not, in any substantial sense, contradict Bellow's other characterizations of women; she like, most other Bellow females, is allowed to occupy only the various spaces that our culture has coded as feminine. India, on the other hand, represents something genuinely different: she represents the "male" half of the binary oppositions that Bellow often uses in his writing; she occupies, in other words, a masculine space. This statement has important implications. One of the most persistent problems for feminist Bellow critics is that the author forces most of his female characters into stereotypically female spaces—thus confirming the arbitrary social distinctions that serve as the basis for all gender inequality. Had "Leaving the Yellow House" actually been India's story, seeing her in this masculine space might force us to conclude that, at least once, Bellow indulged in a bit of feminist-postmodern gender bending. But such an optimistic reading of the story ignores the fact that India's character has been almost completely erased. India's character must be drawn from inferences, suppositions, and from seeing the space around Hattie that she must have once filled.

This brings us to the one vital Derridean opposition that I have consciously avoided so far: the presence-absence binary. India is a powerful character, true, but she is also an absent character; she has been erased from the text in a way that obscures her true importance. Next to Hattie, I would argue, India is the most important character in "Leaving the Yellow House"; however, the reasons for her importance must be re-created from a few fragments. But this reconstruction does not lie beyond our grasp. The ghost of India, though obscured by the text, cannot be completely excised as long as we can see her trace in and around Hattie. The vital terms that we must use to define India exist, albeit inverted, in the terms that Bellow uses to describe his heroine, and the presence that India exerts throughout the story becomes increasingly visible as we survey the lack that surrounds Hattie. The deconstructive techniques that allow us to perceive India throughout the text also allow us to reconstruct the operative dichotomies—such as masculine-feminine, foreign-domestic, master-servant, and absent-present—that pervade the text, resulting in a picture of India as a powerful female character, occasionally obscured by the narrative, but unwilling to be completely suppressed by the text.

Notes

This essay was originally published in *Saul Bellow Journal* 11/12 (1993–1994). It is reproduced here with the author's permission.

    1. Newman quoted in Noriko M. Lippit, "A Perennial Survivor: Saul Bellow's Heroine in the Desert," *Studies in Short Fiction* 12 (1975): 281.

    2. Ibid.

    3. Constance Rooke, "Saul Bellow's 'Leaving the Yellow House': The Trouble with Women," *Studies in Short Fiction* 14 (1977): 185–86.

    4. Jacques Derrida, *Of Grammatology* (Baltimore: Johns Hopkins University Press, 1974), 47.

    5. Saul Bellow, *Mosby's Memoirs and Other Stories* (New York: Penguin, 1971), 21.

    6. Ibid.

    7. Ibid., 7.

    8. Ibid., 40.

    9. Ibid., 43.

4

The Politics of Art: The Colonial Library Meets the Carnivalesque in *Henderson the Rain King*

Daniel K. Muhlestein

> I do not consider myself a racist, and I think that people who call me a racist are very wrong.
> —Saul Bellow

> Not only has Bellow drawn on what Mudimbe has called "The colonial library," he has unfortunately added a work to it.
> —Daniel Lamont, "A Dark and Empty Continent"

Saul Bellow is the author of more than a dozen novellas and novels. He has been awarded both the Pulitzer Prize and the Nobel Prize in Literature and is generally considered one of the greatest writers of the twentieth century. Bellow's work also reflects the aesthetics and ideology and politics of his era, and in recent years critics have begun to explore the possibility that Bellow's most significant novels—many of which were written before and during the civil rights movement—contain elements of racism, either through overt description and characterization or through the strategic omission of black characters or the notion of blackness per se.[1]

Bellow's sexually charged and racially stereotyped description of a black pickpocket in *Mr. Sammler's Planet* has received the most intense critical discussion to date,[2] but while all of Bellow's novels are amenable to analysis in terms of his use—and potential misuse—of black figures and racial stereotypes, the best core sample of Bellow's attitude toward race is

Henderson the Rain King, the one Bellow novel that includes a preponderance of black characters. Critics have evaluated the use of race in *Henderson* from a variety of perspectives, but most contemporary analysis revolves around two related issues: the ways in which the novel uses blackness as a strategic foil against which whiteness can be defined and affirmed, and the extent to which the novel reproduces the racist ideology embodied in what V. Y. Mudimbe and others call "the colonial library."

Toni Morrison raises the first issue in *Playing in the Dark: Whiteness and the Literary Imagination.* In an evidentiary aside near the end of "Romancing the Shadow," Morrison points to *Henderson* as one of a series of American novels in which a racially charged image of blinding whiteness is both contingent upon and called into being by way of its strategic juxtaposition to what Morrison calls American Africanism. American Africanism, Morrison observes, is "a dark and abiding presence that moves the hearts and texts of American literature with fear and longing" and that does so precisely in order to confer upon American whiteness the signal attributes of selfhood and self determination.[3] To Morrison, *Henderson* is an obvious example of the necessary if sometimes repressed connection between American whiteness and its defining, enabling, haunting shadow:

> In *Henderson the Rain King* Saul Bellow ends the hero's journey to and from his fantastic Africa on the ice, the white frozen wastes. With an Africanist child in his arms, the soul of the Black King in his baggage, Henderson dances, he shouts, over the frozen whiteness, a new white man in a new found land: "leaping, pounding, and tingling over the pure white lining of the gray Artic silence."
>
> If we follow through on the self-reflexive nature of these encounters with Africanism, it falls clear: images of Blackness can be evil *and* protective, rebellious *and* forgiving, fearful *and* desirable—all of the self-contradictory features of the self. Whiteness, alone, is mute, meaningless, unfathomable, pointless, frozen, veiled, curtained, dreaded, senseless, implacable. Or so our writers seem to say.[4]

Morrison's brief comment on *Henderson* is echoed in most contemporary analysis of the novel, including Carol R. Smith's "The Jewish Atlantic—The Deployment of Blackness in Saul Bellow," included in this volume, the most complete amplification to date of Morrison's initial insight. Smith's broad-ranging essay includes a lengthy section on *Henderson* in which

Smith uses Morrison's analysis of American Africanism as a framework from within which to rethink the motivation behind Henderson's decision to go to Africa. Henderson goes to Africa, Smith concludes, both because Africa represents for him an "absolute geography of racial difference,"[5] which allows him to highlight his American whiteness by way of contrast with African blackness, and because Africa simultaneously presents him with a convenient symbol of miscegenation which he can joyfully annihilate. In Smith's reading of the novel, the polliwogs in the Arnewi water supply "can be read as barely suppressed . . . and displaced stereotypes of Blackness as sexual, animalistic, and stupid";[6] the frogs' combination of dark bodies and white legs can be interpreted as miscegenation; and Henderson's decision to blow up the frogs can be understood as his response to the threat to his sense of whiteness posed by the actions of his children, one of whom wanted to marry a Central American woman, and the other of whom evidently gave birth to a mixed-race child: "With their central signification of the union between white and black equaling death, both of these narratives threaten the stability and whiteness of Henderson's identity. His journey to Africa can thus be read as much as a flight from the union of black and white as a quest to revitalize his WASP ancestry. . . . In Africa, Henderson can act on and literally kill his fear of the mixing of black and white, which helped prompt his flight from America in the first place."[7]

Smith points out that "Henderson's journey is both related to and carefully distanced from previous European colonial invasions of Africa,"[8] and in "'A Dark and Empty Continent': The Representation of Africa in Saul Bellow's *Henderson the Rain King*," Daniel Lamont works some of the same critical terrain by calibrating the ideological and aesthetic distance between *Henderson* and another important colonial library text, Joseph Conrad's *Heart of Darkness*. Both *Henderson* and *Darkness,* Lamont observes, are obvious examples of colonial discourse, and both are fictional extensions of what Mudimbe in *The Idea of Africa* calls the colonial library: "a body of knowledge constructed with the explicit purpose of faithfully translating and deciphering the African object."[9]

Examples of colonial library narratives range all the way from David Livingstone's journal entries to Rider Haggard's *King Solomon's Mines* and Henry Stanley's *Through the Dark Continent,* include the reports of such disparate adventurers and anthropologists as Sir Richard Burton and Melville Herskovits, and extend as far into the present as Samantha Gillison's

1999 novel *The Undiscovered Country* and such films as *Apocalypse Now*, which reimagines the colonial imperative by re-creating it in war-torn Vietnam. But though the colonial library is so large as to preclude a definitive list of characteristics, the foundation of the genre is a cluster of related assumptions about white superiority and black inferiority. "It is clear," writes Lamont in his summary of the colonial library, "that there has been an Eurocentric construction of hierarchies built around the dichotomy between civilization and barbarism and the consequent of a spectrum which runs: civilization—barbarism, savagery, primitivism. The tropes of savage and primitive are interesting and recurrent. While there has been an element of romanticizing the noble savage, both tropes are used to confirm a sense of racial superiority which diminished the aboriginal inhabitants and devalued their culture" (133).

In Lamont's analysis of *Henderson* and *Darkness*, he argues that although both texts are part of the colonial library, Conrad's novella undercuts the library in ways Bellow's novel does not. After juxtaposing Chinua Achebe's critique of Conrad in "An Image of Africa: Racism in Conrad's *Heart of Darkness*" with Sven Lindqvist's defense of the novella in *Exterminate All the Brutes,* Lamont writes: "I share Lindqvist's reading of the novella; it must be read as a critique of imperialism, even if that critique is somewhat oblique. Marlow is not Conrad and there is a critical difference between the author and narrator which is crucial to a full understanding of the text" (132). In his analysis of *Henderson,* however, Lamont reaches exactly the opposite conclusion. He notes that like Marlow, Henderson uses colonial library terms in ways which reveal "a prejudiced, even racist attitude" (135). But unlike in *Darkness,* in *Henderson* "the reader is not distanced from Henderson by any kind of narrative as in Conrad" (143). The layered narrative structure of Conrad's novella—Lamont concludes—critiques the colonial library in ways the simple narrative structure of Bellow's novel does not.[10]

Neither does Lamont believe that the comic elements in *Henderson* significantly undercut the colonial library upon which the novel is based. Lamont notes that *Henderson* is a "comic fantasy" (146) that has "many elements of the picaresque" (140). He also acknowledges that Henderson is more than a mere reproduction of traditional colonial attitudes; he is also "a parody of them" (141). "Henderson," Lamont reiterates, "is a parodic figure, perhaps even a parodic Marlow" (145). But rather than take seriously the possibility that the parodic and comic elements in *Henderson* work in much the same ways as do the multiple narrators in *Darkness,* Lamont chooses instead to set aside the vexed but important question of the extent to which comic transgressions potentially undercut colonial library ideology. Indeed, from Lamont's perspective, an analysis of the function of the comic elements in the novel represents a dead end at best and a moral failing at worst. "It would be appropriate to read *Henderson the Rain King* as a symbolic fantasy," he acknowledges toward the end of his essay, but then warns: "Such a reading, however, does not absolve Bellow from complicity in imperialist discourse. . . . The question of race is inescapable in the novel and it is too easy to hide behind the fact that the novel is a comic fantasy" (144, 146).

Because *Henderson* slots so comfortably into the colonial library, because unlike *Darkness* it has only one narrator, and because Lamont sets aside the question of the extent to which the novel's comic features potentially subvert its colonial ideology, Lamont concludes that both *Henderson*'s narrator and its author are de facto racists. "From the casual way he uses words such as 'savage,' 'primitive,' and 'barbaric,'" Lamont observes, "it is obvious that Henderson does not really criticize the colonializing point of view" (142). And because there is no clearly articulated gap between the novel's narrator and its author, "Bellow" himself, Lamont concludes, "is implicated in a colonialist discourse" (135): "Bellow has created a romanticized mythical Africa. The novel perpetuates many of the preconditions and stereotypes that I have outlined. The Africans are presented as childlike, charming and ineffectual or duplicitous, primitive and harsh. . . . Bellow seems to recognize this new imperialism and implicates it, but it is not clear that he fundamentally criticizes it. Henderson . . . is an agent of the new Imperium. Not only has Bellow drawn on what Mudimbe has called 'the colonial library,' he has unfortunately added a work to it" (146, 147).

Simultaneously Reproducing and Unsettling the Colonial Library Narrative

In many respects, Lamont's critique of *Henderson* seems justified. In fact, Bellow's novel contains not one but three interwoven iterations of the colonial library narrative, each of which is problematic on its own terms. In two of the three cases, however, Bellow's version of the colonial library narrative does more than merely reproduce the colonial library: it also applies torque to that library in ways which potentially unsettle it and—in certain instances, at least—call it into question. In part this may be because Henderson seems preternaturally aware of how easily his narrative slots into the colonial library. Indeed, he spends much of the first part of the novel attempting to explain and justify his decision to go to Africa.

At the beginning of the novel, Henderson—who is living in Connecticut with his wife, children, and a passel of pigs—is in absolute despair. He knows that his wealth and standing are the ill-gotten gains of exploitation and colonization—"My ancestors," he remarks candidly, "stole land from the Indians. They got more from the government and cheated other settlers, too"[11]—and as a consequence he feels like an interloper who will be secretly relieved to be found out: "When the rightful one appeareth we shall all stand and file out, glad at heart and greatly relieved, and saying, 'Welcome back, Bud. It's all yours. Barns and houses are yours. Autumn beauty is yours. Take it, take it, take it!'" (34). But though Henderson frankly acknowledges both the unearned benefits of colonial theft in specific and the unearned benefits of whiteness in general, he nevertheless asserts that white guilt is not what drives him from his home and wealth and family. Indeed, white colonial guilt is a thing Henderson has become impressively—if not entirely—comfortable with, through long association. "What has that got to do with it?" he asks derisively, when considering the possible connection between his ill-gotten wealth and his desire to flee America (21).

Instead, Henderson considers and provisionally rejects a number of more prosaic reasons for his misery and desire to leave, including the death of his brother and his parents, his dysfunctional family, his bizarre collection of pigs, his temperament, and his general sense of uselessness. But though Henderson remains confused as to the causes of his despair, the sense of loss and longing that despair engenders rings in his ears night and day: "Now I have already mentioned that there was a disturbance in my heart, a voice that spoke there and said *I want, I want, I want!* It happened every afternoon, and when I tried to suppress it it got even stronger. It only said one thing, *I want, I want!*" (24).

For a long time, Henderson tries to fill the void given voice by that relentless *I want!* through commodity fetish, sexual conquest, and communion with his pigs. Eventually, though, he realizes that his attempts to fill the void in his life are bound to fail because they address manifest symptoms rather than the latent cause of his misery, which is his growing awareness of the inexorability of death. When Henderson happens across an octopus, he sees in it a portent of death—"The tentacles throbbed and motioned through the glass, the bubble sped upward, and I thought, 'This is my last day. Death is giving me notice'" (19). And when he discovers the body of an old spinster, he is so shaken by the sight of her corpse that he decides to flee America at once in search of a new beginning, or at least a better end—a land beyond the horizon in which something can be made of nothing and junk can be exchanged for authentic experience:

> Dead! Her small, toothless face . . . was growing cold. The soul, like a current of air, like a draft, like a bubble, sucked out of the window. I stared at her. So this is it, the end—farewell? And all this while, these days and weeks, the wintry garden had been speaking to me of this fact and no other; and till this moment I had not understood what this gray and white and brown, the bark, the snow, the twigs, had been telling me. . . . "So for God's sake, make a move, Henderson, put forth effort, You, too, will die of this pestilence. Death will annihilate you and nothing will remain, and there will be nothing left but junk. Because nothing will have been and so nothing will be left. While something still *is—now!* For the sake of all, get out." (39, 40)

In his desire to absolve himself of ancestral sins, in his desire to make something of himself and test himself and face death in such a way as to transform the dross of his life into something of real value, Henderson fits comfortably within the colonial narrative of the white man who goes to Africa. Indeed, Henderson himself admits as much when he asks, rhetorically, "Is it any wonder I had to go to Africa?" (32). And yet there is still a sense in which Africa is for Henderson a contingent rather than a necessary destination. His decision to go to Africa has as much to do with what he is leaving behind as with where he is headed, and had Charlie—with whom Henderson hitches a ride to Africa—been going somewhere else, Henderson would have likely been willing to have gone there instead: "It was with Charlie that I took off for Africa, hoping to find a remedy for my situation. I guess it was a mistake to go with him, but I wouldn't have known how to go right straight into Africa by myself. You have to have a specific job to do" (41). In that sense, the story of Henderson's journey to Africa cuts against the typical colonial library narrative. He chooses Africa on a mere "whim"—to use Ihab Hassan's provocative word[12]—and he initially views both the continent and its people as contingent others rather than the Demonic Other, his desired destination being "not Africa *per se* but a sphere of reality, or a state of mind, liberated from the tyranny of death."[13]

Indeed, in important respects Henderson initially views the inhabitants of Africa neither as the Demonic Other nor even as contingent others but rather as invisible—or at least irrelevant—others. Henderson does not go to Africa to meet Africans, demonic, angelic, or otherwise. He goes to Africa because a ride is conveniently at hand and because Africa represents for him an apparent opportunity to flee America, to simplify his life, and to escape history. "My object in coming here," he observes shortly after arrival, "was to leave certain things behind" (45), and in his attempt to simplify life, he sheds the bulk of his possessions and parts ways with everyone but Romilayu, welcoming his guide's offer to take him "off the beaten track" (44). Henderson is searching for a land beyond inhabitation and before history, and for a short time he foolishly believes he has found exactly that: "I got clean away from everything, and we came into a region like a floor surrounded by mountains. It was hot, clear, and arid and after several days we saw no human footprints. . . . [I]t was all simplified and splendid, and I felt I was entering the past—the real past, no history or junk like that. The prehuman past. And I believed that there was something between the stones and me" (46). In mythologizing Africa this way, Henderson exemplifies one of the earliest versions of the colonial library narrative: the white search for an undiscovered country—undiscovered, that is to say, in the sense that it is generally uninhabited by Caucasians. Thus far Henderson neither hates the African natives nor wants to save them nor wants to use them as a foil against which he can discover his existential white identity. Indeed, at this point in the novel the natives do not enter into his extended consideration at all. He is blind to their material existence in the most profound sense of that word.

When Henderson stumbles across the Arnewi tribe, however, he shifts from one version of the colonial library narrative to another. Abandoning his quest for the oblivion of a prehistory unencumbered by other humans, he opts instead for Rousseau's strategic reconfiguration of that narrative in the form of the ideology of the noble savage. Henderson is initially disappointed to learn that Prince Itelo speaks English: "You thought first footstep? Something new? I am very sorry. We are discovered" (53). But when Henderson meets Queen Willatale, he becomes obsessed with the notion that the queen can provide him with the answers to life itself. When

Willatale thrusts Henderson's hand between her breasts, he immediately discovers in her heartbeat a pulsation "as regular as the rotation of the earth . . . as if I were touching the secrets of life" (72), and before he has known her for even a day, Henderson resolves to ask Willatale "the best way to live" (81): "I believed the queen could straighten me out if she wanted to; as if, at any moment now, she might open her hand and show me the thing, the source, the germ—the cipher. The mystery, you know. I was absolutely convinced she must have it" (79). In the process, Henderson replaces the search for an undiscovered country with the hoped-for discovery of a primitive oracle, a maternal black other so intimately connected to nature that the land itself can speak to him through her.

As soon as Henderson begins to think of Willatale in specific and the Arnewi in general as noble savages from whom the secret of life might be obtained, he unites that version of the colonial library narrative with its Eurocentric alter ego, the ideology of the white man's burden. Indeed, fragments of this ideology surface even before Henderson meets the queen. When he sees a weeping Arnewi woman, for example, he bursts out in a dramatic monologue even Kipling would have loved: "The poor soul is in trouble? Is there something I can do for her? She's coming to me for help. I feel it. Maybe a lion has eaten her family? Are there man-eaters around here? Ask her, Romilayu. Say that I've come to help, and if there are killers in the neighborhood I'll shoot them" (50).

After meeting the queen, however, Henderson resolves not merely to save a single woman but to rescue an entire tribe. Although Henderson promises to respect the tribe's beliefs, his actual goal is to circumvent those beliefs in such a way as to free the Arnewi from what he takes to be their culturally induced stupidity. When Prince Itelo tells Henderson that frogs have polluted the water cistern, Henderson at first tries to persuade the prince to eliminate them, and when that fails, he resolves to bear the natives' burden himself and kill the frogs: "I realized I would never rest until I had dealt with these creatures and lifted the plague . . . [Itelo] and all the rest of the Arnewi would consider me their very greatest benefactor" (61). Indeed, Henderson is so taken with the thought of rescuing the Arnewi and impressing the queen that he fantasizes about it at length: "I went so far as to imagine that the queen would elevate me to a position equal to her own. But I would say, 'No, no. I didn't leave home to achieve power or glory, and any little favor I do you is free'" (94).

In spite of Henderson's embarrassing tendency to commingle vainglory and wish fulfillment, his attempt to help the Arnewi regain access to their water supply differs from most attempts described in colonial library accounts of the white man's burden in one important respect: in general, Henderson does not view himself as being superior to the Arnewi, but as an equal partner with them. "I thought," he observes in an important moment of reflection and analysis, "this will be one of those mutual-aid deals; where the Arnewi are irrational I'll help them, and where I'm irrational they'll help me" (87). Nevertheless, other aspects of Henderson's account of his time among the Arnewi slot comfortably into the colonial library, including his desire to give the children chocolate (48), the cheap trinkets he offers Itelo and others (73), his assertion that the English and the Arnewi use their different languages to conceptualize the world in radically different ways (56), and his failed attempt to impress the Arnewi women and children by setting fire to a bush: "'How do you think they'd like it if I set fire to the bush with this lighter?' And without waiting for Romilayu's advice I took out the Austrian lighter with the drooping wick, spun the tiny wheel with my thumb, and immediately a bush went flaming, almost invisible in the strong sunlight" (48).

Consequently, Henderson's second iteration of the colonial library narrative—an iteration which commingles the ideology of the glorification of the noble savage with that of the assumption of the white man's burden—produces an account which overlays competing black and white cultural claims in interesting but problematic ways. This hybrid version of the colonial library narrative matches the stories of various medical and missionary colonialists Henderson admires, including Albert Schweitzer (23) and Sir Wilfred Grenfell (78). It is perhaps not surprising, then, that the image which most fully expresses the problematic nature of this version of the colonial library narrative is Henderson's description of Romilayu at prayer, a description which highlights, in the most material way possible, what happens when Rousseau's glorification of the noble savage is grafted—Derrida-like—onto Kipling's notion of the white man's burden: "The scars and mutilations showed that he had been born a pagan, but somewhere along the way he had been converted, and now he said his prayers every evening" (45).

Henderson's third iteration of the colonial library narrative begins when he and Romilayu visit the Wariri tribe and its king, Dahfu. There, as before, Henderson goes in search of the meaning of life. There, as before, he retains at least fragments of Kipling's ideology of the white man's burden. But at the same time, he trades in Rousseau's romantic veneration of the noble savage for a more recent and more overtly antagonistic version of the colonial library narrative: the view of African natives expressed most fully—and most infamously—in Conrad's *Heart of Darkness,* which novella is of course the object of a substantial part of Lamont's analysis.

When Henderson asks his guide about the Wariri tribe, Romilayu responds, "Dem no good people like the Arnewi. . . . Dem chillen dahkness" (114, 115). In Henderson's account of this most secluded and isolated of the African tribes (an isolation which seems intended to suggest that the Wariri represent the truest essence of African blackness), Romilayu's pronouncement proves prophetic. Indeed, within a day of Henderson's arrival, the Wariri of his third iteration of the colonial narrative are presented as though they are a de facto case study in human depravity—a depravity so profound as to border on inhumanity. The first Wariri whom Henderson meets leads him into an ambush. The first group of Wariri whom Henderson meets threatens to kill him. His first night in the Wariri settlement is spent in the company of a corpse, which Henderson interprets as a test of strength and cunning—a test he dares not fail upon pain of death. The next morning he discovers that the Wariri settlement is festooned with the bodies of people who had been hung the day before. The Wariri festival Henderson attends later that day includes both ritual human mutilation and animal sacrifice, an act so commonplace that when the priest slit the cow's throat "Nobody took much notice" (176). Even more shocking is the Wariri method of succession to the throne, a form of ritual strangulation which, when he learns of it, causes Henderson to blurt out in amazement and anxiety, "Oh, no, Christ! . . . Strangled? . . . What sort of outfit is this?" (157, 158). In short, the Wariri of Henderson's account are not noble savages but savages pure and simple—a word Henderson repeats time and again in this part of the novel. They are deceitful. They are violent. They are bloodthirsty. And when Henderson meets them in the light of day in their full festival attire, they dress and act in ways which hearken back to Conrad's strategic use of the term "frenzied":

> Some of the men wore human jaw bones as neckpieces under their chins. The idols and fetishes were being dressed up and whitewashed, receiving sacrifices. An ancient woman . . . had dumped yellow meal over one of these

figures and was swinging a freshly killed chicken over it. Meanwhile the noise grew in volume, every minute something new added, a rattle, a snare drum, a deeper drum, a horn blast, or a gunshot. . . . And the screams, the excitement! The roars, the deep drum noises. . . . The frenzy was so great it was metropolitan. There was such a whirl of men and women and fetishes, and snarls like dog-beating and whines like sickles sharpening, and horns blasting and blazing into the air, that the scale could not be recorded. The bonds of sound were about to be torn to pieces. . . . At least a thousand villagers must have been in this mob, most of them naked, many painted and gaudy, all using noisemakers and uttering screams. (146, 169, 170)

In all those respects, Henderson's account of his time among the Wariri becomes the antithesis of Rousseau's romanticism and the rough equivalent of Conrad's dark tale, just as Lamont argues it does. Nevertheless, although Henderson reproduces many of the motifs favored by the narrator of *Heart of Darkness*, and although in *Henderson the Rain King* the Wariri are represented as being a strange brew of demonic frenzy, overt sexuality, and death, Henderson's third iteration of the colonial literature narrative includes one extremely important mitigating factor. That mitigating factor is Henderson's description of King Dahfu.

To a certain extent, Henderson's account of the king of the Wariri fits the colonial library stereotype of the Demonic Other uncomfortably well. To Henderson, Dahfu's most striking physical characteristic is his black skin, a color so dark that it makes Dahfu seem almost inhuman to the white traveler:

Of course the king's extreme blackness of color made him fabulously strange to me. He was as black as—as wealth. By contrast his lips were red, and they swelled; and on his head the hair lived (to say that it grew wouldn't be sufficient). Like Horko's, his eyes revealed a red tinge. . . . We sat close together, and as I have noted, his blackness made him fabulously strange to me. . . . It didn't seem possible that the black of his face could be exceeded, and yet his hair, visible at the borders of his hat, was blacker. (207, 209, 262)

Further, although Dahfu is intelligent and charming and well educated, Henderson soon begins to worry about the king's soundness of mind. When Dahfu presses Henderson to read various of the king's favorite books, Henderson resists and delays, remarking to himself, "I was afraid to find out that the king might be a crank" (243). And after Dahfu pressures Henderson into spending time with the lion Atti in a vain attempt to have Henderson absorb her characteristics, Henderson—who is frankly terrified during the ordeal—admits: "I came near holding a grudge against the king at that moment. I should have realized that his brilliance was not a secure gift, but like this ramshackle red palace rested on doubtful underpinnings" (269).

In addition, from beginning to end Henderson is never entirely confident that he understands the king, or can trust him. Soon after meeting Dahfu, Henderson frets: "As I couldn't trust him, I had to understand him. Understand him? How was I going to understand him? Hell!" (161). And even after the two men have spent considerable time together, Henderson cautions himself: "And now this powerful black personage who soothed me—but was he trustworthy? How about trustworthy? . . . I felt we were men of unusual dimensions. Trustworthiness was a separate issue" (210, 211). In Dahfu's extreme blackness, then, in his philosophical quirkiness, and in his apparent lack of trustworthiness, the king seems—at least at first blush—to represent the logical endpoint of the kind of pejorative colonial library narrative exemplified by *Heart of Darkness,* which perhaps explains why, midway through the rain king carnival, Henderson says of Dahfu: "When you got right down to it, he was a savage, too. He still dangled a skull (of perhaps his father) by the long smooth ribbon and wore human teeth sewed to his large-brimmed hat" (195). In that sense, Lamont's analysis of Henderson's response to King Dahfu is entirely correct.

But to focus only—or even primarily—on that aspect of Henderson's response to Dahfu is surely to mistake the part for the whole. In the end, the most salient fact about the relationship between the two men is how completely Henderson comes to admire, respect, and love the Wariri king. Although Henderson initially focuses on the king's dark skin, for example, he is not repelled by that blackness, nor does he interpret it as evidence of moral depravity. Rather, Henderson is impressed with the king's sense of dignity and overwhelmed by the king's physical beauty: "I wish to say at this place that the beauty of King Dahfu's person prevailed with me as much as his words, if not more. His black skin shone as if with the moisture that gathers on plants when they reach their prime. His back was long and muscular. His high-rising lips were a strong red. Human perfections are short-lived, and we love them more than we should, maybe. But I couldn't help it. The thing was involuntary" (214). Henderson also eventually realizes that Dahfu has Henderson's best interests at heart, even in—indeed, especially in—the case of the female lion. Watching the king's joyful interaction with Atti, Henderson marvels: "On her own animal level it was clear . . . that she loved the guy. Loved him! With animal love. I loved him too. Who could have helped it?" (227). This friendship between a black king and a white traveler becomes the defining characteristic of Henderson's account of his time among the Wariri. Because of his friendship with Dahfu, Henderson is devastated by the king's death:

> The king had rolled himself from the lion. I pulled him farther away. Through the torn clothing his blood sprang out.
> "Oh, King! My friend!" I covered up my face.
> The king said, "Wo, Sungo." . . . I never took another death so hard. (310, 314)

And because of his friendship with Dahfu, Henderson comes to understand both the necessity of and humanity behind the king's willingness to allow Henderson to be set up to become the next Sungo: "But the king lived under threat of death himself, and what he lived with I could live with. He was my friend" (317).

Henderson's friendship with Dahfu is important because it calls into question one of the grounding assumptions upon which such colonial library narratives as *Heart of Darkness* are typically based. Shortly before his death, Dahfu reminds Henderson that true friends see each other as individuals rather than as racial or ideological categories for which a rubric or template would be appropriate: "Maybe because we are friends. One sees much more in a friend. Rubrics will not do with friends" (300). Henderson's account of Dahfu says exactly the same thing of the Wariri king. Dahfu is not merely—or even primarily—the black king of an exotic African tribe, Henderson's account of Dahfu declares. Dahfu is a unique individual, a human subject, a person worthy of loyalty and love: "I will never regret my feeling toward this man—Dahfu, I mean," Henderson significantly concludes. "I would have done a great deal more to keep his friendship" (288).

The most obvious representation of Henderson's deep regard for Dahfu is his treatment of the lion cub, which he nurses to health and brings to America after the king's death. The lion cub is by no means an unproblematic symbol. Indeed, in important respects it articulates the same double-edged cluster of meanings as does the image of Romilayu at prayer. But as the material embodiment of the friendship between a black king and a white traveler, the lion cub also stands as an implicit rebuke to the colonial library notion that the African other is a Demonic Other. Whatever else King Dahfu is, he is most certainly not *that*. As Henderson observes, shortly after meeting Dahfu: "There was something about this man that gave me the conviction that we could approach ultimates together. . . . My heart proclaimed a holiday" (156, 162).[14]

From Carnival to Carnivalesque to Critique

It seems clear, then, that although *Henderson* does in fact reproduce a cluster of related versions of the colonial library, it simultaneously applies torque to those narratives in ways which deform them and which call into question the racist ideologies upon which they are based. Part of this process of subversive deformation occurs at the level of plot and manifests itself most obviously as a willful rejection of the colonial drive for formal and ideological closure. As we have seen, in *Henderson* colonial ideologies are articulated precisely in order to be subverted, and colonial expectations are raised precisely in order to be dashed. The colonial narratives in the novel are potentially subverted in another important way as well. They are shot through with comedy, the carnivalesque, and grotesque realism, all of which are grafted into *Henderson* in ways which potentially transform this iteration of the colonial library into a de facto celebration of postcolonial perspectives and values.

As Robert F. Kiernan points out, *Henderson* is a parody of quest fiction that is comic in both the general and technical senses of the term.[15] Scenes, incidents, characters, and dialogue are developed and presented for comic effect, and in even the most somber moments in the novel, serious content is intermixed with levity and farce. Like a number of other second-generation postwar authors, Bellow portrays his white traveler protagonist not as a hero but "as clownish, incompetent or powerless,"[16] as what M. S. Bradbury rightly calls "a metaphysical comedian, a supernatural bumbler with aspirations for his soul, a psycho-braggart speaking the romantic vaunt of self."[17] Henderson's prayer during a moment of acute stress and authentic danger illustrates the extent to which *Henderson* commingles high seriousness with comic relief: "And I prayed and prayed, 'Oh, you . . . Something.' I said, 'you Something because of whom there is not Nothing. Help me to do Thy will. Take off my stupid sins. Untrammel me. Heavenly Father, open up my dumb heart and for Christ's sake preserve me from unreal things. Oh Thou who tookest me from pigs, let me not be killed over lions. And forgive my crimes and nonsense and let me return to Lily and the kids'" (253).

The novel typically brackets serious moments and material by enfolding them within a comic framework, and the parts of *Henderson* which most closely approximate colonial library narratives virtually always end in the sort of epic comic failure which calls into question the validity of the narratives themselves. "I was confounded down to the ground," Henderson ruefully confesses, looking back on his initial attempts to impress the Arnewi. "I had been boasting, 'Show me your enemies and I'll kill them. Where is the man-eater, lead me to him.' And setting bushes on fire, and performing the manual of arms, and making like a regular clown. I felt extremely ridiculous" (52, 53). The scene in which Henderson blows up the frogs—which will not be quoted because of its length—is simultaneously "meant to criticize Western good intentions" and played for comic effect,[18] as is his subsequent description of its failure (106–12). And even the climactic moment in which Henderson attempts to become one with the lion Atti is shot through with comedy, farce, and potty humor: "Oh, King, what can I do? My openings are screwed up tight, both back and front. They may go to the other extreme in a minute. My mouth is all dried out, my scalp is wrinkling up, I feel thick and heavy at the back of my head. I may be passing out" (262). The salient point is not merely that *Henderson* is a comic novel, but that the comedy in *Henderson* so often makes fun of the colonial library narratives upon which the novel is based. And in making fun of them, it calls them into question.

The most subversive elements in *Henderson*, however, the parts of the novel which most effectively call into question the colonial library narratives after which the novel is patterned, are not necessarily comic per se, but rather are carnival, or—to be more precise—what Mikhail Bakhtin calls the carnivalesque and associates with grotesque realism. In *Rabelais and His World*, Bakhtin observes that in medieval Europe, officially sanctioned festivals and pageants and other like-minded public occasions engendered a variety of folk-culture comic alternatives which served as both a counterbalance to and implicit critique of the officially sanctioned activities. Bakhtin initially focuses on ritual spectacles, comic verbal compositions, and carnival speech, but over time his exploration of the carnivalesque begins to center on the notion of carnival laughter—the type of voiced

The Politics of Art

communal psychological release which occurs when conventional political and economic hierarchies are temporarily inverted, conventional religious and social mores are temporarily disregarded, and classical notions of order, decorum, and beauty are temporarily set aside in favor of what Bakhtin calls "the sense of the gay relativity of prevailing truths and authorities . . . , a continual shifting from top to bottom, from front to rear, of numerous parodies and travesties, humiliations, profanations, comic crownings and un-crownings."[19]

The search for carnival laughter, and for the important sense of psychological release such laughter simultaneously expresses and affords, is central to *Henderson,* and the novel is so overflowing with examples of the carnivalesque that dissertations have been written on the subject.[20] And though an analysis of the political implications of each instance of the carnivalesque and of grotesque realism would extend well beyond the scope of this essay, two representative core samples will illustrate the extent to which carnival laughter and grotesque realism tend to undermine and call into question the colonial library narratives upon which the novel is based: Henderson's wrestling match with Prince Itelo and the carnival which culminates in the crowning of the new white Sungo.

Henderson's wrestling match with Itelo is an illuminating example of what Bakhtin calls carnival spectacle. In an obvious sense, the match embodies the ideology and perspective of the colonial library. The match is, after all, a de facto competition between cultures and races as well as between Henderson and Itelo, and the match dramatizes—or at least appears to dramatize—white superiority: Henderson wins the match, Itelo is authentically bitter, and the African prince makes himself subservient to the white traveler, all of which fits neatly within the colonial library's narrative of racial superiority: "The prince now got on his knees, scooping dust on his head, and then he took my foot in the suede, rubber-soled desert boot and put it on his head. In this position he cried much harder than the maiden and the delegation who had greeted us by the mud-and-thorn wall of the town" (69).

At the same time, however, Henderson's fanciful and overtly comic description of the wrestling match simultaneously undercuts his purpose for traveling to Africa and calls into question the colonial narrative upon which this part of the novel is based. Although the wrestling match is understood to be an officially sanctioned part of Arnewi culture, Henderson's description of that match transforms it into a carnival spectacle in Bakhtin's sense of that word. During the match, the most obvious symbols of Henderson's colonial status—his white helmet, passport, money, and papers—fly hither, thither, and yon in a comic display of confused agitation. Henderson later strips to the waist—a carnivalesque expression of grotesque realism in its own right—and throws the prince by butting Itelo with his ample stomach, a stomach "on which," Henderson wryly observes, "the name of Frances once tattooed had suffered some expansion" (66). The two men huff and puff in the dust and grit, and in the climactic moment in the match, Itelo's attempt at a leg grab fails not because the prince lacks sufficient strength or skill but because Henderson is so fat that Itelo has to wrap his legs around the wrong part of Henderson's body.

On one level, then, the wrestling match is played entirely for keeps, but on another level—the level of the carnivalesque—it is played entirely for laughs, the sort of carnival laughter which is designed to simultaneously degrade and uplift. And while that laughter implicitly calls into question the Arnewi culture upon which the match is based, in the process it also calls into question Henderson's Arnewi-specific version of the colonial narrative. Henderson came to Africa to discover the essence of life, and to do so by exploring the determinate relationship between truth and power, the relationship—as he puts it—between truth and blows. During the wrestling match, Henderson has an important epiphany about that relationship, an epiphany which potentially justifies his journey to Africa. Midway through the match, Henderson receives a blow to the nose. Rather than angering him, that blow reminds him of an earlier blow and—in the process—produces an insight Henderson appreciates without yet fully understanding:

> I got a bad blow on the nose. . . . But somehow I managed to keep a space clear in my brain for counsels of moderation, which was no small achievement in itself. Since that day of zero weather when I was chopping wood and was struck by the flying log and thought, "Truth comes with blows," I had evidently discovered how to take advantage of such experiences, and this was useful to me now, only it took a different form; not "Truth comes with blows" but other words, and these words could not easily have been stranger. They went like this: "I do remember well the hour which burst my spirit's sleep." (67)

Henderson came to Africa precisely to have such an epiphany—"Your Highness," he reminds Prince Itelo midway through the match, "I am really kind of on a quest" (65)—and the colonial library narrative upon which this part of the novel is based is structured in just such a way as to facilitate it. However—and this is the key point—in describing the wrestling match in terms of carnival, farce, and grotesque realism, Henderson calls into question not merely the validity of the match but also—and as a consequence—the validity of the resulting epiphany. The carnival laughter engendered by the former drowns out the potential insight made possible by the latter, and will continue to do so for the bulk of the rest of the novel. In that sense, the carnival elements in this part of *Henderson* simultaneously authorize and undercut the purpose for Henderson's trip and—by proxy—the unitary language and ideology of the colonial narrative upon which that trip is based.

Soon after arriving in the Wariri village, Henderson participates in a second type of carnival spectacle, one which begins with a critique of the Demonic Other but ends in a celebration of grotesque realism. After talking with Dahfu, Henderson accompanies the king to a native festival. On the way to the arena, Henderson once again emphasizes how loud the Wariri are, how frantic and animalistic they seem: "And the screams, the excitement! The roars, the deep drum noises, as if the animals were speaking again by means of the skins that had once covered their bodies!" (169). The first part of the festival includes ritual mutilation, animal sacrifice, and a skull-tossing contest between King Dahfu and a striking native woman who is painted gold, covered with ritual scars, and naked to the waist. Henderson is taken with the woman and mesmerized by the contest, but his description of the events emphasizes the essential otherness of the Wariri participants and spectators. The woman especially, Henderson concludes, "looked somewhat inhuman" (175), and his response to the contest culminates in a symptomatic moment of free association in which he reminds himself that Dahfu's other female attendants "were wild savages" (176). To this point in the carnival, the Wariri remain for Henderson the Demonic Other.

The first part of the carnival is also a carnival which is not at all carnivalesque from the Wariri perspective. The mutilations and animal sacrifice and skull-tossing contest are all part of official Wariri culture and are overseen and participated in by the king. As such they are part of what Bakhtin would call Wariri culture's "serious official, ecclesiastical, feudal, and political cult forms and ceremonials,"[21] which are precisely that part of a culture against which the carnivalesque responds. Neither does this first part of the carnival serve a carnivalesque function within Henderson's colonial library account, for at this point in the novel he points to the mutilations, the animal sacrifice, and the contest as evidence that the Wariri are truly savages. Henderson's description of these early carnival activities is thus part of unitary language insofar that it affirms the ideology of white superiority upon which the colonial library narratives are based. Carnival does not always equal the carnivalesque, either in culture or in narrative.

The second part of the carnival, however, includes a number of activities which begin to slide toward the carnivalesque, both for the Wariri and for Henderson's narrative. The second set of carnival activities are still sanctioned by the state, but the king does not participate in them, and they seem custom-built to elicit the kind of mockery and laughter which typically call into question dominant institutions and ideologies. The first of these "Roman holiday high jinks"—as Henderson calls them (177)—elicits laughter designed primarily to loosen up the audience: "An old woman wrestled with a dwarf, only the dwarf lost his temper and tried to hurt her, and she stopped and scolded. One of the amazons entered the field and picked up the tiny man; with a swinging stride she carried him away under her arm. Cheers and handclapping came from the grandstands" (177). Once the Wariri audience has been induced to adopt what might be called a carnivalesque perspective, however, carnival laugher is directed at one of the pillars of Wariri society, its gods:

> Several men in black plumes . . . began to lift the covers from the gods. Disrespectfully, they pulled them away. This irreverence was not accident, if you get what I mean. It was done to raise a laugh, and it did exactly that. These bird or plume characters, encouraged by the laughter, started to perform burlesque antics; they stepped on the feet of the statues, and bowled some of the smaller ones over and made passes at them, mockeries, and so on. The dwarf was set on the knees of one goddess and he rocked the crowd with laughter by pulling his lower lids down and sticking out his tongue, making like a wrinkled lunatic. . . .
>
> By and by they began to move the whole pantheon. Bodily. They started with the smaller gods, whom they handled very roughly and with a lot of wickedness. They let them fall or rolled them around, scolding them as if they were clumsy. (180–81)

This unexpected display of carnivalesque disrespect initially shocks and offends Henderson, who declares, "Hell! . . . To me it seemed like a pretty cheap way to behave. . . . I didn't care one bit for this. Grumbling, I sat under the shell of my helmet and tried to appear as if it was none of my business" (181). But by the time only the two heaviest idols remain to be moved, Henderson has embraced the carnivalesque aspects of the carnival so fully that he cheers mightily for the last participant, and when Turombo fails to move the heaviest idol, Mummah, Henderson begs King Dahfu to allow him to move Mummah himself: "Sir, sire, I mean . . . let me! I must" (187).

As Henderson shifts from being a disparaging colonial observer to an enthusiastic spectator to a willing participant, he begins to narrow the gap between himself and the Wariri and—in the process—to call into question the hierarchical binary upon which colonial library narratives most obviously depend: the absolute difference between Africans and Americans, blacks and whites. After he moves Mummah, the Wariri "jumped up and down . . . screaming, singing, raving, hugging themselves and one another and praising me" (192), and for the moment, at least, Henderson is content to bask in their adulation. In doing so, he simultaneously reproduces and intensifies an earlier moment during the carnival, when he had been so taken with the sound and drama of the moment that he "was impelled to make a sound, and therefore I uttered a roar like the great Assyrian bull" (171). Then, as now, the Wariri crowd had roared back its approval. Then, as now, Henderson had been thrilled by the acclaim: "I roared. And the acclaim was magnificent. For I was heard. I was seen gripping my chest as I bellowed. The crowd went wild over this, and its yells were, I have to admit it, just like nourishment to me" (172). And in both instances, the gap between black and white and self and other is at least temporally effaced—carnivalesque moments of considerable significance in a colonial narrative apparently grounded in the notion of absolute difference: "I was so gladdened by what I had done that my whole body was filled with soft heat, with soft and sacred light. . . . My spirit was awake and it welcomed life anew. Damn the whole thing. Life anew. I was still alive and kicking and I had the old grun-tu-molani" (192–93).

Unfortunately, both moments of carnivalesque unity at the Wariri carnival fade quickly. As Henderson watches Turombo, he suddenly realizes that the Bunam has been similarly watching Henderson—an uncanny reversal of the usual colonial gaze—and that the Bunam has been setting up Henderson as Turombo's carnival replacement: "But I understood now why the corpse had been quartered with me. The Bunam was behind it. He sized me up right. He had wanted to see whether I was strong enough to move the idol" (188). And although Henderson remains eager to move Mummah and to receive the further adulation of the crowd, he resents being manipulated, especially by an impudent black man whose wizened face seems to be saying to the white traveler, *"Dummy! . . . Listen! Harken unto me, you shmohawk!"* (187). In playing Henderson for a fool, the Bunam inverts the white/black binary of racial superiority upon which the colonial library narrative is based, but—and this is the key point—he inverts the binary rather than eliminates it, and as the Mummah scene plays out to its conclusion, Henderson's recognition that he is being manipulated by the Bunam begins to bleed the joy out of his impromptu carnivalesque union with the Wariri crowd.

In addition, when Henderson asks permission to move Mummah, he feels compelled to explain his reasons for wanting to do so. The husk of his motivation remains a stale version of the white man's burden, but its kernel is now revealed to be the kind of egotism which effaces the difference between self and other precisely by making the self the de facto center of the universe: "For here was my chance. I knew I could do this, . . . and I flowed, I burned to go out there and do it. Craving to show what was in me. . . . Let these Wariri whom so far (with the corpse in the night and all in all) I didn't care for—let them be worse than the sons of Sodom and Gomorrah combined, I still can't pass up this opportunity to *do,* and to distinguish myself. To work the right stitch into the design of my destiny before it was too late" (185–86).

Thus, although Henderson here frankly acknowledges that egocentrism rather than generosity has become—and perhaps always has been—the driving force behind his recent actions in Africa, his admission paradoxically strengthens rather than undercuts the preexisting ideology of the white man's burden, for his admission reconceptualizes that burden as the strongest possible form of manifest destiny: the manifest destiny of the ego itself. Under the terms of Henderson's most current iteration of the colonial library narrative, he romps through Africa neither to do the Africans good nor because the Africans themselves are good but simply to work out his destiny *through* them, regardless. If the Arnewi and Wariri are no longer seen as the Other (in either its noble or its demonic form), that is not because Henderson has recognized the other's independent selfhood but because to him only the self truly exists. Everything else remains a convenient tabula rasa onto which the majestic self records its history and enacts its destiny.

It is perhaps not surprising, then, that the carnivalesque aspects of Henderson's moment in the Wariri spotlight fade almost as soon as they begin. Within moments of expressing his love for Dahfu—"I was grateful to him. I was his friend then. In fact, at this moment, I loved the guy" (193)—Henderson downgrades his opinion of the Wariri king dramatically, declaring, "When you got right down to it, he was a savage, too" (195). And when the eyes of the Wariri crowd remain upon Henderson after he returns to his seat, he feels not a continued sense of connection and identity but a sudden outburst of anxiety and difference: "And these people had turned on me all the darkness, all the expectancy, all the wildness, all the power, of their eyes. . . . And under all this scrutiny of black eyes I began to worry" (195). Carnivalesque is as carnivalesque does, and at this point in the novel, Henderson's carnival disruptions of the colonial library narrative seem destined to last only a moment or two.

Except, of course, that in accepting the king's wager and moving the idol, Mummah, Henderson unknowingly set off a chain of events which now culminate in the kind of grotesque realism which is—in Bakhtin's view at least—one of the most powerful articulations of the carnivalesque. Because Henderson moved Mummah, he now occupies "a position of rain king of the Wariri. The title of this post is the Sungo. You are now the Sungo, Mr. Henderson" (196). As Sungo, Henderson is immediately forced to endure a cluster of humiliating rituals which, taken as a whole, almost perfectly embody what Bakhtin understood to be the most characteristic literary expression of the carnivalesque: grotesque realism.

Grotesque realism depicts the human body in exaggerated and often comic ways, and in the novel Henderson is depicted in precisely those terms, "as a grotesque: a huge man in knee-pants refusing to let go of his childish place of safety and assurance."[22] His face is repeatedly described in terms simultaneously comic and mythopoetic—"My face is like some sort of terminal," he laments at one point, "it's like Grand Central, I mean—the big horse nose and wide mouth that opens into the nostrils, and eyes like tunnels" (51)—and his body in general and ample stomach in particular are uncovered, examined, poked, prodded, and mocked at regular intervals, all for comic—and carnivalesque—effect.

Henderson always seems to be taking off his shirt (his wrestling match with Prince Itelo is one obvious example), and when he isn't busy stripping down to his skivvies, others frequently prompt him to do so. The Bunam asks Henderson to remove his T-shirt—a shirt which was, Henderson observes with a laugh, "greatly in need of a wash" (143)—and then examines his torso, prompting Henderson to give a comic account of the tattoo which misshapes itself as it traverses his hanging belly (143). Queen Willatale similarly examines Henderson at length, concluding that Henderson has gone to seed in face and body alike:

> "She say now, Mistah Henderson, that you have a great capacity, indicated by your largeness, and especially your nose." My eyes were big and sad as I touched my face. Beauty certainly vanished. "I was once a good-looking fellow," I said, "but it is certainly a nose I can smell the whole world with. It comes down to me from the founder of my family. He was a Dutch sausage-maker. . . ." "She say . . . [y]ou not young, Mistah Henderson. You weigh maybe a hundred-fifty kilogram; your face have many colors. You are built like an old locomotif. Very strong, yes, I know. Sir, I concede. But so much flesh as a big monument. . . ."
> I listened, smarting at his words. . . . And then I sighed and said, "Thank you for your frankness. . . . I want her to read me the whole indictment. . . . Lust, rage, and all the rest of it. A regular bargain basement of deformities." (82, 83)

Even King Dahfu gets in on the act: "'Well,' he said, 'you seem a mos' interesting person. Especially in point of physique. Exceptional,' he said. 'I am not sure I have ever encountered your category'" (155).

In grotesque realism, the body is not merely exaggerated and treated comically; it also suffers what Bakhtin calls strategic "degradation, that is, the lowering of all that is high, spiritual, ideal, abstract."[23] Abstract ideals and religious pieties are made flesh at the bodily level of food, drink, digestion, and sexual activity, and special emphasis is placed on the lower parts of the anatomy—the belly, the sexual organs, the buttocks. Grotesque realism is in that sense a form of ritual humiliation, which is of course exactly what happens to Henderson when he is crowned rain king. He is stripped, shamed, and ritually humiliated, all in precisely grotesque realism fashion:

> The examiner came up behind and lifted off my helmet, while the stiff old generaless . . . removed my shoes. After this, useless to resist, she took off my Bermuda shorts. This left me in my jockey underpants, which were notably

travel-stained. Nor was that the end, for as the Bunam dressed me in vines and leaves, the generaless began to strip me of even the last covering of cotton. "No, no," I said, but by that time the underpants were already down around my knees. The worst had happened, and I was naked. . . . I thought I would give a cry and fall and perish of shame. (197–98)

Pursued by a band of chanting, naked Amazons, Henderson sprints through the streets of the village, crying "Ya-na-bu-ni-ho-no-mum-mah!" (198). When the group reaches the cattle pond, "the women drew up there, leaping and chanting, and then about ten of them threw themselves upon me. They picked me up and gave me a heave that landed me in the . . . water" (198). Extracting Henderson from the water, the women drive him back to the arena, begin whipping the idols, and force Henderson to do the same:

The women about me were dancing, if you can call it that. They were bounding and screaming and banging their bodies into me. . . . And now I wanted to fall on the ground to avoid any share in what seemed to me a terrible thing, for these women, the amazons, were rushing upon the figures of the gods with those short whips of theirs and striking them. "Stop!" I yelled. "Quit it! What's the matter? Are you crazy?" . . . My hand, which had the whip still in it, was lifted once or twice and brought down so that against my will I was made to perform the duty of the rain king. . . . Caught up in this madness, I fended off blows from my position on my knees, for it seemed to me that I was fighting for my life. (200–201)

Throughout the ritual, Henderson is confused and terrified. He is also furious at the Wariri, at one point comparing them to animalistic children of darkness in typical *Heart of Darkness* fashion: "Those children of darkness, the tribe, rose and screamed like gulls on stormy water" (201). In that respect Henderson's account of the concluding ceremony in the Wariri carnival simultaneously draws upon and reinforces some of the very worst aspects of the colonial library narrative. In other respects, however, Henderson's description of the ceremony calls into question the colonial library narrative in precisely the ways Bakhtin thought grotesque realism might. As Henderson is stripped, humiliated, and driven from pillar to post, he begins to lose his old sense of identity: "With swollen throats the amazons cried and howled, and I, lumbering with them, tried to remember who I was. *Me*" (199). He is then effectually reborn in the storm that follows, which rebirth is from Bakhtin's perspective the ultimate point of grotesque realism. "To degrade," Bakhtin observes,

> is to bury, to sow, and to kill simultaneously, in order to bring forth something more and better. . . . To degrade an object does not imply merely hurling it into the void . . . but to hurl it down to the reproductive lower stratum, the zone in which conception and a new birth take place. Grotesque realism knows no other lower level; it is the fruitful earth and the womb. It is always conceiving.[24]

It is perhaps not surprising, then, that Henderson describes the end of the ceremony in terms which gesture toward a type of mental transformation for which physical birth would provide a fit metaphor: "The amazons with their wet bodies began to embrace me. I was too stunned to push them off. . . . Then I met Romilayu, who recoiled from me as if I were dangerous to him. . . . [H]is face showed great fear. 'Romilayu,' I said, 'please man, you've got to help me. Look at the condition I'm in.' . . . Naked, I held on to him" (201, 202). From this perspective, the rain-king ceremony is not demonic but generative. Henderson come to Africa to be transformed, and during the rain-king ceremony he is transformed indeed: he is stripped, humiliated, thrust down into muddy earth, brought back out again, purified by pain, sanctified by ritual, and washed clean by rain—a man effectually born again by way of "his participation in these transforming ceremonies."[25] For that he has the Wariri tribe—and only the Wariri tribe—to thank. Only by becoming an active participant in the Wariri carnival could Henderson become a new man, and in becoming a new man, Henderson proves the worth of Wariri culture.

As a consequence, Henderson's colonial library narrative is born again as well—or if not born again at least transformed in terms of its representation of the relationship between self and other, American whiteness and African blackness. Although Henderson is the one transformed through grotesque realism, Wariri culture is the determinate source of that transformation, and from beginning to end the Wariri call the shots and determine the outcome. Henderson is wrong; the Wariri are right. He is transformed; they affect that transformation and use it to bring water to their land. He loses his bet; they acquire a Sungo. And although as Sungo Henderson is next in line for the throne, ascension to the throne is the one thing most Wariri want desperately to avoid. Making Henderson rain king thus dramatizes how clever the Wariri are and how foolish he is. "I am obliged to tell you, Mr. Henderson," declares King Dahfu when Henderson begs to be allowed to move Mummah, "there may be consequences." "I should have taken him up on this," Henderson responds in a moment of extraordinary understatement, "But . . . a powerful ambition had me and I was a goner" (189).

Henderson the newly minted rain king is thus ultimately two creatures in one: a new man called into being through grotesque realism and an old fool who clings stubbornly to remnants of the colonial library narrative. His foolishness, like his newness, is on perpetual display, and its recurring presence in *Henderson* calls into determinate question the notion of white supremacy upon which the colonial library narrative depends. This is of course a truth that Henderson will not fully apprehend until the very end of the novel, if at all, but as early as the morning after the storm he has at least some inkling of how foolish he has been: "This is how I became the rain king. I guess it served me right for mixing into matters that were none of my damned business" (203). Bakhtin would be proud, both of Henderson's Wariri-inspired grotesque realism transformation and of the extent to which the emergent carnivalesque elements in his account of that transformation threaten to press the residual colonial library narrative aspects of that same account into something approximating chaos.

Contextualizing the Functions of Heteroglossia in *Henderson*

Although the colonial narrative which drives *Henderson* is saturated with heteroglossia in its comic, carnival, and grotesque forms, the political implications of the resulting strange brew of high seriousness and the carnivalesque are not entirely self-evident and depend—at least in part—on which conceptual framework is chosen for their analysis. In Bakhtin's own writings, the carnivalesque, grotesque realism, and heteroglossia are usually—although not invariably—seen as sites of resistance which call into question the force and validity of both unitary language and the political and ideological forces which propagate it. To Bakhtin, heteroglossia is typically dialogical in both the weak and strong senses of that term: weak in the sense that any polyglot text such as *Henderson* embodies a subterranean dialogue between dominate and subordinate languages, ideologies, and power structures; and strong in the sense that over time the persistence of that dialogue demands of the reader the recognition that "the ideological systems and approaches to the world that were indissolubly connected with these languages contradicted each other and in no way could live in peace and quiet with one another—then the inviolability and predetermined quality of these languages came to an end, and the necessity of actively choosing one's orientation among them began."[26] From this perspective, *Henderson* is best understood as an overtly political and potentially radical text, not because it overdetermines the reader's choice between the colonial narratives and the heteroglossia which disrupts them, but precisely because the novel highlights that choice *as* a choice. The text—that is to say—demands of the reader a dialogical response to the competing claims of colonial discourse and its carnival alternatives.

While Bakhtin valorizes the subversive political potential of heteroglossia, Stephen Greenblatt emphasizes the ways in which such potentially subversive impulses can be used—almost against themselves—to reinforce the status quo. In "Invisible Bullets: Renaissance Authority and Its Subversion," Greenblatt points out that in many cases, "subversive insights are generated in the midst of apparently orthodox texts and simultaneously contained by those texts, contained so efficiently that the society's licensing and policing apparatus is not directly engaged."[27] Greenblatt further observes that orthodox texts frequently use any of three related methods to generate subversive insights in such a way as to ensure that those insights end up reinforcing the very orthodoxy with which the text begins: testing, recording, and explaining. In Thomas Harriot's *A Brief and True Report of the New Found Land of Virginia,* for example, Harriot—at least in Greenblatt's reading of the text—tests the subversive Machiavellian hypothesis about the political nature of religion but then proves the hypothesis true in such a way as to guarantee the continuation of the Virginia colony. Harriot also records the Native American's subversive alternative theories about the source of illness but does so in such a way as to encourage white missionaries to flood into the colony. Finally, Harriot explains the ideology of the white colonists in ways which simultaneously call it into question and reinforce its veracity. In every case, subversion is generated in precisely such a way as to ensure that its appearance in the text ultimately strengthens both the text's unitary language and the notion of white supremacy which underwrites Harriot's narrative. "There is subversion," Greenblatt concludes at the end of his interpretation of *Brief and True Report,* "no end of subversion, only not for us."[28]

Seen from this perspective, *Henderson* is best understood as a conservative—and perhaps even reactionary—text. The novel applies torque to several versions of the colonial library narrative and in each case proves that the racist ideologies upon which the narratives are based are pernicious and false. But in an important sense, the same mechanisms of grotesque realism and the carnivalesque by which those racist ideologies are tested and proven false simultaneously undercut the significance of the results of the tests by framing them within a context which is apparently both comic and carnival—in a word, *unserious*. The novel reproduces the potentially subversive perspectives of various African tribes as those perspectives have been recorded by such meticulous and evenhanded twentieth-century anthropologists as Melville Herskovits. But *Henderson* simultaneously contains the potentially subversive aspects of Herskovits's accounts by indiscriminately commingling them with the inflammatory and racially biased accounts of African practices and perspectives written by Sir Richard Burton during the height of the colonial endeavor a full century earlier. Every time Henderson attempts to explain the colonial library ideology which serves as the justification for his actions in Africa, his explanations ring hollow even to himself and are politely ignored by his incredulous African hosts: "'Do you know why the Jews were defeated by the Romans? Because they wouldn't fight back on Saturday. And that's how it is with your water situation. Should you preserve yourself, or the cows, or preserve the custom? I would say, yourself. Live,' I said, 'to make another custom. Why should you be ruined by frogs?' The prince listened and said only, 'Hm, very interestin'. Is that a fact? 'Strodinary'" (61–62). But although Henderson's explanations of his ideology are always entirely inadequate, the form of their expression—which tends always toward comic overstatement—contains the subversive implications of that inadequacy by transforming the explanations themselves into sources of comic relief. From Greenblatt's perspective, then, *Henderson* is best understood as a politically reactionary novel which tests, records, and explains for the same reasons as does Harriot's *Brief and True Report:* both texts generate subversive insights precisely in order to contain them.

There is, however, a third way to conceptualize the relationship between the colonial library narratives upon which *Henderson* draws and the many instances of grotesque realism and the carnivalesque with which the novel is saturated. This third way revolves around a strategic rethinking of the question of means and ends. Thus far the carnivalesque and grotesque realism elements in *Henderson* have been viewed instrumentally, with Bellow being conceptualized as what Derrida, following Levi-Strauss, calls a *bricoleur,* someone who treats a culture's concepts and images and narratives as tools rather than the embodiment of truth, and who uses them as "'the means at hand,' that is, the instruments he finds at his disposition around him, those which are already there, which had not been especially conceived with an eye to the operation for which they are to be used and to which one tries by trial and error to adapt them, not hesitating to change them whenever it appears necessary, or to try several of them all at once, even if their form and their origin are heterogeneous—and so forth."[29] Viewed this way, comedy, the carnivalesque, and grotesque realism are understood to be the literary and cultural tools with which Bellow either reinforces or undercuts the colonial library of which *Henderson* is a part. They are not understood to be important in and of themselves, but rather in terms of how they are used. Their value is instrumental rather than intrinsic, use value rather than truth value.

It may be equally productive, however, to think of the novel's comic elements and of the threads of the carnivalesque and grotesque realism which weave themselves through the text not merely—or even primarily—as the *means* by which racism in general and the colonial library in specific are either reinforced or undercut, but rather precisely as the novel's *end*—its reason for existence. *Henderson* is from this perspective best understood not as a political novel per se but rather as Bellow's most sustained attempt to simultaneously describe and create a sense of the carnivalesque in general and of grotesque realism in specific. In creating and reproducing the carnival, Bellow uses what Derrida calls "the means at hand," which, in 1950s America meant using the colonial library, gender and economic inequality, material signification, repressed homoerotic impulses, and so forth. These remains of the cultural day were not chosen for their truth value—indeed, to a *bricoleur* the question of a tool's truthfulness would be a category error of the first order—but because of their usefulness. To the extent that they facilitated the creation of the carnivalesque, they were useful tools; to the extent that they did not, they were not. And though their relative usefulness would of course be subject to examination and critique, the grounds for that examination would be instrumental and aesthetic rather than political and epistemological. This, in any event, is what Bellow apparently had in mind when he said of *Henderson:* "I don't think the race question enters into *Henderson the Rain King* at all. I think it is too much a comic fantasy to be thought of as having any serious social importance."[30] "People," Bellow observes on another occasion, "write realistically but at the same time they want to create environments which are somehow desirable, which are surrounded by atmospheres in which behavior becomes significant, which display the charm of life."[31]

As long as the comic and carnivalesque and grotesque realism elements in *Henderson* are viewed instrumentally, as a literary means to a political end, the most important images in the novel are the purloined lion cub (which is said to embody the spirit of the dead king) and the starkly white landscape through which Henderson passes on his trip home from Africa. The lion cub is understood to represent the white man's theft—via the colonial library—of Africa's culture and heritage and meaning, and the landscape is understood to represent the colonial library version of white freedom, which is created by way of its fraudulent binary juxtaposition to African blackness. This is of course the conclusion reached by Morrison in *Playing in the Dark* and reinforced by Smith in "The Jewish Atlantic" and Lamont in "Representation of Africa," the conclusion which is at present the standard interpretation of the novel.

But when the comic and carnivalesque and grotesque realism elements in *Henderson* are viewed as an end rather than a means, the most important image in *Henderson* becomes the one found in the novel's culminating scene of instruction and memory: the wild roller-coaster ride in which Henderson both embraces and is embraced by a scruffy old bear named Smolak. Smolak is a literal carnival bear, of course, but it is much more than that as well. The bear is what Kiernan perceptively calls "Henderson's real totem."[32] It is Bellow's material embodiment of the carnivalesque, a symbol which is presented, at novel's end, as *Henderson*'s conclusion and meaning: "Like Smolak, Henderson is a sad clown. . . . His recognition of similarity to the old bear is Henderson's acceptance of the bodily grotesqueness against which he has chafed so long as well as the buffets of external forces."[33] From that perspective, the carnival bear, rather than the lion cub, best represents what might be called the transcendental signifier of *Henderson the Rain King*:

> Whatever gains I ever made were always due to love and nothing else. And as Smolak (mossy like a forest elm) and I rode together, and as he cried out at the top, beginning the bottomless rush over those skimpy yellow supports, and up

once more against eternity's blue (oh, the stuff that has been done within this envelope of color, this subtle bag of life-giving gasses!) while the Canadian hicks were rejoicing underneath with red faces, all the nubble-fingered rubes, we hugged each other, the bear and I, with something greater than terror and flew in those gilded cars. I shut my eyes in his wretched, time-abused fur. He held me in his arms and gave me comfort. And the great thing is that he didn't blame me. He had seen too much of life, and somewhere in his huge head he had worked it out that for creatures there is nothing that ever runs unmingled. (339)

Notes

First epigraph: Saul Bellow quoted in Sukhbir Singh, "Meeting with Saul Bellow," *American Studies International* 35, no. 1 (1977): 19–31. Second epigraph: Daniel Lamont, "'A Dark and Empty Continent': The Representation of Africa in Saul Bellow's *Henderson the Rain King*," *Saul Bellow Journal* 16, no. 2–17, no. 2 (Summer and Fall 2000/Winter 2001): 56–67.

1. The most significant collection of essays analyzing the question of race in Bellow's work is the triple issue of the *Saul Bellow Journal* entitled *Issues of Blackness and Whiteness,* which includes vols. 16, no. 2; 17, no. 1; and 17, no. 2, and which runs through the summer and fall issues of 2000, culminating in the winter issue of 2001. In this seminal collection of essays, Bellow's texts are defended as well as critiqued, with contributors' attitudes toward his novels ranging from conciliatory to disappointed to angry. The most thoroughgoing critique of Bellow's work generally is Alan Rice's important introductory essay, "What Do We Say to Each Other When the Library Is Closed?" In what is perhaps the most controversial part of his analysis, Rice considers the possible connections among Bellow's Jewish roots and his use of racialized discourse: "Bellow's use of a racialized discourse . . . should not be seen as traitorous to his Jewish roots but thoroughly in accord with his white skin privilege, literally the 'price of his ticket' into the canon of American literature" (*Saul Bellow Journal* 16, no. 2–17, no. 2 [Summer and Fall 2000/Winter 2001]: 11).

2. Responses to the description of the pickpocket range from Rice's condemnation of "the outrageously stereotyped black pickpocket in *Mr. Sammler's Planet*" (*Saul Bellow Journal* 16, no. 2–17, no. 2 [Summer and Fall 2000/Winter 2001]: 5) and Emily Budick's assertion that Sammler is, "simply put, a racist" (*Blacks and Jews in Literary Conversation* [Cambridge: Cambridge University Press, 1998], 153) to Aliki Varvogli's extended defense of the scene, in which she distinguishes between Sammler's perspective and Bellow's and argues that "the

symbolic function of the black man was to coax Sammler out of his introspection" ("'The Corrupting Disease of Being White': Notions of Selfhood in *Mr. Sammler's Planet* and *Herzog*," *Saul Bellow Journal* 16, no. 2–17, no. 2 [Summer and Fall 2000/Winter 2001]: 160).

3. Toni Morrison, *Playing in the Dark: Whiteness and the Literary Imagination* (Cambridge: Harvard University Press, 1992), 33.

4. Ibid., 59.

5. Carol R. Smith, "The Jewish Atlantic—The Deployment of Blackness in Saul Bellow," in this volume, 113. Originally published in *Saul Bellow Journal* 16, no. 2–17, no. 2 (Summer and Fall 2000/Winter 2001): 265.

6. Ibid., 114.

7. Ibid., 113, 114.

8. Ibid., 111.

9. Daniel Lamont, "'A Dark and Empty Continent': The Representation of Africa in Saul Bellow's *Henderson the Rain King*," *Saul Bellow Journal* 16, no. 2–17, no. 2 (Summer and Fall 2000/Winter 2001): 133, hereafter cited parenthetically.

10. For a very different interpretation of the relationship between *Henderson* and *Darkness*, one that explores the possible connections among Bellow, Conrad, and Hemingway, see Michael Macilwee, "*Henderson the Rain King*: Translations between Conrad and Hemingway," *Saul Bellow Journal* 20, no. 1 (Winter 2004): 47–71.

11. Saul Bellow, *Henderson the Rain King* (New York: Penguin, 1996), 21, hereafter cited parenthetically.

12. Ihab Habib Hassan, *Selves at Risk: Patterns of Quest in Contemporary American Letters* (Madison: University of Wisconsin Press, 1990), 127.

13. Ellen Pifer, "Beyond History and Geography: *Henderson the Rain King*," *Saul Bellow Journal* 7, no. 2 (Summer 1988): 16.

14. Thomas Rhea explores the relationship between Henderson and Dahfu in detail in "The Metaphysics of Fear in Saul Bellow's *Henderson the Rain King*," *Saul Bellow Journal* 22, nos. 1–2 (Fall 2006/Winter 2007): 35–50. Although the potential homoerotic aspects of their friendship have not yet been examined, the framework for such an analysis has been established by Daniel Muhlestein in "Wrestling with Angels: Male Friendship in *Henderson the Rain King*," *Saul Bellow Journal* 21, nos. 1–2 (Fall 2005/Winter 2006): 41–61.

15. Robert F. Kiernan, *Saul Bellow* (New York: Continuum, 1989), 84–85.

16. John Cullen Gruesser, *White on Black: Contemporary Literature about Africa* (Urbana: University of Illinois Press, 1992), 40.

17. M. S. Bradbury, *Saul Bellow* (London: Methuen, 1982), 59.

18. Dave Kuhne, *African Settings in Contemporary American Novels* (Westport, Conn.: Greenwood, 1999), 91.

19. Mikhail Bakhtin, *Rabelais and His World* (Cambridge: MIT Press, 1968), 11.

20. See Sigrid Renaux, "Bellow's Carnivalistic Vision of the World in *Henderson the Rain King*," Ph.D. diss., University of São Paulo, 1978.

21. Bakhtin, *Rabelais*, 5.

22. Stephanie S. Halldorson, *The Hero in Contemporary American Fiction: The Works of Saul Bellow and Don DeLillo* (New York: Macmillan, 2007), 57.

23. Bakhtin, *Rabelais*, 19.

24. Ibid., 21.

25. Sukhbir Singh, "Bellow's *Henderson the Rain King*," *Explicator* 50, no. 2 (Winter 1992): 119.

26. Mikhail Bakhtin, "Discourse in the Novel," in *The Norton Anthology of Theory and Criticism* (New York: Norton, 2001), 1216.

27. Stephen Greenblatt, "Invisible Bullets: Renaissance Authority and Its Subversion," *Glyph* 8 (1981): 41.

28. Ibid., 57.

29. Jacques Derrida, "Structure, Sign and Play in the Discourse of the Human Sciences," in *Writing and Difference* (Chicago: University of Chicago Press, 1978), 285.

30. Quoted in Lamont, "Representation of Africa," 146.

31. Quoted ibid., 144.

32. Kiernan, *Saul Bellow*, 87.

33. Janis P. Stout, "The Possibility of Affirmation in *Heart of Darkness* and *Henderson the Rain King*," *Philological Quarterly* 57, no. 1 (1978): 126.

5

The Jewish Atlantic— The Deployment of Blackness in Saul Bellow

Carol R. Smith

> Listen, Chuck, there's something I've always wanted that you can buy for me in Europe. A beautiful seascape. I've always loved paintings of the sea. Nothing but the sea. I don't want to see a rock, or a boat, or any human beings. Only mid-ocean on a terrific day. Water water everywhere.
> —Saul Bellow, *Humboldt's Gift*

> Ships also refer us back to the middle passage, to the half-remembered micropolitics of the slave trade and its relationship to both industrialization and modernization. As it were, getting on board promises a means to reconceptualize the orthodox relationship between modernity and for what passes as its prehistory.
> —Paul Gilroy, *The Black Atlantic*

> Through significant and underscored omissions, startling contradictions, heavily nuanced conflicts, through the way writers people their work with the signs and bodies of this presence—one can see that a real or fabricated Africanist presence was crucial to their sense of Americanness.
> —Toni Morrison, *Playing in the Dark*

When Charles Citrine, the central protagonist and narrator of Bellow's 1975 novel *Humboldt's Gift*, makes plans to visit Europe, his brother Julius asks him to bring back to America a painting of the sea. As is apparent from the description quoted above, the image desired by Julius is remarkable for, in

Morrison's phrase, its "significant and under-scored omissions." The wish for such a seascape betokens a resistance to acknowledging the racialized history of Europe and America. What Julius wants in a European painting for his American house is a purified depiction of the sea, without a "rock"—no land; without a "boat"—no carriers of trade; without "human beings"—no historical agents. Such a desire implies not only a refusal to get on board the ship that for Paul Gilroy figures history, but also the wish to deny its existence. Yet in the context of *Humboldt's Gift* this erasure of race from history is itself contained within a highly racialized and ethnically marked structure. The desire for a sublime representation of the sea is presented as a means to fulfill Julius's identity as a successful American of Jewish stock, by adding cultural capital to his established sporting and economic prowess. Paradoxically, the ability of the desired painting to secure this cultural capital is dependent on its being emptied out of racialized historical signification. This decontextualizing move, which isolates the European aesthetic from history, is what enables the wished-for seascape to function as the emblem of Julius's full realization of American identity.

This empty picture is a product of the Romantic Enlightenment, as the closing allusion to Coleridge's *The Rhyme of the Ancient Mariner* emphasizes, but one that shows none of the means of production of modernity. This is the sublime without the terror, through which Europe is constructed as a cultural producer of aesthetic objects and ideas which were and are important to America. In Bellow's work, such ideas and objects symbolize the intellectual link of America to Europe and help to reinvigorate and to reinforce the coupling of liberal humanist ideology and American individuality. Importantly, however, while Julius's desire for an imaginary seascape signals some of the complexities of the connections between race and national identity in Bellow, its embeddedness in *Humboldt's Gift* suggests that the strategy just outlined is only a partial and conflicted element in Bellow's negotiation of these relations.

Julius's desire is doubly frustrated in the novel, both conceptually by its being embedded in American capitalist acquisitiveness (Julius outlines a price range and implies that Charles will operate on commission) and also through narrative. Charles Citrine proves unable to find such an empty picture in Europe. For every seascape, "in all the blue and green, foam and sun, calm and storm, there was always a rock, a sail, a funnel and Julius wasn't having any of that."[1] Instead of fulfilling the quest to realize American identity through European aesthetics, the search for the painting prompts Citrine to dwell on the relationship between European and American identity and migration histories, specifically the Jewish diaspora. Citrine is represented as recognizing the similarities between his own family and the Spaniards from whom he is trying to buy a painting:

"They resembled my parents and my immigrant aunts and cousins. We were parted when the Jews were expelled in 1492. Unless you were very stingy with time, that wasn't really so long ago."[2]

Rather than finding his brother an untroubling aesthetic closure for his American identity, Citrine is shown to uncover a more ancient and "truer" basic narrative of Americanness—that of migration from oppression. The history of elective migration from Europe to America is normalized as historical process, and Jewish experience is presented as being representative of rather than exceptional to this narrative. Citrine's revelation is that his brother's desire to escape from the problematics and oppression of the historical context is actually what defines *History*, in the liberal humanist worldview, thence by extension American history and individuality: "What did a seascape devoid of landmarks signify? Didn't it signify elemental liberty, release from the daily way and the horror of tension? O God, liberty!"[3] The shift in focus away from the narrative fulfillment of the quest for the painting to self-reflexive consideration of the desire motivating that quest exposes the desire for complete American individuality as problematic. "Liberty" is an escape from and possible erasure of (racial) history. By dramatizing this problem through the search for the painting, Bellow signals an awareness of nonwhite, non-WASP histories of migration but positions them within a longer view—from 1492—as just part of an overarching history of the migration from Europe. What coheres non-Black histories is Jewish experience, which by virtue of its originary diasporic history can function as the sign of Americanness. Ironically, then, the painting need not be found, only imagined, for the intellectual history of Europe and the validity of American humanism to be established.

A precondition for this project of imagining remains the omission of histories of migration which are not the result of oppression but of enslavement and not from Europe but from Africa. As Gilroy has pointed out, nineteenth-century European paintings of seascapes do exist, and they very infrequently have "nothing" in them. In fact, as with the famous example of Turner, they portray boats and dead slaves being thrown overboard, while others show rocks or land (Africa) from where the slaves are taken or checked (Liverpool). They represent a historical trace, what Gilroy calls a link to "the half-remembered micro-politics of the slave trade." This "Black Atlantic" is precisely what Bellow works so hard to subsume in the larger Jewish Atlantic as described above, precisely because it calls attention to, in Morrison's terms, the "startling contradictions" between different historical narratives of migration to the United States. The recognition of the problematic intellectual inheritance of modernity plays a crucial role in Bellow's representation of Americanness. The intention behind this essay is to examine the ways in which this problematic is worked through and/or displaced by overwriting the history of the African passage with a history of the Jewish Atlantic.

The figuration of the crisis of American modernity through the representation of the quest of alienated white male figures and the strategic deployment of "Africanist" figures as described by Morrison is central to Bellow's work. While examples of these practices can be found elsewhere, what follows will examine three texts, "Looking for Mr. Green," *Henderson the Rain King*, and *Mr. Sammler's Planet*. In these, Bellow invokes Blackness as Africanness relative to other ethnic identities (such as, primarily, Jewishness) in order to police a distinction between race and ethnicity that underwrites a model of American history as elective assimilation. Bellow thereby anticipates Gilroy's insistence on a racialized understanding of the Enlightenment, but in contrast to Gilroy's use of racial difference to reconceptualize the liberal humanist inheritance, Bellow's construction of racial difference operates to reify a positive notion of the Enlightenment as central to assimilated (white) America. This belief is consonant with a philosophical affiliation with liberal humanism, despite the horrors of the Jewish Holocaust, as a response to the politically divided America of the civil rights period and after. Such a position is articulated by Bellow in a 1963 interview, in which he situated the specific slave history of African Americans as a closed narrative in the longer history of progressive historical Enlightenment: "Our period has been created by revolutions of all kinds—political, scientific, and industrial. And now we have been freed by law from slavery in many of its historical, objective forms. The next move is up to us. Each of us has to find an inner law by which he can live. Without this, objective freedom only destroys us. So the question that really interests me is the question of spiritual freedom in the individual—the power to endure our own humanity."⁴ For Bellow, the revolutions have freed "us" to contemplate our spiritual future. The past, with its history of slavery, is to be passed over since it is completed, and with its closure comes the guarantee of the universality of individual freedom. Any contingent or problematic relationship between this concept of "spiritual freedom" and slave past must be disavowed and is here as elsewhere in Bellow elided by a separation of the "historical" from the "spiritual." Traces of the material and cultural history of these revolutions, which latterly spur Gilroy and others to review the diaspora of Africans as problematizing a belief in liberal humanism and allowing its productive reformulation, have to be elided to preserve the progressive trajectory of the Enlightenment. I will argue that this separation allows Bellow to view all such troubling "historic" forms, even the unique horror of the Holocaust, as closable episodes of this past and therefore not disabling to belief in Enlightenment notions of the self and modernity.

Of course, the growing national attention to the historical specificity of African migration to the Americas—slavery rather than elective assimilation—and the dissemination of literature and political movements concerning contemporary oppression of African Americans work directly against this humanist stance. Rather, the treatment of African Americans and their representations in this period can be read to operate as marking the limit of the conceptualization of American identity as a process of assimilation by consent. Simply put, the middle passage cannot be treated as an elective voyage of migration. Bellow's 1963 statement of intent to retain the aesthetics and ideals of the modern period, which has and arguably still guarantees Americanness, thus cannot help but engage him in this process of the deployment of Blackness. Even when, as in *Humboldt's Gift,* in which the relationship with Europe is configured positively in terms of the transportation of culture rather than of slaves, this is, in Morrison's terms, "an underscored omission." The violence of this displacement calls attention to itself and serves in my reading to reinvoke the repressed history of the middle passage. Here and elsewhere, the more Bellow attempts to disengage the "historic" from the "spiritual," the more they are shown to be inextricable.

Moreover, Bellow's liberal agenda, as the last quotation implies, constrains him more often to name Blackness and to distance it from Americanness, rather than to work it as a constitutive absence. This requires a further series of strategies for the containment of Black identity. As will be analyzed and described below, Blackness is therefore either massified, criminalized, and contained in the ghetto to serve as a passive example of modern alienation (as in "Looking for Mr. Green"), or displaced to a symbolic, colonial geography where the (white) male American finds his self (*Henderson the Rain King*), or stereotypically oversexualized and silenced to allow an epiphanic moment of revelation (*Mr. Sammler's Planet*).

Each of these texts shares a common concern, by implication and example, with the ways in which intellectual links with Europe can be narrativized as American and normalized as the past and future of the conceptualization of American identity. The passages from *Humboldt's Gift* discussed previously can be read both as further evidence of this project and as a revealing trope of how difficult it is to sustain, since they contain within them both the promise of the European intellectual and aesthetic inheritance, and a recognition of the troubling and potentially disabling material circumstances of its production—slavery and the middle passage. That descriptions of Bellow's work as archetypally American and his characters as symptomatic of modern American man's alienation are commonplace, despite this deployment of Blackness, underlines the importance of this project in securing his literary and cultural status.[5] His main characters—male, if ethnically marked usually Jewish but racially white—embark on literal and/or symbolic journeys which through modernist narrative conceits reveal the continued need for and importance of moments of transcendence. That these protagonists are so commonly considered to be representative Americans while being so obviously Jewish (as, for example, in "Looking for Mr. Green" and *Mr. Sammler's Planet*) is at least in part symptomatic of the desire on the part of Bellow and the academy to maintain that European heritage be unrevised, by strategically employing Jewishness as a sign of the intellect and the passage from Europe. Hence Bellow's self-description as "an American of Jewish heritage,"[6] rather than as a hybrid Jewish American, thereby eschewing the language of the civil rights movements but echoing the assimilationist narrative. This is not to suggest that Bellow represents his characters as denying their Jewishness, or that he himself writes from a racialized position. Rather, it is the preeminent status of Jewishness as a sign of elective immigration that allows Bellow and his Jewish characters to so securely represent Americanness, just so long as Blackness is otherwise deployed.

Such a reading begins to explain what an American author—Jewish or not—is doing during the accentuated period of racialized U.S. politics from the 1950s through to the 1970s invoking negative stereotypes of Blackness and images of the middle passage without slaves. It is certainly not because Bellow is unaware of or fails to represent African Americans/Negroes.[7] In fact, in "Looking for Mr. Green," he can be seen to typify the tendency of authors of the 1950s to represent the Negro as a passive victim of modernization in the urban landscape.[8] First published in *Commentary* (1951) and then in *Mosby's Memoirs and Other Stories* (1968), the short story concerns a government worker who tries to deliver a welfare check to the eponymous Mr. Green. The alienation of the central figure is established through his identity in comparison to the otherness of African Americans. Thus he is Jewish (by surname—Grebe) and white (by physical description),[9] and his place in society is represented by his movement into the ghetto of Chicago: "He was delivering relief checks in the Negro district, and although he was a native Chicagoan this was not part of the city he knew much about—it needed a depression to introduce him to it."[10]

The quest for Mr. Green is at first narrativized as a realistic search for an actual person in the recognizable historical context of the Depression, albeit one which underlines the separation of white from Black. However, this quickly develops into a metaphysical search typical of earlier Bellow.[11] What is different here is the way in which ethnicities are described and deployed. African Americans are represented as othered both from Grebe's narrative point of view and from that of a white coworker, and in overtly racist terms from an Italian shopkeeper and first-generation Polish immigrant.[12] Grebe is never represented from the point of view of African Americans, who are themselves presented almost always by sketchy outlines of unindividuated groups, as, for example, in this description of a communal room entered by Grebe during his search: "It was full of people, and they were silent as he entered—ten people, or a dozen, perhaps more, sitting on benches like a parliament. There was no light, properly speaking, but a tempered darkness that the window gave, and everyone seemed to him enormous, the men padded out in heavy work clothes and winter coats, and the women huge, too, in their sweaters, hats and old furs."[13] This room is a domestic space with no domestic or familial detailing. The relationship between each member of the group is not described; the only attempt at differentiation is the split into gender. The invocation of some kind of hell-scape, calling up a Miltonian parliament of fallen angels, and the size of these Black people render them as Other than Grebe and arguably Other than the reader.

The two exceptions to this racialized presentation are significant: an old man, Mr. Field, and a naked, drunken woman who is crucial to the story's final closure. The representation of these two introduces a gendered dynamic to the race/gender economy seen elsewhere.[14] Thus placed in opposition to the nameless groupings and the mysterious Mr. Green is Winston Field, who is represented as a worthy recipient of his welfare check. This is represented through the official paperwork recording his life: "Social Security card, relief certification, letters from the State hospital in Manteno, and a naval discharge dated San Diego, 1920."[15] The implication here is clear: Winston Field is an assimilated American with a paper life history to prove it. His internalization of the American Dream narrative is emphasized by Field's explicit articulation of a capitalist reworking of the Du Boisian notion of the "talented tenth." The terms in which he describes this are central to the representation of race in the story: "There ain't no little ways to make things better, and the only big thing is money. That's the only sunbeams, money. Nothing is black where it shines, and the only place you see black is where it ain't shining. What we colored have to have is our own rich."[16] With money, black can become white; lightness contrasts positively with the gloomy communal room described earlier. If Field's argument owes something to Du Bois, it eschews a politics of positive intellectual separatism that might end in the goal of racial assimilation, in favor of capitalist transformation. Be white and rich and be American: this is the "inclusive" system of elective assimilation. Notice, though, that it is a process of assimilation to the narrative of (white) capitalism and not to social integration. As will be seen, a similar symbolic deployment yet separation of black and white can also be found in later Bellow.

Otherwise the ghetto and its inhabitants, as with the communal room discussed above, are deployed as illustrative material in a meditation on the evils of the disintegration of both the modern city and consensus politics in the United States. Marianne Friedrich is representative of the critical tradition in this: "The sequence of realistic images and impressions from Chicago's ghetto increasingly takes on symbolic, metaphysical dimensions, as the reader learns to interpret the "camouflage" of realistic impressions."[17] Friedrich, like other critics, focuses on the symbolic quest and in doing so simply accepts the deployment of nonwhites as "camouflage," with any comment on this deployment of Blackness firmly within Bellow's place in literary rather than imperialist history. Thus this dominant critical tradition follows the internal textual politics of the use of Blackness. The transcendence, which these critics are so quick to isolate and praise, is of course that of the alienated modern (white) man. This of course secures Bellow his position in the canon of modern American literature. Yet while the quest for Mr. Green might not be on the same scale as that for Moby Dick, its use of color to guarantee its Americanness is comparable. What has been regarded, and arguably dismissed, as "camouflage" is therefore useful only insofar as what it can be stripped away to reveal: Grebe's self-revelation, which can be seen in Morrison's terms as central and indivisible from the definition of American national literature and identity. As Morrison reflects: "These speculations have led me to wonder if the major and championed characteristics of our national literature—individualism, masculinity, social engagement versus historical isolation; acute and ambiguous moral problematics; the thematics of innocence coupled with an obsession with the figurations of death and hell—are not in fact responses to a dark, abiding, signing Africanist presence."[18]

Hence at the end of "Looking for Mr. Green" when Grebe is unable to find Mr. Green, he gives the check to an African American woman, whose naked and drunken horrifying state signals and emphasizes the seeming failure of his quest. However, the story finishes with the following: "And though the self-ridicule was slow to diminish, and his face still blazed with it, he had, nevertheless, a feeling of elation, too. 'For after all,' he said, 'he *could* be found!'"[19] The actual existence of African Americans is useful insofar as their excess physicality—here represented in Conradian horror—is the mode of transcendence to the epiphany of selfhood of Grebe at the end. It is thus understandable why Friedrich et al. can read the figure of the woman as mere "camouflage," especially when Mr. Green need never have existed at all for white selfhood to be affirmed—surely an extreme example of Morrison's "signing Africanist presence." Grebe can be representative of "everyman" despite his ethnic difference because *that* difference—Jewishness—can be transcended through the othering of Blackness described above. This mode of securing the presence and primacy of whiteness at the expense or even denial of Blackness can, like Julius's seascape, be read as revealing the importance of Blackness through the extremity of its figuration as much as it tries to efface or deny it. As will now be shown, the deployment of Blackness—whether through strategies of disavowal, fragmentation, or sexual objectification—remains central to Bellow's Americanness in the later and more prestigious novels *Henderson the Rain King* and *Mr. Sammler's Planet*.

The critical reception of *Henderson the Rain King* is similar to that of "Looking for Mr. Green" in that it focuses on its typification as quest narrative and firmly situates it in the Western canon of such novels from *Don Quixote* to Kerouac's *Big Sur*.[20] Whether or not the critics read Bellow as writing within or parodying this quest narrative, the importance of Africa as the site of the quest remains. The following comments illustrate typical readings of the figurative relationship between America and Europe: "Eugene Henderson, a middle-aged millionaire who feels like a displaced person, flees from the piled-up burden of his life and from the unredeemed death he sees before him. He decides to find salvation not in civilization but in the primal, savage state: he leaves his wife and goes to Africa."[21] Henderson's journey to Africa is an attempt to get back to that lost condition—the Africa of the imagination which, since Conrad and Hemingway, has stood as the place where man discovers the truth about himself and, by generic extension, about mankind itself.[22] Henderson succeeds in satisfying his desire. His final celebration of life is his answer to the voice that cried "I want, I want, I want," which sent him to a symbolic Africa of the soul in the first place.[23]

Thus Africa is understood as the primal savage state of the imagination or of the symbolic, explicitly, or by implication in opposition to America as the civilized state, of the actual or real. As with Mr. Green in "Looking for Mr. Green," it would seem that the actual physical existence of the African continent is not necessary, so long as it could exist. Any historical relationship outside these literary/aesthetic or philosophical discourses of Africa and America is suppressed. The trade in anything beyond ideas is omitted; the relationship between the trade in Africans and these Enlightenment ideas is repressed.

One notable exception is the work of Judie Newman, for whom Henderson rejects the European past, and that of his WASP ancestors, refusing to take his place in their portrait gallery. He typifies the American belief in the ability to wipe out the past and begin again in a new world where salvation from inherited guilt is a product of salvation from inherited tradition and history.[24] Newman at least argues for a recontextualizing of Bellow within the cultural histories of America and Europe, which leads through American exceptionalism directly into a materialist historiography. This reading persuasively suggests an understanding of the markedly ideological structural positioning of America versus Africa seen above in other critics. The situating of Africa as a new world needs further examination. While Newman rightly emphasizes that Henderson is represented as an exemplum of the new frontiersman and the narrative strategy does seem to be that of a repression of the past, there is an equally important strategy at work. The more the novel seems to displace and to deny the history of the slave triangle, the more the renewal of Henderson's and America's identity (the end of the quest) is dependent on renegotiating these historical relations between America, Africa, and Europe.

Consonant with this sense of renegotiation, Henderson's journey is both related to and carefully distanced from previous European colonial invasions of Africa. Hence he travels with a honeymoon couple and afterwards alone with a native guide rather than as a missionary for religion or capitalism in the massed ranks of a church or army. His search is not for land, minerals, or slaves but for the answer to "I want, I want, I want."[25] Hence also the text is littered with symbolic remnants of European colonialism—a British shoe, an Italian cap[26]—and allusions to the literature of the period from Keats to Conrad.[27] Such references are, as this list implies, highly self-conscious and knowing and could be said to evidence an ongoing, if not humorous critique of colonialism by Bellow. Given this narrative positioning, Henderson's quest is represented as being able to remain naive and originary to himself and ironic to the reader. Hence the inclusion of scenes of revelation on encountering the native settlements which have been critically marked as "neither conscientiously symbolic nor artificial":[28]

> From these coverings smoke went up into the silent radiance. Also an inanimate glitter came off the ancient thatch. "Romilayu," I said, stopping him, "isn't that a picture? Where are we? How old is this place anyway?"
> Surprised at my question he said, "I no know, sah."
> "I have a funny feeling from it. Hell, it looks like the original place. It be older than the city of Ur . . . I have a hunch this spot is going to be good for me."[29]

Even without the reference to a picture—another painting?—no reader could miss the presence of an imperialist gaze here. In comparison with the ghettos of Chicago described in "Looking for Mr. Green," the aestheticizing picture frame, the detailing of the glitter, the silence, and the mythic allusions relate to a very different stereotype and a different deployment of Blackness. The primacy and invasive position of the white gaze remain more sharply defined here and more obviously reminiscent of the mind-set employed by previous colonialists to distance themselves from the actuality of their brutality. The sense that this spot is going to be good for Henderson relies also on his sharing a colonialist power position, the resources of this spot or country having been "good" for previous invaders.

It is precisely this type of scene that encourages critics' acceptance of the representation of the African continent as a symbolic space for the self-actualization of Americanness. That this positions America as unsuitable for regeneration while at the same time typifying Henderson "as a symbol for America itself—an American in need of change" tends to escape comment.[30] Yet the question of what kind of America(n) needs to go to Africa for what kind of change is central to Bellow's deployment of Blackness in Africa, and consequently to what kind of Americanness returns.

Henderson is represented as fleeing an America where he can find no fulfilling identity in either a personal or national frame. Despite an illustrious family heritage, wealth, and war service, he can find nothing in America to answer that "I want, I want, I want." He explains the situation of contemporary America as the lack of opportunity: "You have to think about white Protestantism and the Constitution and the Civil War and capitalism and winning the West. All the major tasks and big conquests were done before my time. That left the biggest problem of all, which was to encounter death."[31] This is the history of WASP America, especially of the white male American; those killed, conquered, or enslaved to enable this history to be completed are not mentioned. Of course, for these groups Henderson's America has several major tasks to encounter in the latter half of the twentieth century—a guarantee of full civil rights for African Americans being perhaps the major struggle. Other contemporary authors do engage explicitly with the relationship of white and black histories of the time albeit in a manner where the white narrative remains the dominant.[32] As will be argued, Bellow's commitment to troping America through the stories of existentially troubled white males such as Henderson avoids direct engagement with this mixed American history, suppressing it or displacing it as a search for self, the "encounter [with] death." This symbolic economy can deal with people of African descent *if* and *only if* they remain in Africa and therefore reiterate a belief in American history as the uncontested history of white success.

However, this absolute geography of racial difference is by no means the sole determinant of race in *Henderson the Rain King*. At the same time that Henderson is clinging to a belief in the purity of this American history in the national frame, his family is represented as engaging with nonwhite Americanism through a series of encounters with Africanist presences. Both of his children are shown to have relationships with nonwhite Americans. Henderson's son Edward wants to marry a woman from Central America whose physical description is racially marked: "an Indian with dark blood, a narrow face, and close set eyes."[33] On hearing this, Henderson automatically assumes he is being forced to marry because she is pregnant and that she will be a danger to Edward: "If I leave him with this gift she will eat him in three pieces."[34] Henderson's thought conflates two negative stereotypes of black femininity, that of excessive sexual and procreative fecundity and that of a symbol of death to white masculinity.

Ricey, Henderson's daughter, is caught up in a similar racialized dynamic. A child is found in the valise in her room. At first Henderson pretends to go along with the story of his wife and Ricey that the noise he hears is a cat, ignoring the evidence of the bottle-sterilizing kit in the kitchen. It is only when Henderson finds the child, "a colored child," that he acts, employing a private detective and demanding that the child be removed from his house. The clear implication is that the child is Ricey's, given not only the behavior of Ricey and her mother but also Henderson's fear of involving the police and his persistent belief that it is a foundling even when the headmistress states, "'She claims to be the mother.'"[35] Having committed the "social death" of miscegenation, Ricey is banished to live with an aunt. With their central signification of the union between white and black equaling death, both of these narratives threaten the stability and whiteness of Henderson's identity.[36] His journey to Africa can thus be read as much as a flight from the union of black and white as a quest to revitalize his WASP ancestry.

These two possible narratives of the construction of American identity, and the desire to keep them separate, govern Henderson's encounters in Africa. Africa is the place where his identity as white is most guaranteed by its imperialist positioning, as is his power to keep white and black separate and in their respective places. Yet it is also precisely the origin of that which he fears is destroying America—Blackness represented as Africans/Africanist presences. The novel attempts a negotiation and a defusion of this doubled knowledge through various set-piece episodes in which the deployment of Blackness works to stabilize Henderson's white Americanness.[37]

Hence, after entering the Arnewi village as described above, Henderson finds that due to an infestation of frogs in the water supply their cattle are dying. In a comic inversion of the usual colonial practice of enslaving or killing indigenous peoples, he employs Western technology, represented as a bomb, to help the Arnewi by blowing up the frogs. Unfortunately, while the frogs are killed, the cistern is also destroyed, so Henderson's intervention actually leaves them worse off. Despite this conclusion, his imperialist position remains secure: there is no questioning of whether this benign interference is needed or whether Western technology is invasive; Henderson simply employed it wrongly. The implication is that America's intervention in Africa is thus equally benign: no one suffers, is enslaved, or loses their land or traditions.

No one except the frogs. The Arnewi are represented as stereotypical "good natives"—peaceful, emotionally connected to nature (the cows), and nontechnologically aware—and by this they are in their right position in terms of the imperialist narrative, useful but separate. The frogs are described thus: "Through the webbing of the light I saw first polliwogs with huge heads, at all stages of developments, with full tails like giant sperm and budding feet. And then great powerful frogs, spotted, swimming by with their neckless thick heads and long white legs, the short forepaws expressive of astonishment."[38] These "polliwogs" (tadpoles) can be read as barely suppressed (golliwogs) and displaced negative stereotypes of Blackness as sexual, animalistic, and stupid. The ways Western and specifically American culture represents peoples of African descent have been examined.[39] The cartoon grossness of this representation draws attention to this Africanist presence, though it is an Africanist presence with white legs. As with his son's mixed-race marriage and Ricey's baby, signs of hybridity signal death here—quite literally for the Arnewi since the frogs threaten their cows that produce milk, which is the staple of their diet.

In Africa, Henderson can act on and literally kill his fear of the mixing of black and white, which helped prompt his flight from America in the first place, through the massacre of these frogs. That they function in such a symbolic manner in the novel is emphasized by the way in which their death is likened to Hiroshima and that "the sun was already beginning to corrupt the bodies of the frog dead."[40] Not dead frogs, which would be the more usual formation, but "frog dead" as if "frog" were a marker of nationality or ethnicity. Newman has noted that the frogs are the Arnewi's taboo animals and that Henderson's destruction of them represents his Americanness: "In typical American fashion Henderson pins his faith on the annihilation of custom and taboo, and a new beginning."[41] If the frogs are also representative of America's taboo, the fact of miscegenation and the history of slavery, then he is also trying to annihilate or suppress that history. Just as there were no slaves or ships in *Humboldt's Gift,* here the sexually excessive and predatory Blackness which produces deformed (neckless, thick heads) and mixed-raced offspring are destroyed. Henderson journeys to the origin of slavery to literally wipe it out.[42]

Obviously, though, this does not mean that African Americans cease to exist or to be represented; it is only the troubling (for white America) historical signs of slavery that are erased. The rest of the novel deals with the writing of an alternate history/myth of the relationship between America and Africa to replace that of the actual imperialist history, in a similar strategy to the revisioning of the painting in *Humboldt's Gift*. This narrative consolidates the position of whiteness as the default sign of Americanness. It does so through yet another Africanist presence but one whose forms— a young white child and a lion cub—are not destabilizing for American identity, as were the hybrid forms discussed so far.

Henderson travels to another tribe, the Wariri, and becomes involved in their customs. At the resolution of a complicated narrative containing a highly detailed description of the rituals of this tribe, he is crowned the Rain King. As part of this, he is represented as developing a relationship with the Wariri king, Dahfu, and partaking in a symbolic rite of lion worship. The latter takes the form of Henderson becoming or communing with a lion.[43] Dahfu is killed and is, by local belief, reincarnated in a lion cub. Henderson returns to America by plane via Newfoundland with the cub and at the end of the novel is represented running in the white landscape with the cub and an orphaned, white American child who speaks only Persian. The novel closes with his reflection: "I guess I felt it was my turn to move, and so went running—leaping, leaping, pounding and tingling over the pure white lining of the gray Arctic silence."[44]

Here, finally, Henderson is fulfilled and represented in a spectacularly white moment of liberation and epiphany and self-presence. Morrison comments on the whiteness of this ending and other endings by white American authors, noticing that Henderson's self-reinvention is contingent on a deployment of Blackness: "If we follow through on the self-reflexive nature of these encounters with Africanism, it falls clear: images of Blackness can be evil *and* protective, rebellious *and* forgiving, fearful *and* desirable—all of the self-contradictory features of the self. Whiteness, alone, is mute, meaningless, unfathomable, pointless, frozen, curtained, dreaded, senseless, implacable."[45] Certainly the images of Blackness that are employed at the end of *Henderson the Rain King* would seem to confirm the double nature of Morrison's reading, though they are ultimately so far removed from the negative part of the equation as to make them safe enough to be related to whiteness. Thus the lion cub in its infantile state is nonthreatening, and its potential to become a man-eater is defused by its probable captivity in a zoo. This is Blackness in its acceptable and "pure" animalistic form, rather than as polliwog or mixed-race child. The lion cub is a Black presence that can be imported to America and acknowledged as important to it because of the safety of its signification: "Then my daughter brought home a baby. Of course we had to take it away from her. I hope she will consider this lion as a replacement. I hope I can persuade her."[46]

The reason a lion cub is preferable to and safer than a child is that in Henderson's familial narrative it can sign or stand for the Africanist presence, which Morrison argues is needed for the health of whiteness. It is a presence which, in its displaced figuration as the product of neither enforced migration nor subsequent miscegenation, can represent a positive reciprocation between Africa and America. The history of slavery is displaced behind the story of Henderson's rescue of the cub and the affection it shows for him. Henderson's love for it is central to his liberation, and in turn Ricey's acceptance of it instead of her "colored child" enables her to reenter the family. The need for a "suitable" Africanist presence to bring personal health is confirmed by the representation of the white, Persian-speaking child Henderson meets on the plane home whom he describes thus: "Your face is too white from your orphan's troubles. Breathe in this air, kid, and get a little color."[47]

The representation of color bringing or giving life to a white landscape is also central to the ending of the novel in terms of Henderson as figuring the national narrative. His return journey is of course a passage home, but one which touches on Newfoundland—new found land—whose whiteness can be read to signify not only the deathly negative of Morrison's reading but also the potential for a new beginning, one which can acknowledge the symbolic need and status of the Africanist presence but not the slave history from where this presence comes. Hence the importance of this white land that has no significant slave history, unlike those more southerly islands and landfalls of the Atlantic coast. Henderson's passage home is the last stage in the remaking of the link between Africa and America. The slave passage, ship deaths, and islands of the Carolinas are displaced by the white nothingness of Newfoundland.

It is in and through this new found land that Henderson brings in the Africanist presences detailed above. That these are displaced signs of Africa and slavery rather than actual Africans and their history preserves the racial economy of the novel. Blackness is smuggled into America in the fragmented and displaced forms of the cub and the orphaned child. The former is clearly readable in terms of the white stereotype of Blackness as animalistic and natural strength. Morrison calls the latter "an Africanist child" but gives no further exegesis.[48] Certainly this child, like the cub, does function as a sign of Blackness in the service of white Americanness, but as a significantly fragmented one. In the case of the child, the fragmentation is not employed to import blackness as strength as it was with the cub but, more crucially for the Bellovian project of overwriting the "Black Atlantic," to recuperate the slave narrative. The child in its orphaned state, its removal from its homeland and protectors, and its lack of the English language might be read as a displaced presence of the narrative of many enslaved Africans. They, too, were through enslavement brought from their homes, lost family, culture, and language. Of course, as with the cub, the figuration of such a narrative of Black experience—through the body of a white child—functions yet again to contain Blackness safely within a white symbolic centered economy as it is literally within a white body. Both the child and the cub in their helpless infantile state are represented as being rescued and protected by Henderson and being saved by coming to a new life in America. As with the painting in *Humboldt's Gift*, these Africanist presences are used to write all passages from Africa to America as elective. These representations of Blackness, disconnected from its history and from hybridity, can be safely (from a WASP point of view) exchanged for the "Blackness" of Ricey's baby and thence disperse color and health into (white) America.

The successes of this strategy might be measured by noting that while the normal critical response has been to recognize the Atlantic as the site of Henderson's rebirth, it has not explored the implications that this construction holds for American national identity. Thus Donald W. Markos unquestionably states that "The sight of the Atlantic Ocean thrills him because it is a symbolic reflection of the newly discovered depths in him."[49] That the Atlantic can only be calm and empty enough to produce an unthreatening reflection if its status as the mode of transport for Africans has "disappeared" is not mentioned.

Henderson's and America's relationship to Africa is rewritten, but once again from a white American point of view. Admittedly this relationship retains the Africanist presence as noted by Morrison, but at the expense of the history of the passage, of overwriting the negative inheritance of modernity to gain the same kind of epiphany as at the end of "Looking for Mr. Green." Henderson can arrive back in America, to a new America, having travelled to Africa and disconnected America from the "problems" of its African inheritance. As long as he remains in Newfoundland, he is in control of the kinds of Blackness brought to America. To move away from this privileged landfall, isolated from the historic and geographical sites of slavery, into the contemporary America of the 1960s and 1970s is to enter the more contested space of *Mr. Sammler's Planet*.

If *Henderson the Rain King* attempts to renew and revise the link between American national identity and the ideas of modernity by myth-making in Africa, in *Mr. Sammler's Planet* a similar strategy of renewal is enabled by the deployment of a negative stereotype of Black sexuality in America. The novel centers on Artur Sammler, a Jewish Holocaust survivor, who lives with the remnants of his family in New York. Sammler's perception of America is of the collapse of American civil society and by extension civilization. This is particularized in a similar narrative strategy to that of *Henderson the Rain King*, in which Sammler's personal and familial identities and encounters can be interpreted as symptomatic of the national debate. Stanley Crouch is representative of critical praise for the text in his defense of Bellow: "Bellow was addressing the dangers that arrive whenever the authority that comes of disciplined and responsible quality is pushed aside. As those dangers applied to the United States, the writer saw clearly the jagged quest for power from the people in the street to the talk show hosts of the mass media."[50]

Crouch's reading of the novel pivots on the above conservative interpretation of this period. His negative particularization of who or what are these sources of "quality" is tellingly patrician. Quality by definition does not mean "people in the street" or "talk show hosts of the mass media"; by elimination, then, quality's guardian is WASP, male America. The membership of the two groups—civil rights protestors on the streets, black, female, gay; the hosts of talk shows which from a right-wing agenda focus on the "triviality" of the personal—and their fighting for equal rights are demonized as anti-American. His invocation of the culturally powerful myth that the ideas of modernity, discipline, responsibility, and control were totally distinct from and under threat from the civil rights movements echoes Bellow's own recorded views of the time on these movements: "Maybe civilization *is* dying, but it still exists, and, meanwhile we have our choice: we can either rain more blows on it, or try to redeem it. [On female liberation] I'm all for freedom, short of degeneracy. As John Stuart Mill foresaw, women today show all the characteristics of slaves in revolt. They're prone to the excesses of the lately servile, the newly freed. I'd like to see their increased freedom accompanied by human development."[51]

For Bellow, then, as for Crouch, civilization might be under threat, but it must be protected. By the use of similarly humanistic and patrician language—"redeem," "freedom" versus "degeneracy," and allusion to Enlightenment philosophy—Bellow represents the modernist dilemma as a moral choice between civilization or degeneration. By implication, acceptance into American civilization is gained by accepting the mission of redemption rather than through the reevaluation of American identity argued for by the civil rights movements. Those who wish to enter this American civilization are represented as needing to curb their "natural" instincts and be taught to be human—civilized—because by implication they are those slaves and women who were not and are not yet fully developed. That entry into full American citizenship equates to acquiescence in the figuration and linking of these groups (women and slaves) as excessive or negative is unquestioned, as the neo-Darwinist link between freedom and development in the last sentence implies. They are certainly so linked and figured in *Mr. Sammler's Planet*, as an examination between Sammler's encounters with a black pickpocket and his view of his daughter Shula's behavior shows.

The novel is framed by Sammler's encounters with a pickpocket he first encounters stealing on a bus, by whom he is subsequently confronted, and whom, at the end of the novel, Sammler watches being bludgeoned by his son-in-law. In one of many parallel narratives in the text, Sammler's daughter steals a manuscript to aid him in his research. Her theft is represented as a prime example of the collapse of America and civilization: "Then suddenly she too was like the Negro pickpocket. . . . Millions of civilized people wanted oceanic, boundless, primitive, neck free nobility, experienced a strange release of galloping impulses, and acquired the peculiar aim of sexual niggerhood for everyone."[52] This is a description of contemporary 1970s America in the process of contamination and degeneration—a return to the primeval swamps rather than Bellow's wished-for human development. Or it is, at least, a description of white male America's fear of such, a fear which is particularized and disavowed through a deployment of a negative stereotype of Black male sexuality. Marian Russell comments on this deployment of Blackness, pointing out that in *Mr. Sammler's Planet*, "the Black man becomes a convenient metaphor for the disturbing elements in white society and is, in the last analysis, not an image of black culture, but a mirror image of the prevailing white culture."[53] Moreover, this figuration functions more integrally in delimiting the assimilationist norms of white culture and (white) America. Rather than providing a passive mirror of white culture, the representation of the black pickpocket facilitates the redemption of modernity and civilization advocated by Bellow in the 1970 interview, through its being positioned in contrast to Sammler's ethnicity.

Thus the pickpocket is not the type of safe Africanist images deployed at the end of *Henderson the Rain King* which, if not contained, will transform America as it already has Shula to "sexual niggerhood." That the threat should be so explicitly represented as sexual is symptomatic not only of the period's negative stereotyping of Black masculinity but also of the sexual/ethnic economy identified in Bellow. The most important encounter is when the pickpocket follows Sammler home after he has been seen by Sammler stealing on a bus and shows him his penis: "The black man had opened his fly and taken out his penis. It was displayed to Sammler with great oval testicles, a large tan-and-purple uncircumcised thing–a tube, a snake; metallic hairs bristled at the thick base and the tip cured beyond the supporting, demonstrating hand, suggesting the fleshy mobility of an elephant's trunk, though the skin was somewhat iridescent rather than thick or rough. Over the forearm and fist that held him Sammler was required to gaze at this organ. No compulsion would have been necessary."⁵⁴ The Black man does not speak at any point. The excessive and animalistic detailing is reminiscent of the description of the polliwogs and of course reduces him to a huge savage sexual object, one which Sammler is compelled to view. This is, though, a penis rather than a phallus; it signs the Black man through the white, imperialist gaze. Susan Gubar situates the scene in a longer history of the representation of Black masculinity she outlines as follows: "Since American culture denied most black men 'the name of the Father'—the genealogical, linguistic, economic authority traditionally signified by the phallus—the black man excommunicated from the symbolic suffered an iconographic devolution into the penis incarnate and then was pathologized by whites fearful or ashamed about their own representational violence."⁵⁵ However convincing Gubar's reading is in its psychoanalytical frame, here rather than the representation being evidence of shame at the violence of representation, it could be argued that such detailing is being deployed precisely to draw attention to the animalistic and therefore nonhuman nature of the action of the Black man. Draw attention to it and imply the need to counter its threat to American civilization.

This incident serves as a nexus of the familial and national narratives generated through Sammler. It thereby functions to threaten not only Sammler but also the redemption of civilization which his survival of the Holocaust and emigration to America promises. Here as elsewhere in the text it is this deployment of Blackness to represent the "sexual ways of the seraglio and of the Congo bush" that is shown to threaten the Enlightenment inheritance Sammler has striven to preserve.⁵⁶ And it is this threat which provokes Sammler to remember his war experiences and how his countering and killing the enemies of civilization was important then and should be now. There is no attempt to displace and incorporate Blackness as in *Henderson the Rain King*; it has to be eliminated from the text—as it is when the pickpocket is attacked with sculptures made from iron pyrites from the Dead Sea by Sammler's son-in-law at the end of the novel. Only with him thus removed from the text is the familial narrative finally closed and thus the national narrative completed. The importance of the ethnic symbolism here, that a Jewish, Israeli immigrant eliminates the Black man, is underlined by the description of the weapon: "Stars of David, branched candelabra, scrolls and rams' horns, or inscriptions flaming away in Hebrew: *Nahamu!* 'Comfort ye!' Or God's command to Joshua: *Hazak!*"⁵⁷

These signs of Jewishness are deployed to excise that which threatens the status quo of American civilization: the symbolic Black male as the sign and origin of criminality and sexual license has to be strategically eliminated. In contrast to the representation of Jewishness as passive or mad in the face of the Holocaust, typified by the retelling of the story of Rumkowski, the mad Jewish King of Lodz, which disables its function of guaranteeing European humanism, here Jewishness is shown to work actively and violently to maintain Americanness. Eisen's actions at Sammler's prompting guarantee their status as Americans through their choice to fight to restore order.

The novel ends with the death of Elya, who has financially supported the family and is understood by Sammler to have done what all men should, that is "to do what was required of him."[58] This belief in the importance of the action of the individual is what signifies Americanness in the novel. Sammler warns against the modern predilection for revolution for special groups: "It is clear that this revolution, a triumph for justice in many ways—slaves should be free, killing toil should end, the soul should have liberty—has also introduced new kinds of grief and misery, and so far, on the broadest scale, it has not been altogether a success."[59] The American Revolution was and should continue to be the revolution of the ordered individual. Sammler argues that an excess of individuality allows the corruption and evasion of the ethical stance and results in such horrors as the Holocaust. The ideas of the Enlightenment, the notion of selfhood, the ethical duty to family and nation are not themselves at fault. The problem is that in the contemporary period duty has been replaced by personal desire. The diminishing relationship between the individual and an ethical life is described thus: "In business, in professions, in labor; as a member of the public; as inhabitant of the cities, these strange pits; as experiencer of compulsions, manipulations; as endurer of strain; as father, husband obliging society by performing his quota of actions—the individual seems to feel these powers less, less and less."[60]

If Henderson symbolizes a quest for American identity in his "I want, I want, I want," then Sammler equally represents the answer of personal duty over personal excess and desire. In opposition to the civil rights movements in their invocation of the politics of the personal, Sammler is represented as a symbol of continuity with modernity and duty. This continuity can be assured only if slavery is read through the progressive history of the Enlightenment, which is secured by the strategies described above. If slavery can be thus represented as an exceptional aberration of modernity, then those who are now free should fit in by performing their quotas of actions, like Sammler, rather than arguing for special rights or turning to excess crime or sexuality as the Black pickpocket does. Again we are returned to a conception of American identity as a process of elective migration and assimilation. This is the representation of migration as a long history of choosing to flee from oppression, the history of the Jewish diaspora, which is shown to be preeminently American.

Having thus, post-Holocaust, reaffirmed the importance of liberal humanism, remade its links to Africa (*Henderson the Rain King*) and America (*Mr. Sammler's Planet*), Bellow writes *Humboldt's Gift*. The search for the painting, the final deployment of Blackness in this reading can be read as the fulfillment of the project of the Jewish Atlantic. As has been shown, that the painting can only be imagined rather than found is precisely the point; there is no need for such a representation once you have actually made the passage to America. The Jewish Atlantic is a strategic positioning created by the deployment of Blackness, its function as guarantor of the inheritance of European liberal humanism need last only until the European inheritance is translated securely into the American present and future. Then, in retrospect, from the American shore, the Jewish Atlantic disappears through assimilation, and the Atlantic and America whiten. It is such complex negotiations of race, ethnicity, and nationality which also guarantee Bellow his place in American literature.

Notes

Originally published in *Saul Bellow Journal* 17 (2000): 253–79. This essay has been reproduced here with the author's permission.

First epigraph: Saul Bellow, *Humboldt's Gift* (London: Penguin, 1975), 390. Second epigraph: Paul Gilroy, *The Black Atlantic: Modernity and Double Consciousness* (London: Verso, 1993), 17. Third epigraph: Toni Morrison, *Playing in the Dark: Whiteness and the Literary Imagination* (London: Pan, 1993), 6.

1. Bellow, *Humboldt's Gift*, 140.
2. Ibid.
3. Ibid., 411.
4. Bruce Cook, "Saul Bellow: A Mood of Protest," *Perspectives on Ideas and the Arts* (February 12, 1963), reprinted in *Conversations with Saul Bellow*, ed.

Gloria L. Cronin and Ben Siegel (Jackson: University of Mississippi Press, 1994), 17–18.

5. Bellow's criticism of the 1970s best exemplifies this; see esp. John J. Clayton, *Saul Bellow: In Defense of Man* (Bloomington: Indiana University Press, 1979); and M. Gilbert Porter, *Whence the Power? The Artistry and Humanity of Saul Bellow* (Columbia: University of Missouri Press, 1974), as does the historical overview of Bellow and others framed by Gerhard Bach, ed. *The Critical Response to Saul Bellow* (Westport, Conn.: Greenwood, 1995); and Gloria L. Cronin and Ben Siegel, eds., *Conversations with Saul Bellow* (Jackson: University of Mississippi Press, 1994).

6. Michiko Kakutani, "A Talk with Saul Bellow: On His Work and Himself," *New York Times Book Review*, December 13, 1981, reprinted in *Conversations with Saul Bellow*, ed. Gloria L. Cronin and Ben Siegel (Jackson: University of Mississippi Press, 1994), 185.

7. The use of terminology is obviously problematic since the term *Negro* is little used outside academic work on historical material, with the terms *African American* or *Black* the more accepted forms. I have followed Bellow's usage and deployed *African American* or *Black* when invoking a contemporary reading. See Susan Gubar, *Racechanges, White Skin, Black Face in American Culture* (New York: Oxford University Press, 1997), 40–43, for a clear elucidation of the problematics of terminology in dealing with similar texts.

8. As Susan Gubar and others have noted, these authors are predominantly white and can be seen to fit into a tradition of what she names as "racechange" (Gubar, *Racechanges,* 1997). See also Hazel V. Carby, *Race Men* (Cambridge: Harvard University Press, 1998), esp. chap. 2, on the representation of modernism and the body of Paul Robeson. For a thorough collation of critics who read "Looking for Mr. Green" in terms of the crisis of modernity, see Marianne M. Friedrich, *Character and Narration in the Short Fiction of Saul Bellow* (New York: Peter Lang, 1995).

9. Bellow, "Looking for Mr. Green," 83. "[H]is face was red from the sharpness of the weather . . . , with grey eyes. . . . He wore side burns that surprised you somewhat by the tough curl of the blond hair" (Saul Bellow, "Looking for Mr. Green," in *Mosby's Memoirs and Other Stories* [New York: Viking, 1968], 86). This is not, of course, to suggest that these physical characteristics could not be shared by someone of African American descent—they of course could—but as will be argued, they are not in the racial economy of Bellow.

10. Ibid.

11. See Friedrich, *Character and Narration,* 47ff., for a resume of the themes in the critical articles. This overview shows that if the story receives any critical attention it is for the way in which it is a prototype of the metaphysical quest for

self and identity in the later novels rather than an example of deployment of race in Bellow.

12. Bellow, "Looking for Mr. Green," 96–97.

13. Ibid., 88.

14. The Conradian horror of the woman who refuses to be named or clothed and thus puts at stake Grebe's ordered world is a common negative stereotype of black female sexuality. See especially, in *Henderson the Rain King*, where the African female characters such as Princess Mtalba are described in terms of the body and sex as in "Looking for Mr. Green" but with no command of English and therefore are coded as more natural and can be unproblematically desired and consumed by the white male. The central male African characters such as the guide Romilayu and King Dahfu speak English and have cerebral conversations with Henderson.

15. Bellow, "Looking for Mr. Green," 98.

16. Ibid.

17. Friedrich, *Character and Narration*, 53.

18. Morrison, *Playing in the Dark*, 5.

19. Bellow, "Looking for Mr. Green," 105.

20. Clayton, *Saul Bellow: In Defense of Man*, 166.

21. Ibid., 166–67.

22. D. W. Markos, "Life against Death in *Henderson the Rain King*," *Modern Fiction Studies* 17, no. 2 (1971), reprinted in Gerhard Bach, *The Critical Response to Saul Bellow* (Westport, Conn.: Greenwood, 1995), 110.

23. M. Gilbert Porter, *Whence the Power? The Artistry and Humanity of Saul Bellow* (Columbia: University of Missouri Press, 1974), 129.

24. Judie Newman, "Saul Bellow's Sixth Sense: The Sense of History," in *Saul Bellow in the 1980s*, ed. Gloria L. Cronin and L. H. Goldman (East Lansing: Michigan State University Press, 1989), 16.

25. Saul Bellow, *Henderson the Rain King* (London: Penguin, 1959), 12.

26. Ibid., 141, 153.

27. See ibid., 105, for a Keatsian nightingale, not to mention the wholesale allusions to *The Heart of Darkness*.

28. Richard G. Stern, "Henderson's Bellow," *Kenyon Review* 21, no. 4 (1959), reprinted in Gerhard Bach, *The Critical Response to Saul Bellow* (Westport, Conn.: Greenwood, 1995), 103.

29. Bellow, *Henderson the Rain King*, 47.

30. Markos, "Life against Death in *Henderson the Rain King*," 109.

31. Bellow, *Henderson the Rain King*, 276.

32. It's not only money Henderson inherits but an intellectual and literary tradition of service to the American nation. See the discussion of *The White Negro* by Norman Mailer in Gubar, *Racechanges*, 176ff.

33. Bellow, *Henderson the Rain King*, 125.

34. Ibid., 126.

35. Ibid., 37. It is not only the mixing of Black and white which Henderson is represented as equating to death but any disturbance of one order by another. Hence his killing of the male cat "with brown and grey smoky fur" (90) lest it go wild and disturb the order of or kill the other animals. Given the human/animal interchanges throughout this novel, the function of this image as a negative stereotype of Black male sexuality and the relationship to Ricey's unnamed partner—for this child to be "colored," Ricey's sexual partner has to have been Black—need not be underlined. See also the way in which these hybrid taboo objects are linked throughout the novel: for example, the cat with the death of the frogs (89), and the baby, a seal, and "a chimpanzee who was dressed in a cowboy suit" at the end of the novel (335).

36. The equation of the mixing of black and white equating death to whites is by no means original to Bellow. See Gubar, *Racechanges*, chaps. 2 and 3. Of course, experience of mixed-race relationships for African Americans, given the history of lynching and other forms of cultural and political suppression, has sometimes meant actual death rather than existential angst.

37. See Sukhbir Singh, "Meeting with Saul Bellow," *American Studies International* 3, no. 5 (1997): 19–31, for a more laudatory reading of Bellow's treatment of ethnicity and a disavowal from Bellow that *Henderson the Rain King* is actually about race.

38. Bellow, *Henderson the Rain King*, 58.

39. See Patricia A. Turner, *Ceramic Uncles and Celluloid Mammies* (London: Anchor, 1994), especially for how nonhuman creatures are used to reinforce anti-Black stereotypes. See also the discussion of Richard Wright's concept of the "frog's perspective" as an analogy of the consciousness of Black men in *White Man Listen!* by Paul Gilroy, *The Black Atlantic* (Cambridge: Harvard University Press, 1993), 147. Of course, since *White Man Listen!* was not published until 1964, Bellow, like Wright, would have to be using the concept from Nietzsche; still, the usage of such symbolism despite the radically different politics is typical of the period.

40. Ibid., 110.

41. Newman, "Saul Bellow's Sixth Sense," 17.

42. That this central character is of WASP ethnicity rather than Jewish is only strategically important since such erasure of the "Black Atlantic" passage can thus be represented in Bellow's ethnic/national identity politics as a nonpartisan process which clears the way for the further strategic deployment of Jewishness in *Mr. Sammler's Planet* and *Humboldt's Gift*. As stated previously, the argument here is that Bellow positions representations of Jewishness to guarantee the assimilationist model of white America rather than to gain a separatist distinctiveness for Jewish Americanness.

43. A potential reading of the relationship between Henderson and Dahfu

as one of homosocial or even homosexual attraction with the lion acting as a symbolic signifier of disavowal might be developed especially alongside the reading of blackface in Eric Lott, "White Like Me," in *Cultures of United States Imperialism*, ed. Amy Kaplan and Donald E. Pease (Durham, N.C., and London: Duke University Press, 1993).

44. Bellow, *Henderson the Rain King*, 341.
45. Morrison, *Playing in the Dark*, 59.
46. Bellow, *Henderson the Rain King*, 335.
47. Ibid., 340.
48. Morrison, *Playing in the Dark*, 59.
49. Markos, "Life against Death in *Henderson the Rain King*," 116.
50. Stanley Crouch, "Introduction to Saul Bellow," in *Mr. Sammler's Planet*, by Saul Bellow (London: Penguin, 1995), xi.
51. Bellow quoted in Jane Howard, "Mr. Bellow Considers His Planet," *Life Magazine* (April 2, 1970), reprinted in *Conversations with Saul Bellow*, ed. Gloria L. Cronin and Ben Siegel (Jackson: University of Mississippi Press, 1994), 77–78.
52. Saul Bellow, *Mr. Sammler's Planet* (London: Penguin, 1995), 162. Notice the similarity between, in terms of vocabulary (neckless) and general description of the polliwogs, the negative Africanist presence in *Henderson the Rain King*, a similarity underscored by the equating the pickpocket's penis later in the text with an elephant trunk. It has been argued that such an equation in jokes of the period (elephants substituting for Blacks) showed an increase of anti-Black feeling during the civil rights movement but allowed such feelings to be safely articulated away from the charges of racism.
53. Marianne Russell, "White Man's Black Man: Three Views," *College Language Association Journal* 17 (1973), reprinted in *Saul Bellow in the 1980s*, ed. Gloria L. Cronin and L. H. Goldman (East Lansing: Michigan State University Press 1989), 201–2.
54. Bellow, *Mr. Sammler's Planet*, 49.
55. Gubar, *Racechanges*, 175.
56. Bellow, *Mr. Sammler's Planet*, 32.
57. Ibid., 172.
58. Ibid., 313.
59. Ibid., 228.
60. Ibid., 235.

6

"Washed Up on the Shores of Truth": Saul Bellow's Post-Holocaust America

Victoria Aarons

In a 1987 letter to the American Jewish writer Cynthia Ozick, Saul Bellow, Nobel laureate and novelist of vast intellectual depth and complexity, acknowledged what for him was a failure of reckoning. The overwhelming event of the Holocaust, in Bellow's words, "a crime so vast that it brings all Being into Judgment," was met by American intellectuals in the years following the war with an unconscionable silence, a reprehensible disregard for that which defined the failure of the civilized world.[1] For Bellow, the silence imposed upon the known events of the Holocaust, "the destruction of European Jewry," amounted to an unforgivable restraint among those who should have assumed the censuring voice of America's conscience. In the immediate aftermath of the war, writers, intellectuals, and artists might have brought to the forefront of modern sensibilities what was surely an irrevocably defining moment of the twentieth century.[2] In exposing the appalling brutality and pathology of German anti-Semitism and Nazi legislation—in Bellow's words, the "forces of deformity that produced the Final Solution"—as well as criticizing the belatedness of America's intervention in a war that might have been averted or at the very least abbreviated, the voices of American writers, and, as Bellow cautions, in particular, "Jewish Writers in America," heedlessly missed the opportunity to shape public response to the incalculable loss of human lives and to the atrocities instituted by the Nazi regime.[3] Inexplicably, those whose influence helped shape modern thought and whose censure might have created a public moral reckoning remained silent. And this turning away from what, in Bellow's words, was "the central event of their time," constituted a personal as well as a shared failure for Bellow and his generation of writers.[4]

In writing to Cynthia Ozick, whose own literature challenges the limitations of expression in Holocaust narratives, Bellow admits to a failure of moral and literary courage: "I can't say how our responsibility can be assessed. We ... should have reckoned more fully, more deeply with [the Holocaust]. Nobody in America seriously took this on and only a few Jews elsewhere (like Primo Levi) were able to comprehend it all ... but in the matter of higher comprehension ... there were no minds *fit* to comprehend.... All parties ... are passing the buck and every honest conscience feels the disgrace of it."[5] For Bellow, the omission of the Holocaust in literary discourse in the direct aftermath of the war remained disquieting. His lingering sense of ambivalence, not about the nature of the events of the Holocaust—for him "the most atrocious [war] in history"—but about the value of literature in performing any useful function in explaining those events seems something of an uncharacteristic hesitancy from a writer such as Bellow, an intellectual whose critical commentary on the transgressions and pathologies of twentieth-century life and thought have defined him throughout his career.[6] But this nagging ambivalence seems to have shadowed Bellow throughout a half century of prolific literary accomplishment and enormous influence on twentieth-century American letters. As late as 1990, Bellow persisted in asking, "What would writing about [the Holocaust] have altered?"[7] In so doing, Bellow raises the persistent question of the representation of the Holocaust in literature and, more generally, of the role of the artist in the expression of atrocity.

As Bellow candidly confesses, his priorities, not unlike America's collective opportunism in the increasing plenty of the years following World War II, might be characterized as self-interest at the expense of conscious awareness, not only of the political events of his time, but of the human condition forever altered by, as Bellow put it, "a singular kind of madness."[8] Of course, for the intellectual, self-deception, a willful and willed obliviousness to a higher consciousness, is the most unforgiveable deceit as well as the one most difficult to maintain. And Bellow was, after all, in his own characterization, a writer of utmost honesty, critical probing, and ironic, self-critical reflection. As Bellow readily acknowledges,

> I was too busy becoming a novelist to take note of what was happening in the Forties. I was involved with "literature" and given over to preoccupations

with art, with language, with my struggle on the American scene, with claims for recognition of my talent, or, like my pals of the *Partisan Review,* with modernism, Marxism, New Criticism, with Eliot, Yeats, Proust, etc.—with anything except the terrible events in Poland. Growing slowly aware of this unspeakable evasion I didn't even know how to begin to admit it into my inner life. Not a particle of this can be denied. And can I really say—can anyone say—what was to be done, how this "thing" *ought* to have been met? Since the late Forties I have been brooding about it and sometimes I imagine I *can* see something. But what such brooding may amount to is probably insignificant. I can't even begin to say what responsibility any of us may bear in such a matter.[9]

Bellow's expiation here is both moving and, in no small part, a little maddening because, despite these remarks, the Holocaust emerges in the sweep of Bellow's fiction, if at times indirectly, as a motivating presence in some of his best work.

All such rationalizations and disclosures aside, Bellow was, contrary to his own heartfelt disclaimer, deeply engaged with politics at home and abroad. As part of "the *Partisan Review* crowd"—New York intellectuals of the 1930s and 1940s, such as Irving Howe, William Phillips, Philip Rahv, Delmore Schwartz, and Lionel Trilling—Bellow, like his colleagues, was committed to revolutionary political ideologies, to Marxism, socialism, Trotskyism, and the like. The critic Alan Berger describes those years as a time of intoxicating literary freedom for the New York intellectual, a "political hothouse" defined by "radical politics and modernist culture."[10] Bellow and his fellow intellectuals, whose ever-widening voices were gaining ground in the 1940s—voices that came to define the American literary scene, in defiance of provincial conservatism—were committed to the life of the mind outside of the confining borders of the manuscript page. They were actively and unreservedly engaged with the affairs of their world, but they were also committed to modernism and its autonomous self-expression and freedom of thought. Therefore, there seems to be something curious about Bellow's regretful admission to his son Gregory that he "came late" to the Holocaust, that somehow the Holocaust escaped his notice, a political reality he failed to engage as he did with so many other political exigencies of the time.[11]

Given Bellow's interest in global politics, in internationalization, and in the European political-cultural scene, turning from events affecting millions throughout Europe strikes one as an enigmatic and not uncomplicated exception. It is almost unthinkable that the Holocaust, for a Jewish intellectual of such compassionate and impassioned expression as Bellow, engaged as he was in the world of revolutionary thought and action, could possibly have been, as he admits, one of those "things that got away from me."[12] There was clearly, or not so clearly, something about the Holocaust that separated itself from other political interests for Bellow. His own comments suggest two possibilities: it may have been his own vision of himself as a rising intellectual refashioning possibilities for primarily literary expression as he mined the understandably exhilarating narcissism of his own swift trajectory on the literary scene; it may also have involved the headiness of American life for Jews in the middle of the twentieth century, including the dissociation from his Jewish immigrant roots characteristic among the first-generation American-born of his time. As Bellow explained, "I never considered it a duty to write about the fate of the Jews. I didn't need to make that my obligation. I felt no obligation except to write—what I was really moved to write. . . . I don't know why. There it is."[13] Such explanations are historically plausible and are suggestive, in a cautionary way, about the relation between novelistic commitments and political engagement. However, despite the seeming regret imbedded in his remarks, Bellow emphatically responded to the Holocaust throughout his career; indeed, some of his more subtle fictional modes of representation significantly influenced the ways in which we talk and think about the Holocaust well into the twenty-first century.

In fact, Bellow's insistence that his obsession with America—"so absorbed by my American life that . . . I wasn't ready to think about Jewish history"—eclipsed his undertaking of the Holocaust is a remarkable admission from a writer whose engagement with the Holocaust early on was so effectively rendered in his fiction and brought to the fore in unnerving and insidious fashion.[14] This admission, however, partakes less of abdication than of uncertainty. Indeed, despite the clear sense of regret expressed in his letter to Cynthia Ozick about the decades of "brooding" that followed the war, and despite his own conviction that it was not until "I went to Auschwitz in 1959 that the Holocaust landed its full weight on me," Bellow explored the possibilities of living in a post-Holocaust world in his novels with a deceptively restrained immediacy in the midst of what he rightly perceived as a profound and challenging cultural silence.[15] As S. Lillian Kremer has suggested, "Bellow was at the forefront of American literary readiness to address anti-Semitism and the *Shoah* in fiction. . . . a subdued yet ever-present component, rarely at the dramatic center, but often surfacing in the thought and speech of characters haunted by its specter."[16] Writing in a virtual vacuum, without literary precedent, Bellow exposed the social and moral disfigurement that brought about the catastrophic events of the Holocaust and the fear left in its wake. With narrative indirection mirroring and commenting on the tortuously oblique conditions of America's own comportment toward Jews, Bellow's fiction creates an America where the Holocaust is a fact of his characters' lives, lives shaped by the unwelcome knowledge of the human capacity for evil, a "fictional, yet mimetically accurate, post-Holocaust world," as Thomas Rhea puts it, "in which the horrors exceed the limits of language."[17] Bellow's post-Holocaust universe is so powerful in large part because of its indirection, its ongoing presence in the interstices of ordinary human action. Bellow exempts no character from the ethical weight of living in a post-Holocaust world. In many ways, the Holocaust forms an absent presence in Bellow's fiction; it lives not only as historical fact, but also in its immediacy. In Bellow's fiction, a literary enterprise spanning a half century, the Holocaust remains uncannily present, just below the surface of everyday thought and action, breaking through in moments of frightening recognition.

Bellow was, as he acknowledges, gaining literary recognition during the war years at a time when millions of Jews throughout Europe were being rounded up, deported to death camps, and systematically murdered. His first novel, *Dangling Man,* was published in 1944, the year of the Nazi occupation of Hungary and the deportation of Hungarian Jews, as well as the first transports of Jews from Athens to Auschwitz and the liberation by the Russians of the first concentration camp, Majdanek. In 1944, President Roosevelt created the War Refugee Board in response to political pressure to help Jews under Nazi control. This was the year that discussions of bombing the death camps took place in both Washington, D.C., and London, proposals that were ultimately rejected. Roosevelt issued a statement in 1944 condemning the ongoing "crimes against humanity" by the Germans and Japanese. As the war drew to a close, Americans could no longer claim ignorance of events taking place throughout Europe. Yet Bellow's first novel, *Dangling Man,* curiously enough set during World War II and described by the critic Edmund Wilson in the *New Yorker* as "one of the most honest pieces of testimony on the psychology of a whole generation who have grown up during the Depression and the war," pays scant attention to the devastating events taking place across the Atlantic and then only in veiled references, as if through a scrim of oblique recognition.[18] Readers and critics generally agree that Bellow's literary milieu was America, that the centers of gravity for Bellow and his anxiously fixated protagonists were the urban settings of Chicago and New York, places of heightened self-awareness and unrestrained discourse. When reference is made to the appearance of the Holocaust in Bellow's fiction, readers generally point to *Mr. Sammler's Planet,* published in 1970, and to *The Bellarosa Connection,* a novella published in 1989. But as early as 1947, with the publication of his second novel, *The Victim,* Bellow introduces what will become a distinctive and recurring trademark of his writing, a deceptive indirection that ultimately exposes its despairing center.

In *The Victim* and *Mr. Sammler's Planet,* we see an evolution in Bellow's thinking about the events of the Holocaust. These two novels pose what for Bellow is the central and defining conundrum confronting his uncertain protagonists: how to live in a post-Holocaust world. Bellow navigates, through narrative indirection, a fictive response to the silence imposed upon the Holocaust in its immediacy and aftermath. In doing so, Bellow poses the following questions: How can a Jew live after the events of the Holocaust? What are the imperatives and requirements for living in post-Holocaust America? What does it mean to live responsibly, to live and write ethically in response to the Holocaust? What is involved in negotiating a world in which we have such knowledge, not only of the capacity for evil, but of the systematized, legislated organization of mass murder? In approaching these questions, Bellow takes us through a world of shards and fragments, of vulnerability, predatory threat, and imperiled conscience.

To be sure, Bellow was writing in something of a literary vacuum regarding the Holocaust. It was not until the early 1960s that American writers, and in particular American Jewish novelists, took on the Holocaust as an explicit literary landscape. And even then, the Holocaust was approached cautiously by American Jewish writers, with a guarded concern that to write about the Holocaust would be to trespass on perilous, uneven, and uninvited territory. Unarguably, the earliest notable "Holocaust novel" written in America was Edward Lewis Wallant's *The Pawnbroker,* published in 1961. In this novel about a displaced Holocaust survivor relocated in Harlem, past experiences are reenacted in a series of dream sequences; the reader is only taken *there*, to the site of this survivor's undoing, through a canopy of flashbacks, momentary, fleeting, images seared on the imagination. And although Wallant draws the pawnbroker's dream-state reliving of the horrors of his experience with terrifyingly clarity, the Holocaust, he reminds us, is the stuff of someone else's nightmares and thus takes place at some remove, not only geographically, but psychically as well. The novel's setting is not the concentration camps; neither is it war-torn Europe or Nazi Germany. Instead, it takes place in New York, the self-contained space of Harlem, one that for Wallant exists outside of real time, so much so that one of his characters will wonder aloud about the origin of the survivor's concentration-camp tattoo: "Hey, what kind of tattoo you call that?" the young man with no knowledge of history will ask the pawnbroker.[19] This compartmentalization of the experience of the Holocaust renders the tone of the experience paradoxically horrific and somehow distant, apart, with the effect that the character of its evil is somehow blunted, even domesticated.

So, too, in Philip Roth's early story "Eli, the Fanatic," published in the 1959 collection *Goodbye, Columbus*, the Holocaust "appears," in this instance, by way of suburban Woodenton, New York, as a remote event, one that happened to another people in a distant place. In this story, the suburban pastoral of Woodenton is disturbed by uninvited refugees of the Holocaust, survivors who have lost everything and whose presence at the yeshiva and obvious "Jewishness" threaten the supposed peace of the assimilated Jews living there in uneasy armistice with the gentiles and in willful obliviousness toward the fate of European Jews. Of Roth's beleaguered Jewish protagonist, Eli Peck, whose defense of his fellow Jews-in-hiding is wearing thin, the head of the offending yeshiva will accusingly ask: "No news [of the Holocaust] reached Woodenton?"[20] To be sure, for American Jewish novelists in the two decades following the end of the war, the Holocaust was approached tentatively and indirectly. In this literature, the Holocaust exists in absentia, in what might be considered forms of avoidance. Not surprisingly, America, not Europe, forms the dramatic setting for the inclusion of the Holocaust, so that the Holocaust is engaged, as it were, on safer ground.

Bellow, like Wallant and the early Roth, came to the Holocaust indirectly and made America center stage for exposing, in retrospect, the horrors of the Holocaust, an event that, as an American Jew, could indeed only be imagined—and then inexpertly—from a distance. There is a deeply rooted sense in Bellow's work of the impossibility of "getting it right," complicated, perhaps, by his own ambivalence about taking on the Holocaust as subject matter. Is literature the appropriate medium for the expression of atrocity? This question, a continuing source of contention, was beginning to be contested in the direct aftermath of the war. Should a writer take a political position on the Holocaust? For Bellow, the issue of responsible public discourse, a reckoning on the part of America, of the American literati, of the Jew-who-got-away, the Jew whose fate might well have been otherwise, remained a source of anxious and recurrent concern. In many ways, Bellow's perception of a personal and political failure to expose the tragic collapse of morality for the sake of political and perhaps artistic expediency becomes the failure, not only of the intellectual, but the failure of America as well, suggesting America's inadvertent accountability for the prolonged, devastating effects of the Holocaust. Bellow's hesitant grappling with the events of the Holocaust, events escalating in stunningly proximate relation to his own arrival on the American literary scene, might well be seen as a metonymic measure of America's own inadequate and delayed response. And perhaps four decades of "brooding," as Bellow reveals in his letter to Cynthia Ozick, yields only the sure knowledge of the limitations of the intellect, the impossibility of understanding the events that resulted in such incalculable loss as well as the inadequacy of giving a voice to the unspeakable.

To this end, Saul Bellow's Holocaust exists just beyond the articulation of its horrors. As the frighteningly real presence of anti-Semitism haunting urban cityscapes, the Holocaust comes to life in Bellow's work in the lurking menace of the lingering specter of annihilation. Most notably in *The Victim* (1947) and *Mr. Sammler's Planet* (1970), the Holocaust emerges as the backdrop against which Bellow's uneasy protagonists negotiate their lives in the deceptive clarity of America. For Bellow, the Holocaust exposes not only the bankruptcy of the civilized world, but also the failure of the intellect to imagine a world where ideas and culture are regenerative. For Bellow, the Holocaust marks the end of the intellectual's self-delusion of the talismanic properties—the saving powers—of culture and thought. For Bellow's post-Holocaust protagonists—from the neurotically phobic Asa Leventhal in *The Victim* to the more restrained intellectual and survivor Artur Sammler in *Mr. Sammler's Planet*—the Holocaust exposes the failure of reason, decency, and compassion; it is demonstrable proof that human beings are capable of unlimited forms of pathological self-justification and atrocious acts. Indeed, as Bellow's Artur Sammler, a transplanted survivor in New York City, puts it, the facts are the facts; the Holocaust occurred: "Why speak of it? Things that happen, happen."[21] In a voice that clearly speaks for its author, Bellow's protagonist Sammler will, even as he holds forth, resign himself to the inevitable failure of words: "Arguments! Explanations! . . . All will explain everything to all, until the next, the new common version is ready. This version . . . will be, like the old, a fiction" (19). Here Bellow links the making of certainties, of collective convictions, with the making of fiction, convenient narratives of compensation and reprieve.

The Victim might be considered Bellow's initial foray into the dangerous landscape of the Holocaust. Published in 1947, only two years after the end of the war and the liberation of the concentration camps, and in the midst of the continuing Nuremberg trials, *The Victim* tells the story of Asa Leventhal, a Jew living in New York in the years immediately following the end of the war. Leventhal is antagonized by a certain Kirby Allbee, whose anti-Semitism takes on an increasingly predatory and accusatory hostility throughout the course of the novel. Allbee is to Leventhal what the specter of the Holocaust is to the Jews, and the interactions between the two men—the one predatory and the other victimized—are shown by Bellow to be a microcosmic reminder of anti-Semitism's prelude to murderous impulses. It is, after all, the anti-Semite Allbee who, toward the novel's end, will turn the gas on in Leventhal's flat, causing the Jew to run choking and gasping from his room.

In *The Victim*, the presence of the Holocaust constitutes a defining rupture in the very existence, not only of European Jewry, but of the real conditions of life for American Jews. Set far from the ruins of the Nazi devastation, the Holocaust haunts the postwar America of Bellow's harrowing novel. New York City is transformed into a Kafkaesque world of phobic disorientation for Leventhal, a man plagued by "the feeling that he really did not know what went on about him . . . strange . . . savage things. They hung near him all the time in trembling drops, invisible, usually, or seen from a distance. But that did not mean that there was always to be a distance, or that sooner or later one or two of the drops might not fall on him."[22] A tangible fear leaves Leventhal victimized by his own sense of impending dread, but also by this immediate, inexpressible, and irrepressible history, in the form of Albee, that threatens him still.

Bellow's post-Holocaust America is aggressive and menacing, and it is against this landscape—psychic and terrestrial—that Leventhal finds himself vulnerable to forces out of his control, dangers localized in the singular figure of Kirby Allbee. For Allbee is far too much a stock character to be other than a representation of generalized anti-Semitic threat. He blames Leventhal for being dismissed from his job, and Leventhal thus becomes a convenient—and not without precedent—scapegoat for Allbee's own incompetence. Although Allbee conveniently sees himself as the victim, in his way of thinking, having been intentionally persecuted by the perfidious Jew, it is really Leventhal who is made the victim by the self-serving Allbee. "Why me?" Leventhal will ask of Allbee's accusations of betrayal, quickly assessing, "Of course, he has to have someone to blame; that's how it starts" (76). And Allbee's stalking advance upon the apprehensive Leventhal is just indistinct enough to be vaguely uncertain. Is Allbee really predatory, hatefully seeking out to destroy Leventhal, to make Leventhal pay for what Allbee considers Leventhal's underhanded attempts to get him fired from his job? Or is Leventhal so unhinged, so unreasonably suspicious, drawing upon some ancient sense of persecution, that his reaction is one of paranoid obsession? Bellow creates such intentional ambiguities, at least in the initial pages of the novel, in order to bring the reader to the uncomfortable conclusion that, indeed, Leventhal is in a vulnerable position as a Jew whose history lingers over him, just as the smoke from the chimneys hovered like a canopy over the ruins of Europe. In positing the tension between these two singular men, ordinary in scope and circumstance, Bellow shows us a crazy kind of dance, the two working in tandem, so that the one man's fear impels the other man's barbaric, anti-Semitic vitriol, emboldening him, unwittingly encouraging his actions, giving license to Allbee's escalating anger. The motivation and all-too-willing participation that allowed the events leading up to Hitler's Final Solution, Bellow cautions, are not contained in its European theater. Rather, the irrational hatred, loathing, maniacal deception, and pathological acts of cruelty and ill will that put into action the events of the Holocaust also define the Jew's experience of living in the immediacy of a post-Holocaust world.

Grafting images suggestive of Holocaust Europe onto New York City, Bellow gives us an urban landscape that shimmers in the undulating heat, hostile and menacing to his unnerved protagonist. The opening scene of *The Victim* sets the stage, with considerable urgency, for Leventhal's mounting disorientation and subsequent persecution. Leventhal emerges from the subway to find the very landscape to have shifted, "the whole continent . . . to have moved from its place and slid nearer the equator" (11). The very shape of the world is transformed, skewed, made all the more oppressive by the reiterative references to the overpowering heat of the day and the heavy, sun-soaked cityscape—"the street . . . deadened with heat and light," "clouds . . . heavily suspended and slow," "brackish air . . . chalky." The suffocating conditions of Leventhal's relentless claustrophobia make all the more emphatic his ubiquitous fear and ill-defined anxiety (40, 158). Such descriptions of the claustrophobic heat and crowded airways become a rhythmic patterning in the novel, the beat of despair, creating a kind of background noise against which Leventhal's escalating apprehension and dread become real.

Bellow thus places his protagonist in an ominous, nightmarish landscape surrounded by a very real threat of anti-Semitism, which presents a barrier to his social mobility and interaction. Leventhal is the target of, as Bellow's Mr. Sammler might have put it, "historical stupidity . . . the persistence, the maniacal push of certain ideas, themselves originally stupid, stupid ideas that had lasted for centuries," and that here, in post-Holocaust America, show themselves to be unshakably fixed (143). From the vulgar Mr. Beard, Leventhal's boss, whose crudely offensive remarks reveal his deep-seated prejudice—"Takes unfair advantage . . . Like the rest of his brethren. I've never known one who wouldn't. Always please themselves first" (13)—to the anonymous woman in the movie theater whose muttered epithet, "the gall of Jews," in response to a polite request from Leventhal's wife to remove her hat, renders Leventhal infuriatingly impotent. And even though Leventhal is an American Jew living in the presumed safety of cosmopolitan New York, his identification with "the lost, the outcast, the overcome, the effaced, the ruined" casts his lot with those catastrophically subject to circumstances beyond their control and suggests his conviction that it's by chance alone that he was born in America, that he escaped the Europe of his immigrant parents, escaped, that is, the horrifying fate of European Jewry (26).

As Allbee indefatigably pursues Leventhal through the streets of New York, the nightmarish quality of Leventhal's existence increases; the already oppressively overbearing heat takes on a fiery hue, and the crowds of people amass into an indistinguishable throng herded through the streets against their will. And it is very clear that this is a collective destination, one eerily made all the more intolerable by Bellow's sinister description of the mode of transit. For, amid this ominous terrain, against the "redness in the sky, like the flame at the back of a vast baker's oven . . . gaping fierily over the black of the Jersey shore . . . the trains rushing by under the gratings . . . the cumbersome busses crawled groaning," Bellow transforms New York hideously into a Holocaust landscape of imminent danger and entrapment (28). Bellow's descriptions of the constant, harshly rumbling sounds of the trains, "numbing," groaning with the heavy burden of crowds of people packed together, augur impending doom (28). Suggestively, such instances of claustrophobic panic for Leventhal take place on modes of transit. The subways, trains, and busses, recalling the cattle cars taking masses of Jews to their destruction, pass through the novel indifferently, unaffected by the lives of their passengers, who are squeezed uncomfortably together with insufficient air to breathe. The constant reference to the subway disturbs all the more because of its subterranean position; it's a hidden, menacing mechanism of deportation. In *The Victim,* the trains and their conductors seem to be part of a labyrinthine network, an underground maze of intricate, unstoppable design. The steady subterranean reverberation of the trains exists under the streets of New York and also just beneath the surface of Leventhal's consciousness, a dissociative terror that pulls him under, choking in the brackish, insufficient air.

And above ground, too, the specter of the Holocaust transforms the cityscape: "the factories were beginning to smolder and faced massively . . . into the sun" (40). Against the backdrop of the smoldering chimneys, the threat of the Holocaust exists in the immediacy of Leventhal's, as well as the reader's, perception. The towers of the buildings "scorched, smoky, gray," emerge into the sky as warnings, beacons of disaster. The very landscape is dangerous, ready to strike: "the light over them and over the water was akin to the yellow revealed in the slit of the eye of a wild animal . . . something inhuman that didn't care about anything human" (52–53). In a stunning moment, one the novel has been propelling itself toward all along, Leventhal awakes from uneasy dreams to "gas . . . pouring from the oven," the air acrid and hard to breathe (246). Such references to trains, to towers, to suffocation, to the mechanisms of destruction, and to nightmarish images of terror and agonizing loss are significantly more ominous than mere representations or symbols of annihilation. Rather, here the constant undercurrents of such recognizable Holocaust markers are gestures of collective transference and images of collective rupture. As Leventhal will desperately cry out to the indifferent Allbee, "millions of us have been killed. What about that?" (133). Leventhal, although separated from the events of the Holocaust, fears its legacy. His identification with the millions of murdered Jews defines his experience of living in post-Holocaust America, which Bellow shows to be a deceptive oasis, transitory, just one more stop along the tracks of diasporic Jewish history.

If the central problem in *The Victim* involves the repercussions for American Jews living in a post-Holocaust universe in the initial years after the war, then the uncertainties Bellow poses in *Mr. Sammler's Planet* revolve around living in the wake of the Holocaust for the survivor of, in Bellow's words, "the greatest disaster of [Jewish] history."[23] What happens in the years between *The Victim* and *Mr. Sammler's Planet?* Initially published serially in the *Atlantic Monthly* in 1969 and in book form in 1970, *Mr. Sammler's Planet* stages its central character, a seventy-year-old Polish Jew, a survivor of the Holocaust, against the backdrop of New York. Here Bellow's displaced Artur Sammler, former journalist in London, finds himself relocated in America, "advertised throughout the universe as *the* most desirable, most exemplary of all nations," and at its very center, New York, "the soul of America " (14, 146). But it's here in America that Sammler, a man who literally scrambled from the grave, buried under a pile of bodies and left for dead, finds another kind of madness. For in America, "a glorious planet," Sammler discovers a universe "at grips with historical problems, struggling with certain impossibilities, experiencing violently states inherently static" (135, 146). Bellow's New York in the late 1960s and early 1970s is a place of debauchery, depravity, criminality, profligacy, self-indulgence, and grasping excess, a place wherein "everything [was] being done to make it intolerable to abide here, an unconscious collaboration of all souls spreading madness and poison" (135). But Bellow's America, epitomized by New York, is also a place of paradoxes, in which is revealed, as Artur Sammler discovers, the undulating "magic of extremes" (135).

Bellow's description of post-Holocaust America in *The Victim* both resembles and does not that in *Mr. Sammler's Planet*. The time from 1945, when Bellow began work on *The Victim*, his second novel, to 1970, when *Mr. Sammler's Planet* was published in book form, were important years in American history. These decades were a time of socioeconomic change and cultural upheaval, increasingly a time of excess and restless reassessment, a seemingly endless period in which political, cultural, and social authorities were challenged and upended. This period saw radical swings in political thought. This shift in political climate was characterized, perhaps, by more candor, by a more honest assessment of America's failures and possibilities. Not surprisingly, then, the twenty-plus years since the liberation of the concentration camps demonstrate a shift in how we think about and navigate the events of the Holocaust. And we find this shift in Bellow's depiction in *Mr. Sammler's Planet* of his central character's ability to step back and critically assess the repercussions of the Holocaust on twentieth-century life and to attempt to define the terms and requirements necessary for living responsibly.

What happens, then, in Bellow's ideas about the Holocaust between *The Victim* and *Mr. Sammler's Planet?* Bellow moves from the Holocaust eerily hovering in the backdrop of his protagonist's consciousness, its hauntingly sinister presence rising in the towering infernos of the smokestacks blackening New York's skyline, to a more direct engagement with the events of the Holocaust. With the publication of *Mr. Sammler's Planet,* enough time seems to have passed so that the Holocaust, itself no longer proximate and thus teetering into America in its devastating aftermath, has become part of history. Thus Bellow can go back to the Holocaust. He can return to Poland at war, to Zamosht Forest into which his protagonist fled only to be attacked by Polish partisans. He can go into the mausoleum in which Artur Sammler was forced to hide, into the mass graves, the extermination by gas, the death of his wife, "when everyone is murdering everyone. . . . When [Sammler] and sixty or seventy others, all stripped naked and having dug their own grave, were fired upon and fell in. Bodies upon his own body. Crushing. . . . Struggling out much later from the weight of corpses, crawling out of the loose soil," and Sammler's own desperate killing, "without pity," of the German soldier in the forest (92, 140). In portraying a man who "had actually gone through it," who survived the Holocaust, "one of the doomed who had lasted it all out," and whose unhappy legacy gives him both legitimacy and experience to speak, Bellow can directly turn to that which only hovers anxiously over Asa Leventhal's New York (15, 140).

Between 1947 and 1969, then, some of the darkness lifts, and Artur Sammler, blinded in one eye, ironically can emerge into the light of New York City, despite "the breath of wartime Poland passing over [his] damaged tissues," with something resembling the kind of equanimity that Leventhal lacks (5). Perhaps like Bellow himself, who, after so many years, imagines that he "can see something," Sammler, a man betrayed by the failure of reason and an enlightened intellectual culture, comes into the light of New York City with some knowledge of human motivation, some sense of possibility for a future.[24] But it's a light off-kilter, a light too bright, disingenuous, contrived, not entirely without mockery: "the sun, relatively bright for Manhattan—shining and pouring through openings in his substance, through his gaps . . . an intensification of vision" (43). Walking the streets of New York, Artur Sammler is assaulted; the "particles in the bright wind, flinging downtown, acted like emery on the face" (44). For Sammler, "separated from the rest of his species, if not in some fashion severed" by such knowledge and experience, can never again see the world made right (43).

To be sure, the world in which Artur Sammler, with "zero instincts, no grasp of New York," finds himself is not all that different from Asa Leventhal's uneasy universe (10). America is still on the brink of something, poised now between knowing and assessing the conditions within which one must calculate and negotiate the horrors of mid-twentieth-century history. Indeed, for both of Bellow's troubled protagonists, life after the Holocaust is irrevocably altered. Something is always off, uneasily tilted, skewed. For Bellow's protagonists, the Holocaust remains the point of origin, that against which everything must be measured and observed. As the novel opens, Artur Sammler awakens "shortly after dawn, or what would have been dawn in a normal sky" (3). In a scene mirroring an occasion in *The Victim* where Asa Leventhal emerges from the subway to find the landscape to have shifted, "the whole continent . . . to have moved from its place and slid nearer the equator," Bellow's Sammler wakes to the uneasy knowledge that even the natural world has been forever altered by his history (11). Such disquieting moments of disorientation speak to Bellow's conviction, voiced by Sammler, that "existence was not accountable to him" and that knowledge, faltering even under the best of circumstances, has its unfortunate limitations (277).

For Bellow's post-Holocaust characters, the world can never be "normal," never righted. And, although Sammler is a much more sophisticated, mature, and controlled character than his predecessor Asa Leventhal, he, too, survives in a wounded world, a universe in which everything is amiss and where he is misled by his powers of observation so much so that the very quotidian deceives him, as he awakens to "the books and papers of his West

Side bedroom and suspected that they were the wrong books, the wrong papers" (3). The repetition of "wrong . . . wrong" resounds with and sets the scene for the conditions in which Sammler finds himself. And, to be sure, Mr. Sammler's planet is Bellow's universe, a landscape shaped by the events of the Holocaust and the knowledge that follows, knowledge undiminished by time. To this end, Gregory Bellow recollects his father's unsettling words spoken in conversation some five years before his death: "Not a day goes by that I do not think of the horror of those last moments as the gas was released in the showers, the yelling, the screaming, the suffering."[25]

In creating the voice of a survivor as the moral center of a novel that contends with the aftermath of the Holocaust and the arguments left in its wake, Bellow invokes the experiences of one survivor, a man who has "lasted" more than he has "survived," for Sammler "hadn't even done that, since so much of the earlier person had disappeared. It wasn't surviving, it was only lasting. He had lasted. For a time yet he might last" (91). Sammler is not, for Bellow, a representative figure. He does not stand for "the survivor." He is, instead, one man who has lived through the worst of times by chance and desperate fortune alone. "Where," Sammler wonders, "was the achievement? He had clawed his way out [of the mass grave]. If he had been at the bottom, he would have suffocated. . . . There was no special merit, there was no wizardry. There was only suffocation escaped. And had the war lasted a few months more, he would have died like the rest. Not a Jew would have avoided death" (10). Instead, Sammler escaped and reemerged into these demoralized times. And the mystery for Sammler and, I suspect, for Bellow, involves the difficulties in reconciling a post-Holocaust world with the events that preceded it. For "the sun," in Sammler's planet, "shone as if there were no death," the modern world and its inhabitants oblivious to one of the greatest crimes of the century, instead propelling themselves into an unknown future (44). Thus, *Mr. Sammler's Planet* is Bellow's meditation on the ways in which the Holocaust has shaped American life and thought. And it is in Artur Sammler's meditations that we hear the voice of Bellow, eloquent, cogent, erudite, and philosophical, the deeply introspective Jewish intellectual of the twentieth century.

There is a stunning moment in *Mr. Sammler's Planet* when Bellow casts aside the fictional mode and directly addresses the controversy surrounding German political theorist Hannah Arendt's argument in *Eichmann in Jerusalem*. In that book, Arendt puts forth the idea of the banality of evil: that the Nazis acted not from some monstrous evil but rather from banal, unexamined motives of obedience to authority. In commenting on the nature of criminality, Bellow's Mr. Sammler speaks with the authority, not only of a survivor, but of a European man of letters, one who has spent some thirty years reflecting on his experiences and on the nature of the human condition. Sammler directly opposes Arendt on the question of Nazi criminality, of the motivations of those Germans who perpetuated and carried out the Final Solution, and of how we are obligated to understand such acts. He disagrees with Arendt's argument that the Nazis enacted their plans under the most ordinary and mundane of motives and that those who carried out the actions of annihilation did so merely as a banal yielding to authority, an act of following orders. Sammler, although confirmed in his belief in the futility of theorizing, argues unequivocally that Arendt gets it wrong:

> The idea of making the century's great crime look dull is not banal. Politically, psychologically, the Germans had an idea of genius. The banality was only camouflage. What better way to get the curse out of murder than to make it look ordinary, boring, or trite? With horrible political insight they found a way to disguise the thing. Intellectuals do not understand. They get their notions about matters like this from literature. They expect a wicked hero like Richard III. But do you think the Nazis didn't know what murder was? Everybody . . . knows what murder is. That is very old human knowledge. The best and purest human beings, from the beginning of time, have understood that life is sacred. To defy that old understanding is not banality. There was a conspiracy against the sacredness of life. Banality is the adopted disguise of a very powerful will to abolish conscience. (18–19)

Sammler's argument raises again the question of whether one can entertain a political position on the Holocaust, on the nature and motivations upon which human beings act in atrocious and unconscionable ways to other human beings. The fact of the Holocaust exists; it altered the ways in which we understand the human capacity for evil and for the pathology of criminal intent. Murder—and the extent of mass murder at the center of Nazi ideology and execution—violates the most basic of prohibitions. And the scale of annihilation executed by the Nazis is evidence, not of ordinary, unthinking compliance, but rather of a deliberately calculated act of transgression and desecration. To see it otherwise, Bellow suggests through Sammler, is to deny the obvious and to expose oneself to pathological deception.

Bellow's attack on Arendt's discussion of the nature of Nazi criminality is meant to expose the intellectual's tendencies to theorize at the expense of clear, straightforward reckoning. For Bellow, as Sammler insists, to theorize the Holocaust is to fail to make the necessary "acknowledgment of social descent. Historical ruin, Transformation of society" (7). A certain kind of intellectual, Bellow proposes, shows the propensity to reason oneself into positions that can barely be tolerated in decent, civilized society. Bellow thus exposes such intellectualizing as a deeply unfortunate and dangerous matter of distortion, of inadvertently twisting the truth through a labyrinthine process of analyzing actualities—"the roots of this, the causes of the other, the source of events, the history, the structure, the reasons why . . . superstructures of explanation"—so that they no longer resemble themselves (3). Realities thus become abstractions; certainties, facts, the obvious morphed into ideologies, theories, models, and concepts. The danger, Bellow implies, is that we no longer see the thing for what it is; it thus loses its authenticity, its immediacy, and its basic human component.

Bellow further explains Hannah Arendt's failings in a 1982 letter written to the writer and critic Leon Wieseltier, suggesting that her own philosophical blindness sadly, tragically even, resulted in her defense of the indefensible:

> Much of her strength went into obstinacy, and she was the complete intellectual—i.e. she went always and as rapidly as possible for the great synthesis and her human understanding, painfully limited, could not support the might of historical analysis, unacknowledged prejudices, frustrations of her German and European aspirations, etc. She could often think clearly, but to think simply was altogether beyond her, and her imaginative faculty was stunted. . . . I once asked [Warsaw Ghetto survivor] Alexander Donat, author of *The Holocaust Kingdom,* how it was that the Jews went down so quickly in Poland. He said something like this: "After three days in the ghetto, unable to wash and shave, without clean clothing, deprived of food, all utilities and municipal services cut off, your toilet habits humiliatingly disrupted, you are demoralized, confused, subject to panic. A life of austere discipline would have made it possible for me to keep my head, but how many civilized people lead such a life?" Such simple facts—had Hannah had the imagination to see them—would have lowered the intellectual fever that vitiates her theories.[26]

What Arendt seems to ignore, in Bellow's assessment, are the basic requirements of surviving in this world. All her philosophizing, the attempts to contextualize the Nazi crimes in some larger abstraction about the nature of the human condition, ironically detracts from that which is most human. By complicating motives and patterns of behavior, Arendt paradoxically reduces the essential decencies of living to obscurities; elaborate paradigms replace simple yet indispensable matters of worth. Essentially, Bellow accuses Arendt of talking herself into an impossible corner. In opting for the cerebral over the instinctual, she thus inadvertently adopts the dangerous language of German mythmaking. As Sammler ironically maintains, "You had to be a crank to insist on being right" (3).

Finally, Bellow seems to suggest that, if the Holocaust teaches us nothing else, it is that words, uttered irresponsibly, distort essential truths. "What was gone," Bellow's Sammler ultimately discovers, "was the old words . . . terms beaten into flat nonsense. Not compassion; but what was a compassionate utterance? And compassionate utterance was a mortal necessity. Utterance, sounds of hope and desire, exclamations of grief. Such things were suppressed, as if illicit" (261). Words can no longer be trusted. Language in the post-Holocaust world of theories, explanations, and rationalizations, in Bellow's thinking, have come to replace truthful accounting, even if such accounting becomes the acknowledgment that we cannot fully explain the events, the motivations and actions that brought about the tragedy. What seems very clear is that Bellow faults the very cultural, social, and political institutions meant to serve and protect its citizens from harm. The atrocities perpetuated upon the Jews and others considered expendable by the Third Reich happened in part because of anti-Semitic and tyrannical fervor. But, as Bellow reminds us, such mass destruction was made possible by law, by systematized, legislative degree, laws of the land that were methodically revised to promote and execute tyranny, to make politically and socially acceptable heinous criminality at the expense of morality and decency. And no institution in the modern world, for Bellow, is without blame. Perhaps Bellow's position is best summed up in the words of his protagonist Sammler: "He was not against civilization, nor against politics, institutions, nor against order. When the grave was dug, institutions and the rest had not been for him. No politics, no order intervened. . . . But there was no need to thrust oneself personally into every general question—to assail Churchill, Roosevelt, for having known (and surely they did know) what was happening and failing to bomb Auschwitz. Why not have bombed Auschwitz? But they didn't. . . . they wouldn't. Emotions of justified reproach, supremacy in blame, made no appeal to Sammler. The individual was the supreme judge of nothing. . . . Existence was not accountable to him" (277).

Perhaps not. But, for Bellow, human beings are accountable to existence, to the landscape we formed and now live in, for the history to which we are bequeathed. The problem, Bellow suggests, is in taking the short view, in failing to recognize and act upon the continuing threat posed by the dangers of primeval myth—"the persistence, the maniacal push of certain ideas, themselves originally stupid, stupid ideas that had lasted for centuries"—and of hypocrisy, bigotry, small-mindedness, and stratagems of defeat (142). How must one live, Bellow's novels ask, with history so scarred? Can humankind continue on this planet without further madness, disgrace, and suffering? In both *The Victim* and *Mr. Sammler's Planet*, Bellow poses the continuing threat of anti-Semitism, "maniacal ideas" that have endured "for centuries" and that stand alongside the fears, compulsions, self-indulgences, delusions, and barbarity of the modern world, a society marred by, as Sammler mourns, "a kind of impunity, because no one cared what happened" (144).

But, for Bellow's Sammler, all is not quite lost. For, after all, humankind has, for better or worse, survived. "There is," as Sammler concedes, "still such a thing as man. . . . [T]here are still human qualities. Our weak species fought its fear, our crazy species fought its criminality. We are an animal of genius" (305). Despite the lingering threat of anti-Semitism—"There are always humans beings who take it upon themselves to represent or interpret the old savagery, tribalism, the primal fierceness of the fierce, lest we forget prehistory, savagery, animal origins" (227)—Bellow's America is not prewar Poland. Instead, Bellow's characters, like Artur Sammler, find themselves "washed up on the shores of truth" (124). America is, throughout his novels, the stage upon which human beings might be able to reinvent themselves. Despite its many absurdities and incongruities, America is where the unimaginable is finally imagined, offering, as Sammler puts it, "the charm, the ebullient glamour, the almost unbearable agitation that came from being able to describe oneself as a twentieth-century American" (73). The dark undercurrents of anti-Semitism and the detritus of the Holocaust that we find in *The Victim* dissipate in *Mr. Sammler's Planet*. This is not to say that such threats are no longer real. Rather, they are continually challenged by America's regenerative possibilities and the many assaults on human endurance.

If Bellow poses the seemingly impossible question of how we might live an informed, educated, meaningful existence in a post-Holocaust world, the answer, deceptively simple, might well be found in the character of Dr. Elya Gruner, Artur Sammler's nephew, who sponsored Sammler's arrival and subsequent life in America and over whose dead body, at the novel's close, Sammler prays. Elya Gruner is a man who, according to Bellow, managed to meet "through all the confusion and degraded clowning of this life through which we are speeding . . . the terms of his contract," a covenant established well before him, but nonetheless pertinent to the modern world (313). In Elya Gruner, Sammler finds the basic requirements for civilized, responsible living. Here the covenant is rescripted, Genesis rewritten for the modern, enlightened era, where America is the new point of origin, beginning not with Eden, but with the Fall, with the certain knowledge that we are a corrupted, shameful species. Bellow, not unironically, presents in his fictional universe the Edenic Fall in reverse order: from the depths, expulsion and worse, to the fertility, fecundity, and promise of America, the new world. This rebirth, of sorts, is not without its Bellovian pitfalls, its ironic, misguided, and maniac transgressions, its failures and often comical catastrophes. But, as Artur Sammler reckons, humankind, after the Holocaust, has been given, unbelievably, another chance, human beings "who had been sent back again to the end of the line. Waiting for something. Assigned to figure out certain things, to condense . . . some essence of experience" (274). Just when it seemed that human beings had come to the end of the line, wherein "this too great demand upon human consciousness and human capacities . . . overtaxed human endurance. . . . not . . . only of moral demand, but also of the demand upon the imagination to produce a human figure of adequate stature," Bellow, in his fiction, offers us another chance (232).

In short, the "assignment" for Bellow is felt in the simple desire of Sammler's nephew Elya Gruner to be good, to be kind, "to do what was required of him," and these efforts, in Bellow's way of thinking, distinguishes him from others, from, in fact, the host of characters who inhabit Bellow's novels (313). Elya Gruner, contrary to all expectations, is a man who lives without pretense or madness, without malice or self-deception, recognizing instead his limitations and failures, but also his obligatory responsibility to others. In both Bellow's and Sammler's planet, basic human decency defines responsible living in a post-Holocaust world. And there is, for Bellow, a kind of courage in proceeding through life with the Holocaust as legacy, a life of exhaustion and confusion, but also of plenty. As the poet laureate Howard Nemerov put it, "consider the courage in all that."[27] For Bellow, there is a kind of courage in facing life after the Holocaust, in ordinary, determined, honest living, ever conscious of the past. Should a novelist be political in the strictest sense of the word? The novel, for Bellow is not a political platform. Bellow was not a politician; nor are his novels political treatises. Art, for Bellow, is not a platform for dogmatic exposition. Nonetheless, there can be no doubt that Bellow was deeply affected by the events of the Holocaust and that we see in all his work the artful attempts to navigate such events honestly and ethically, demonstrating, as Thomas Rhea suggests, the fundamental principle that "a responsibility persists not only for those who survive atrocities but also for everyone who lives on this post-Holocaust planet."[28] Despite the requirements of restraint for the novelist, especially a modernist such as Bellow, the Holocaust, in his fiction, is contrasted with this simple prescription for ethical living in a post-Holocaust world. Cocooned in an impossible silence, both literary and political, Bellow, despite his own sense of regret and retreat, like Nemerov's persona, "Advanced into the silence and made it verbal."[29]

Notes

1. Saul Bellow, *Saul Bellow: Letters*, ed. Benjamin Taylor (New York: Viking, 2010), 439.
2. Ibid., 438.
3. Ibid., 439.
4. Ibid., 438.
5. Ibid., 438–39.
6. Saul Bellow, *It All Adds Up: From the Dim Past to the Uncertain Future* (New York: Viking/Penguin, 1994), 41.
7. Saul Bellow, "A Half Life: An Autobiography in Ideas," in *Conversations with Saul Bellow*, ed. Gloria L. Cronin and Ben Siegel (Jackson: University Press of Mississippi, 1994), 276. Originally published in *Bostonia*, November/December 1990, 37–47.
8. Saul Bellow, *To Jerusalem and Back: A Personal Account* (New York: Viking, 1976), 161.
9. Taylor, *Letters,* 439.
10. Gregory Bellow and Alan Berger, "Blinded by Ideology: Saul Bellow, the

Partisan Review, and the Impact of the Holocaust," *Saul Bellow Journal* 23, nos. 1–2 (2010): 9–10.

11. Ibid., 7.
12. Bellow, "Half Life," 276.
13. Ibid.
14. Ibid.
15. Ibid.
16. S. Lillian Kremer, "Saul Bellow," in *Holocaust Literature: An Encyclopedia of Writers and Their Work,* vol. 1, ed. Kremer (New York: Routledge, 2003), 124–25.
17. Thomas Rhea, "The Dual Nature of Duty in Saul Bellow's *Mr. Sammler's Planet,*" *Saul Bellow Journal* 2, nos. 1–2 (2010): 56.
18. Edmund Wilson, "Doubts and Dreams: Dangling Man under a Glass Bell," *New Yorker,* April 1, 1944, 78.
19. Edward Lewis Wallant, *The Pawnbroker* (New York: Harcourt Brace Jovanovich, 1961), 20.
20. Philip Roth, "Eli the Fanatic," in *Goodbye, Columbus and Five Short Stories* (New York: Modern Library/Random House, 1966), 264.
21. Saul Bellow, *Mr. Sammler's Planet* (1970; repr., New York: Penguin, 1984), 137, hereafter cited parenthetically.
22. Saul Bellow, *The Victim* (1947; repr., New York: Signet, 1965), 89, hereafter cited parenthetically.
23. Bellow, *It All Adds Up,* 15.
24. Taylor, *Letters,* 439.
25. Bellow and Berger, "Blinded," 20.
26. Taylor, *Letters,* 391.
27. Howard Nemerov, "Life Cycle of Common Man," in *The Collected Poems of Howard Nemerov* (New York, Chicago: University of Chicago Press, 1981), 221.
28. Rhea, "Dual Nature of Duty," 54.
29. Nemerov, "Life Cycle," 221.

7

Mr. Sammler's Planet: Saul Bellow's 1968 Speech at San Francisco State University

Andrew Gordon

Saul Bellow was never a systematic political thinker. An autodidact, stubborn and independent, never much of a joiner, like Augie in his novel *The Adventures of Augie March,* he preferred to "go at things as I have taught myself, freestyle."[1] As James Atlas writes, "always he resisted the party line."[2] Bellow's views on politics and the writer he outlined in his essay, "Writers, Intellectuals, Politics: Mainly Reminiscence." There he traces his political development from the influence on his thinking as a young man of Marx, Lenin, and Trotsky—he was a Trotskyist in the 1930s—through his gradual rejection of Marxist politics and a feeling that the proper subject matter of the writer was not politics but the soul. In the 1940s, "although I now drifted away from Marxist politics, I still admired Lenin and Trotsky."[3] "The more clearheaded of the Village intellectuals toward the end of the thirties were beginning to understand that the Revolution was a disaster. Few of them, however, turned away from Marxism."[4] Bellow's final rejection of revolutionary politics took place in Paris from 1948 to 1950. There he found that postwar European writers "accepted politics as their absolute."[5] But Bellow reacted strongly against that notion of the role of the writer, rejecting Sartre: "His [Sartre's] hatred of the bourgeoisie was so excessive that he was inclined to go easy on the crimes of Stalin."[6] From the 1950s on, Bellow felt that "politics as a vocation I take seriously. But it's not my vocation. And on the whole, writers are not much good at it."[7] He felt that the true subject matter of the writer was not politics but "the powers of soul, which were Shakespeare's subject.

... [A]mong ourselves, in the West, the forces are not acknowledged, they cannot even be recognized."[8]

Bellow may have been right that most writers are not much good at politics. But it does not then follow that Bellow's fiction is apolitical. Shakespeare's subject may have been the human soul, but he was also centrally concerned with politics and history, and so is Bellow. Every Bellow novel comments on the culture and history of the time in which it is written and makes a political statement, if only implicitly. *Mr. Sammler's Planet* (1970), although it has a strong religious streak and begins and ends by referring to "the soul," is actually Bellow's first explicitly political novel.

In the turbulent 1960s, as in the 1930s, American writers were often asked to declare themselves on the vital questions of the day, including civil rights, women's rights, and, perhaps the overriding issue of the decade in America, the war in Vietnam. But when Bellow was asked to take a political stand, his impulse was to head for the exits: "Vietnam, civil rights meant writers were 'pressed'—if not quite in the old sense—to line up with the Mailer group, or *Commentary* group, lashed into one ideological column or another. I got tired of having my arm twisted to sign statements insulting Lyndon Johnson and so on. I got out."[9] Bellow's major political fiction of the late 1960s is *Mr. Sammler's Planet*. But there is a significant void at the center of the novel: unlike other major American political novels of the period, such as Norman Mailer's *The Armies of the Night* (1968), Kurt Vonnegut's *Slaughterhouse-Five* (1969), John Updike's *Rabbit Redux* (1971), or E. L. Doctorow's *The Book of Daniel* (1971), which reference the then ongoing war roiling the American scene, *Mr. Sammler's Planet* never mentions Vietnam. Although the book features vivid description of a Nazi massacre in World War II, of Artur Sammler's killing of a German soldier, and of the 1967 Six-Day War in Israel (like Bellow, Sammler goes there as a journalist), the war in Vietnam does not exist in the novel. "Sammler does not perceive, nor is it pointed out in the novel, that the real cause of political disruption in America was not protesting college students but government prosecution of a disastrous war in Asia."[10] The absence of any mention of the Vietnam War, the motor for much of the widespread political protest and questioning of authority during the late 1960s, turns the young radicals in the novel into lunatics, running amok and tearing down the universities for no apparent reason.

Gregory Bellow calls *Sammler* a "watershed novel" that "signaled a shift on his part from the position of the son to that of the father. His embrace of patriarchy, which colored the last forty years of his life, was cemented by a turn to the political right and an embrace of Judaism. . . . Shocked by the political excesses of the late 1960s, particularly the attack on the universities by radicalized students, my father voiced increasingly conservative social and political views—particularly as they applied to women and blacks."[11] Morris Dickstein calls *Mr. Sammler's Planet* a "rank, embittered" novel,[12] and Mark Shechner terms it "the superego's book."[13] Critics such as Joseph McCadden and Gloria Cronin have dealt at length with misogyny in *Sammler*, and many other critics have commented on Bellow's treatment of the sole black character in *Sammler*, a pickpocket.[14] What I want to argue here is the falsity of *Sammler* as a portrait of the late 1960s in America by focusing on the only scene in the novel that represents the New Left in action: Bellow transforms a real-life incident in which he was heckled while giving a speech in 1968 at San Francisco State University into a scene in which Artur Sammler is heckled while giving a speech in 1969 at Columbia University. This scene dramatizes Bellow's view of "the attack on the universities by radicalized students."

In the course of the novel, Artur Sammler, an elderly Holocaust survivor, doesn't do much; mostly he meditates and cogitates and reacts to the crazy behavior of those around him in New York City in 1969. He also acts as a father confessor to many of the characters, although he finds their conduct distasteful and really doesn't want to hear about it. He is aloof and judges almost everyone harshly. The young have low morals: his grandniece Angela Gruner is spoiled and oversexed; his grandnephew Wallace Gruner is spoiled and rebellious; the student and entrepreneur Lionel Feffer, who invites Mr. Sammler to speak at Columbia, is a devious operator; and the rest are rude, foul-smelling, ignorant, would-be revolutionaries, like the radical who heckles his speech. Women are also no good: femmes fatales like Angela; or foolish and messy, like his niece Margotte Arkin; or social climbers, like his dead wife Antonina; or domineering, like Elya Gruner's dead wife; or batty eccentrics, like his daughter Shula. And minorities are criminals: the sole black character is a thief and a flasher.

The distance between the author and his creation is often narrow in this novel, so that at times the two merge. Ruth Miller notes that "Bellow lent to Sammler fragments of his personal experience, the fiasco of his lecture at San Francisco State, the hurried trip to Israel to report on the Six-Day War, the spells of tachycardia . . . and soon Sammler borrows from Bellow . . . Bellow's reaction to Hannah Arendt's theory of the banality of evil, Bellow's distaste for New York . . . his perceptions of women, his judgments of youth. . . . Sammler borrows the accusations and protests and recriminations of Bellow's prose pieces."[15] In part, Sammler was Bellow's mouthpiece to vent his spleen. But also in part, as he aged, Bellow was turning into Sammler. Writes Mark Harris, "Dr. Braun [in the story "The Old System"] and Mr. Sammler were the figures Bellow was trying out now. They were who he was becoming or who he was becoming closer to."[16]

Apart from Sammler, Elya Gruner, and Dr. Lal, the characters in *Mr. Sammler's Planet* are grotesques and lunatics. As Mark Shechner observes, these caricatures are "humors" characters, flat figures with one or two exaggerated tendencies, as in the plays of Ben Jonson.[17] Sammler, the elderly Holocaust survivor, is an unimpeachable moral arbiter, so that the disorder of New York in the late 1960s is likened to the horrors of Europe under the Nazis, as if the world is collapsing once again.

One of Sammler's nephews, Walter Bruch, survived Buchenwald and tells Sammler about a prisoner in the camp who fell into the latrine. "No one was allowed to help him, and he was drowned there while the other prisoners were squatting helpless on the planks. Yes, suffocated in the feces."[18] Symbolically, Sammler too feels he is suffocating in shit, drowning in the ugly, morally disordered, chaotic society that surrounds him in New York in the late 1960s.

Mr. Sammler's Planet purveys many of the same themes as other Bellow novels: the dangers of playacting, the need to believe in humanity, to maintain human connections, and to be responsible toward others. But there is a contradiction between the overt message of the novel, its defense of humanistic values, and the covert, emotional message, which is one of almost unremitting disgust and contempt. Says Daniel Fuchs, "Humanistic, liberal affirmation seems not to survive the novel's air."[19]

An interviewer noticed that "Bellow the public figure can be acerb, aloof and elusive. But in private he is different"—that is, much warmer and more generous.[20] Bellow sometimes split these opposite sides of his personality into two separate characters in his novels, which one could call "the father" and "the son": Dr. Adler, the cold, detached, judgmental, and unsympathetic father in *Seize the Day*, versus Tommy Wilhelm, Dr. Adler's warm, oversensitive, sloppily sentimental, nostalgic, and family-loving son.

Sammler, as Gregory Bellow notes, was Saul Bellow's first novel in which the hero was the father rather than the son. It is also his first novel in which the hero resembles the cool and aloof Dr. Adler. The qualities of the son are relegated to Sammler's nephew Elya Gruner, who is kind, nostalgic, and filled with love of family. Yet Elya Gruner's goodness is asserted by Sammler more than shown; he is dying in the course of the novel, and we barely see him.[21]

I want to focus on a crucial scene in the novel which was based on a real event, to see how Bellow transforms it from its original context into something implausible, distorting the history of the American 1960s. Bellow's being heckled when he spoke at San Francisco State in May 1968 inspired the scene in *Sammler* where Mr. Sammler is rudely interrupted and denounced while he is delivering an invited lecture at Columbia University.

A bit of context may help to establish the volatile atmosphere at San Francisco State when Bellow spoke there. Then called San Francisco State College, now San Francisco State University, it was a commuter school, largely working-class, multiethnic, including some black, Chicano, and Filipino students who banded together under the label of the "Third World Liberation Front" (echoing the North Vietnamese National Liberation Front, or NLF) and called for black studies and ethnic studies programs. The protest movement at San Francisco State lasted a year, from March 1968 until March 1969, including demonstrations and a strike. "In March of 1968 the Third World Liberation Front took over the YMCA office at State. The administration cracked down. Not just on students but also on their progressive teachers." After the firing of a teacher who was a member of the Black Panther Party, in November 1968 students walked out of classes, "led by Black and Third World students and supported by the radical and mostly white Students for a Democratic Society.... The police were called in, in large numbers and clad in riot helmets."[22] A series of college presidents resigned before S. I. Hayakawa, a Japanese American professor, took the position. Hayakawa shut down the campus; he later rode his notoriety as a conservative hard-liner who got tough on students to a term as Republican senator from California.

The strike at San Francisco State inspired students elsewhere. In January 1969, students at UC Berkeley also struck for black and ethnic studies departments, and movements for black and ethnic studies spread to other American campuses. The strike at San Francisco State ended successfully in March 1969 with the formation of an ethnic studies department and a pledge by the administration "to admit hundreds of new black and third world students." The legacy of the strike was community control of many campuses and the establishment of programs in ethnic studies in colleges and universities across America.[23]

In 1968 and 1969, when I was a graduate student at UC Berkeley, I participated in demonstrations at both campuses in favor of departments of ethnic studies. The tension over the issue was greater at San Francisco State, perhaps because there was a higher percentage of minority students at State than at Berkeley. Hayakawa was despised as an Asian American "Uncle Tom" doing the bidding of the white power structure against Third World students. He ripped the wires out of the speakers used by the student demonstrators, trying to silence their speech, and he accused the protestors of being hopped-up drug addicts. I was in the cafeteria at State in the fall of 1968 when a young man marched through, loudly chanting, "Hayakawa is unfit; Hayakawa mainlines shit." Soon a demonstration started outside the cafeteria, and the riot squad closed in. I raced to catch a streetcar as the mounted police charged, swinging their clubs like Cossacks.

It was into this cauldron of a campus about to erupt that Bellow walked when he spoke at San Francisco State in May 1968. The protests there had already been going on for two months. His subject was "What Are Writers Doing in the Universities?" According to James Atlas, "Bellow made no secret of his contempt for student radicals. . . . In the women's movement, the Black Power movement, the student uprisings on campuses across the country, he saw an insurrection against all the things he valued. . . . There was something about the new liberation movements that infuriated him."[24] For Bellow, the New Left of the 1960s resembled the fascists or Stalinists of the 1930s, and he had to struggle against them. He was not alone in this attitude, for other Jewish intellectuals of his generation, members of the *Partisan Review* crowd, had travelled the same path as Bellow between the 1930s and the 1960s, from the left to the right.[25]

Bellow was also influenced by the climate of political conservatism among some faculty at the University of Chicago, home of Leo Strauss, the guru of the neoconservatives. Bellow's close friend and intellectual mentor in the late 1960s was his colleague at the Committee on Social Thought, the conservative sociologist Edward Shils. Bellow and Shils even threatened to take away a fellowship from a graduate student in the Committee on Social

Thought at the University of Chicago because of the student's New Left political activities. Shils, an acerbic, aloof intellectual, may have provided one model for the character of Sammler; Shils also heavily annotated the manuscript of the novel.[26]

Bellow was described by one member of the audience at San Francisco State, Hannah Koler, as "an exciting speaker—witty, entertaining and definitely cynical—A packed to the doors audience—all went well until the question period."[27] Some of the questions were hostile, and Bellow answered sharply. One of the questioners, Floyd Salas, was a Mexican American ex-con, ex-boxer, a San Francisco Bay Area political activist, novelist, and teacher of creative writing at San Francisco State. (Salas was still alive in 2011; he has published many volumes of poetry and fiction and won numerous awards, including an NEA Fellowship.) Salas was then thirty-seven; Bellow was fifty-three. Salas is small and tough, described by the writer Don Herron as "a quick, bantam-like guy."[28] The exchange between Salas and Bellow grew heated.

The bone of contention was their vastly different views of the relationship between the writer and the university. Salas reportedly asked Bellow, "Are you saying the university should offer writers a haven from the vulgarities of the contemporary world? . . . I want to challenge you if that's the case."[29] Bellow refused to answer, so Salas reportedly began to curse, accusing Bellow of "trying to make the university a genteel old maid's school."[30] Bellow moved on to another questioner, who proved equally hostile. "At this point, Salas went berserk, in the words of one witness, and began ranting: 'You're a fucking square. You're full of shit. You're an old man, Bellow. You haven't got any balls.'"[31] Bellow responded, "I think this meeting is pretty well broken up now. I don't mind answering questions, but it's not hospitable to insult your speakers, so let's call it off."[32] And he left.

Since there is no transcript, accounts differ as to what exactly Salas said. Salas told an interviewer, "'When I had that thing with Bellow, I'd read everything he'd ever written.' He believes that Bellow's *Henderson the Rain King* and *The Adventures of Augie March* are the best books by a man he still calls a great writer." As to the obscenity, "Floyd swears that never happened, but does admit that he finally shouted out to the crowd, 'Do you realize what you're doing, worshiping that effete man down there in that expensive suit? I bet he can't even come!'"[33]

Whatever his exact words, Salas's outburst was a provocation, deliberately rude and offensive, and Bellow was understandably shocked. Considering the violent history of the twentieth century, a writer in 1968 would have had reason to be fearful of mob rule or of being shouted down by bullies. Surprisingly, though, some in the audience criticized both Salas and Bellow. Writes Hannah Koler: "Somehow I felt Bellows [sic] invited this by reacting very sharply to questioners—he lacked graciousness, courtesy or an attitude of sympathetic understanding."[34] A reporter in the *San Francisco Chronicle* described Bellow as "prematurely old and cranky" and "an alienated super-intellectual afflicted with defensiveness and hostility."[35]

Bellow's letter to Mark Harris about the incident is worth quoting at length:

> The thing was offensive though. Being denounced by Salas as an old shit to an assembly which seemed to find the whole thing deliciously thrilling. Being told furthermore that 'this is an effete old man—he can't come!' My impulse was to say "Let's choose a young lady from the audience for a trial heat and see about this." But the young lady wouldn't have known the difference between one man and another. One glance at the audience told me this. So I left the platform in defeat. Undefended by the bullied elders of the faculty. While your suck-up-to-the-young colleagues swallowed their joyful saliva. No, it was very poor stuff, I assure you. You don't found universities in order to destroy culture. For that you want a Nazi party.[36]

Bellow's letter to Mark Harris, written October 22, 1968, shows him five months later still smarting from the incident because Salas had belittled his manhood, he hadn't defended himself well, and no one else there had risen to his defense. He felt isolated and betrayed. Perhaps he was so angry at the women in the audience because he had been humiliated in front of them, his masculinity questioned.

In the late 1960s, Saul Bellow began to see himself as an embattled defender of the university and high culture against the barbarian hordes. At the same time, Floyd Salas was a working-class Chicano writer in the vanguard of a movement of students and teachers who were trying to transform the university and the society to make it more culturally inclusive. No question that Salas was insulting and way out of line. Like many 1960s radicals, Salas deliberately defied middle-class standards of civility and decorum: that meant sometimes being impolite, confrontational, and even obscene toward your opponents.[37] Yes, Salas was trying to attract attention to himself as an aspiring young novelist with the temerity to challenge a famous, older literary lion. But most of all, in his expensive suit, Saul Bellow must have looked to Floyd Salas at that moment, rightly or wrongly, like "The Man," the representative of the white establishment come to San Francisco State to champion the idea of the university as an "ivory tower" which should protect the writer and intellectual from the vulgar world outside. But the tower had been breached: demonstrations were happening on the campus and students had recently occupied an office. So Salas was going to be deliberately vulgar in a university setting in order to prove to Bellow that Bellow's notion about the role of the writer in the university was wrong.

What is more, Salas was a fighter, an ex-boxer who had challenged an opponent. Bellow's refusal to answer him, to accept the challenge, infuriated Salas. He assumed that Bellow was "chicken" and insulted his manhood. Bellow was right to be shocked and offended; he was a guest of the university, an invited speaker, and the students showed him no respect. But the heckling did not mean that Salas was "a Nazi" trying to tear down Western civilization. Salas had always worked within the university; he just wanted to change it.

In any case, the incident at San Francisco State became the basis for the scene in which Sammler's speech at Columbia University is interrupted by a student radical:

> He was interrupted by a clear loud voice. He was being questioned. He was being shouted at.
> "Hey!"
> He tried to continue. "Such attempts to draw intellectuals away from Marxism met with small success . . ."
> A man in Levis, thick-bearded but possibly young, a figure of compact distortion, was standing shouting at him.
> "Hey! Old Man!"
> In the silence, Mr. Sammler drew down his tinted spectacles, seeing this person with his effective eye.
> "Old Man! You quoted Orwell before."
> "Yes?"
> "You quoted him to say that British radicals were all protected by the Royal Navy? Did Orwell say that British radicals were protected by the Royal Navy?"
> "Yes, I believe he did say that."
> "That's a lot of shit."

Sammler could not speak.

"Orwell was a fink. He was a sick counterrevolutionary. It's good he died when he did. And what you are saying is shit." Turning to the audience, extending violent arms and raising his palms like a Greek dancer, he said, "Why do you listen to this effete old shit? What has he got to tell you? His balls are dry. He's dead. He can't come."[38]

Sammler then exits the auditorium without saying another word.

Now, like much of *Mr. Sammler's Planet,* this is vivid writing. Changing the setting from San Francisco State to Columbia works. Columbia is middle-class, Ivy League, and eastern, whereas State is working-class and western, but both schools were radical hotbeds: Columbia was the scene in April 1968 of a student strike led by SDS in which administration buildings were occupied.

So the setting is appropriate. And the details, such as "raising his palms like a Greek dancer," help bring it to life. Moreover, the student's accusation "He's dead" relates thematically to the novel, for Sammler is a Lazarus who crawled out of a mass grave in Poland during the Holocaust and later hid in a cemetery. The novel's central question becomes: Is Sammler so detached that he is more dead than alive?

The problems with the incident begin with changing the target of the heckling from Bellow to Sammler. In the late 1960s, Saul Bellow was a famous writer known for his increasingly neoconservative views and who had contempt for student radicals. He would be an obvious target, whereas Sammler is harmless, completely unknown to the audience. Moreover, Bellow was fifty-three when he gave his speech at State, but Sammler is seventy-five; to verbally bully an elderly man (and a Holocaust survivor, to boot) is much crueler. It is to revictimize an old man who has already been a victim of history.

A second problem of lack of verisimilitude stems from changing the incident into an argument over the politics of George Orwell, which might make sense in the 1930s but not so much in the 1960s. Sammler's subject is not the trendy "What Are Writers Doing in the Universities?" but "The British Scene in the Thirties," not exactly a hot topic with much relevance to the New Left. In the late 1960s, only an Old Leftie, or an Old Leftie converted to staunch anticommunism—like Bellow—would be emotionally invested in such thirty-year-old ideological quarrels. There seems to be a historical displacement occurring here.

Perhaps it can be explained by Gregory Bellow's insight: "Mr. Sammler's growing shame at having so readily identified with the English.... was my father's metaphor for his own youthful affinity with Marx and his Trotskyite idealism. Further, the Bloomsbury group is the English equivalent of the circle of radicals that comprised the *Partisan Review* crowd."[39] Orwell then stands in for Bellow's own political evolution. Orwell, an Englishman, fought with POUM (Partido Obrero de Unificación Marxista: Workers' Party of Marxist Unification) in support of the Spanish republic and against Franco's fascists during the Spanish Civil War, and then watched in horror as POUM was attacked and destroyed by the Communists. POUM was accused by the Stalinists of being Trotskyist and secretly fascist. Orwell fled Spain and became one of the first intellectuals in England to break ranks with "fellow travelers" who supported the Communists.[40] By lecturing on Orwell, Sammler is making a statement about breaking ranks. Orwell then justifies Bellow's turn toward neoconservatism and against the New Left in the 1960s, which was also a reaction against his guilt and shame over his revolutionism in the 1930s. The radical's attack on Orwell is a disguised attack on Bellow.

Finally, in Bellow's fictional version, the heckling is not only implausible but also sudden and unprovoked. At San Francisco State, Bellow was allowed to finish his speech. Salas's verbal assault came not during the lecture but afterward, during the question-and-answer session. The effect of the changes from the incident at San Francisco State to the fictional scene is to heighten the craziness of the interruption. Unlike Sammler, Bellow was neither blindsided nor rendered speechless by the heckler. In fact, Bellow got in the last word before calling a halt to the proceedings. Sammler is the innocent victim of an assault by a disturbed individual with "violent arms." Floyd Salas was a Mexican American writer in the midst of a political struggle to make the university accept increased cultural diversity; the man who interrupts Sammler's speech is simply a rigid ideologue scoring a point, a bearded fanatic—a stereotype. As Daniel Fuchs writes: "Perhaps Bellow succeeded too well in creating an old man who is out of it. Someone closer to the action could have seen that the young in the late sixties were not only contemporary versions of Dostoyevsky's possessed ... but people with a legitimate sense of grievance.... [O]ne cannot help wondering about the strategy of a writer with such gifts for humanistic possibility in presenting us with a character so alone that that the younger generation seem to him a form of strangeness."[41]

Of course, fiction does not have to correspond exactly to real life, but it should at least seem true to life. Bellow defines African Americans in this novel by a single character: a pickpocket and a flasher. Similarly, he defines student radicals by a single character: a foul-mouthed, raving fanatic. The radical who interrupts Sammler is described as "a figure of compact distortion." But the distortion is Bellow's. By ignoring the context in which the original incident occurred—the struggle against the Vietnam War, the widespread questioning of authority, plus the superheated atmosphere on the campus of San Francisco State during a student strike—Bellow turns the heckling of Mr. Sammler at Columbia University into a senseless assault. As Morris Dickstein writes, "Unlike the Old Left, with its tenacious illusions about a mass-murderer like Stalin, the New Left and the counterculture did few people any harm—except at times, themselves."[42] Floyd Salas was extremely rude and insulting to Saul Bellow, but he was neither a fascist nor a Stalinist nor a barbarian out to destroy the university and Western civilization.

Notes

1. Saul Bellow, *The Adventures of Augie March*, Fiftieth Anniversary Edition (New York: Viking, 1953, 2003), 1.
2. James Atlas, *Bellow: A Biography* (New York: Random House, 2000), 334.
3. Saul Bellow, "Writers, Intellectuals, Politics: Mainly Reminiscence," in *It All Adds Up: From the Dim Past to the Uncertain Future: A Nonfiction Collection* (New York: Viking, 1994), 101.
4. Ibid., 104.
5. Ibid., 106.
6. Ibid., 107.
7. Ibid., 109.
8. Ibid., 113.
9. Saul Bellow quoted in Susan Crosland, "Bellow's Real Gift," in *Conversations with Saul Bellow*, ed. Gloria L. Cronin and Ben Siegel (Jackson: University Press of Mississippi, 1994), 233–34.
10. Joseph F. McCadden, *The Flight from Women in the Fiction of Saul Bellow* (Washington, D.C.: University Press of America, 1981), 171.
11. Gregory Bellow and Alan L. Berger, "Blinded by Ideology: Saul Bellow, *The Partisan Review*, and the Impact of the Holocaust," *Saul Bellow Journal* 23, nos. 1–2 (Fall 2007–Winter 2008): 16.
12. Morris Dickstein, *Gates of Eden: American Culture in the Sixties* (Cambridge: Harvard University Press, 1997), 103.

13. Mark Shechner, *After the Revolution: Studies in the Contemporary Jewish American Imagination* (Bloomington: Indiana University Press, 1987), 148.

14. See McCadden, *The Flight from Women*; and Gloria L. Cronin, *A Room of His Own: In Search of the Feminine in the Novels of Saul Bellow* (Syracuse, N.Y.: Syracuse University Press, 2001).

15. Ruth Miller, *Saul Bellow: A Biography of the Imagination* (New York: St. Martin's, 1991), 185–86.

16. Mark Harris, *Saul Bellow: Drumlin Woodchuck* (Athens: University of Georgia Press, 1980), 110.

17. Shechner, *After the Revolution*, 146–47.

18. Saul Bellow, *Mr. Sammler's Planet* (New York: Viking, 1970), 58.

19. Daniel Fuchs, *Saul Bellow: Vision and Revision* (Durham, N.C.: Duke University Press, 1984), 227.

20. Jane Howard, "Mr. Bellow Considers His Planet," in *Conversations with Saul Bellow*, ed. Gloria L. Cronin and Ben Siegel (Jackson: University Press of Mississippi, 1994), 78.

21. See Shechner, *After the Revolution*, 147.

22. Bay Radical: A History of Radical Activism in the Bay Area, http://bayradical.blogspot.com/2008/04/san-francisco-state-on-strike.html.

23. Ibid.

24. Atlas, *Bellow*, 374, 387–88.

25. G. Bellow and Berger, "Blinded," 19.

26. Atlas, *Bellow*, 386, 390–91. On Shils's political philosophy and his critique of modernist utopianism, see Fuchs, *Saul Bellow: Vision and Revision*, 34–36.

27. Quoted in Harris, *Saul Bellow: Drumlin Woodchuck*, 119.

28. Don Herron, "Collecting Floyd Salas," www.donherron.com/?page_id=208.

29. Atlas, *Bellow*, 375.

30. Ibid.

31. Ibid.

32. Ibid.

33. Herron, "Collecting Floyd Salas."

34. Harris, *Saul Bellow: Drumlin Woodchuck*, 120.

35. Atlas, *Bellow*, 376.

36. Harris, *Saul Bellow: Drumlin Woodchuck*, 124.

37. See Kenneth Cmeil, "The Politics of Civility," in *The Sixties: From Memory to History*, ed. David Farber (Chapel Hill: University of North Carolina Press, 1994), 263–90.

38. Bellow, *Mr. Sammler's Planet*, 42.

39. G. Bellow and Berger, "Blinded," 14.

40. See George Orwell, *Homage to Catalonia* (New York: Harcourt, Brace, 1952); and Richard Crossman, *The God That Failed* (New York: Harper, 1949).

41. Fuchs, *Saul Bellow: Vision and Revision*, 231.

42. Morris Dickstein, "After Utopia: The 1960s Today," in *Sights on the Sixties*, ed. Barbara L. Tischler (New Brunswick, N.J.: Rutgers University Press, 1992), 23.

8

Biography, Elegy, and the Politics of Modernity in Saul Bellow's *Ravelstein*

Willis Salomon

Saul Bellow's *Ravelstein* is a biographical roman à clef, an undisguised fictive account of the life and death of Bellow's friend Allan Bloom. At the time of his death in 1992 from complications related to HIV/AIDS, Bloom was an infamous University of Chicago political philosopher, classicist, student of Leo Strauss, and cultural provocateur, who had infamously penned *The Closing of the American Mind* in 1987, for which Bellow had written a foreword. *Ravelstein* is an elegy for Bloom, a first-person fictive meditation on the significance of Bloom's life and death, mediated in part by Bellow's fictionalized account of his own brush with death after a toxic dinner in St. Maarten. It is also, if implicitly, a defense of Bloom and his intellectual and political values, a defense seemingly occasioned by Bellow's own fraught encounters with the American cultural Left of the 1990s.

The intersection of biography and elegy govern the unfolding narrative of Bellow's novel. The generic interests of biography and elegy complement each other in *Ravelstein,* especially in Bellow's construction of character. Character, as even a casual reader of Bellow knows, has theoretical consequence in his novels. Bellow's characters almost always project a sense of realism, not only because he often bases them on real people, as he so evidently does in *Ravelstein,* but also because he gives them speaking life in the closely met way that we encounter personal affect. He does so in a way that inverts traditional realism, as speech takes precedence over narrative, and dialogue contains much of a novel's narrative information. Uniformly, Bellow's fictive universe bases itself strongly on the observation of affect, both structurally and thematically. Affect for Bellow amounts to a metonymy for ethical choice, for the energetic hotwires of personhood that give the keen observer a measure of another's character, as well as of the character of otherness. Such measures of character in turn imply judgments about American culture, and so the biographical basis for *Ravelstein* serves Bellow's usual purpose of exploring character as the ground for exploring the excesses and vicissitudes of American life, here most challengingly, perhaps, because of Bellow and Bloom's intense friendship.

Yet the biographical element of *Ravelstein* also reveals a larger elegiac purpose, one comprised of an implied high-modernist intellectual response to Bloom's and Bellow's detractors on the cultural Left, especially during the early 1990s, the period of "political correctness." Chick, Bellow's narrator and stand-in, describes their detractors condescendingly as the "campus 'free spirits,'" whose job "was to make you aware of the bourgeois upbringing from which your education was supposed to free you."[1] With distaste, he refers to the "liberated teachers" who "offered themselves as models, sometimes seeing themselves as revolutionaries" and who "sometimes spoke youth gibberish . . . Ph.D. hippies and swingers" (50). For Bellow, such behavior amounts to a juvenile abuse, in the form of theatricalized self-indulgence that turns away from both philosophical rigor and political prudence, of the moral seriousness of the Left's historical position. The substance of Bellow's response to what is for him the noisy, self-congratulatory Left comes in *Ravelstein* in the form of an elegy to what for Bellow is its opposite: the intense, aestheticized intellectual engagement that, in the novel, Abe Ravelstein represents. Bellow thus makes Ravelstein's death signify, not only the end of a very large life, but also the end of an era, one that is here given the philosophical weight of Ravelstein's (and, of course, Bloom's) Platonic preoccupation with "the purpose of our existence: . . . the correct ordering of the human soul" (44).

Of course, this philosophical heft comes with the expected Bellovian irony about anything as serious as death since, after all, "death does sharpen the comic sense," as Chick says on beginning his story about coming to write a biography of Abe Ravelstein (14). The biography that Chick discusses with Ravelstein is self-reflexively the biography that we read, but self-reflexivity is very much not Bellow's theme here. Rather, it is only a narrative pretext. Bellow is more concerned with showing Ravelstein, and thus Bloom, as a living person, whose otherness confronts the reader with a sense of its truth.

Bellow's realism concentrates on what might be called an aesthetic of great personhood, with "greatness" revealing itself metonymically as aestheticized relational energy, in the way that "dining, drink, conversation, Athenian-style" consumed Ravelstein (40). "We aren't doing psychobiography here," Chick says almost defiantly, but Bellow *is* constructing, in the character of Abe Ravelstein, a representative anecdote of a highly unique, eroticized intellectual comportment (17). Chick says that, at the conclusion of the novel's introductory section on Ravelstein as a subject of biography, in "approaching a man like Ravelstein, a piecemeal method is perhaps best," a method that both assembles character and takes it apart (16). The understatement of "perhaps" aligns with Bellow's usual mixing of high intellectual culture and "the living creature and his needs" (31). The greatness of Ravelstein, his greatness of soul, is, for Bellow, a lesson in the aesthetic brilliance of the mundane, in the way that, as Chick declares, "The simplest of human beings is, for that matter, esoteric and radically mysterious" (22).

At the root of Bellow's defense of Bloom is his sense that the life of the mind is necessarily above, necessarily transcendent of, politics. Bloom, for Bellow, was both a superior intellectual and a scapegoat for the politically correct attitudes of the 1990s, the early years of the culture wars. In his eulogy for Bloom in *It All Adds Up,* Bellow says this of his old friend and ally, in terms that might interchangeably be said of Bellow himself: "He had the nerve to show American society to itself nakedly, and for this he was denounced—he was blasted, he provoked deadly hostility and became the enemy, the bête noire of armies of kindly, gentle, liberal people here and abroad who held all the most desirable, advanced views on any public question: people who did good works but, through some queer inexplicable shift of psychic currents, were converted into a killer mob."[2] The bitterness behind the irony is evident here—the "kindly, gentle, liberal" doers of good works become a "killer mob," one attacking someone they thought to be a "rigid conservative bound to a traditional canon" but who is—and for Bellow this is an incontestable matter of fact—a world-class intellectual whose philosophical speculations and lifelong work were not reducible to "a camouflage for partisanship."[3] Of course, exposing "American society to itself nakedly" was also Bellow's most fervent novelistic commitment, his modernist belief, as asserted in a 1990 interview with *Bostonia* magazine, that "conceptualization is a weak substitute for this sort of feeling for things and beings as they are immediately perceived."[4]

The tone of this passage, with its dig at the self-righteousness of Bloom's critics on the cultural left, shows to what extent Bellow felt that Bloom had been misunderstood and at what cultural cost. This skepticism about the Left of his youth is always evident in Bellow, along with his ready admission of his own involvement. In the same lengthy 1990 interview with *Bostonia*, Bellow remarks that, though he saw immediately that Kristallnacht was "evil and dangerous," he accepted as his reason to support the war the Trotskyist line that World War II would advance "the historical cause of socialism" because it was a war against "the whitest of white regimes, a white guard, anti-revolutionary regime."[5] In this way, he says, he "belonged to a special group of cranks that knew a little history and some Marxist doctrine and used to discuss matters on an 'elevated plane,'" one that, he implies, traded awareness of an uncomfortable reality for the urgency of ideals.[6] Similarly, in a 1998 letter to Phillip Roth commenting on a manuscript of Roth's *I Married a Communist*, Bellow addresses the question that bedeviled the Old Left and that, in the form of beliefs about the across-the-board depredations of "American exceptionalism," still emerges persistently in the discourse of the contemporary American Left.

Of course, the question directed to the late-twentieth-century Left, is, "How were they able to accept Stalin—one of the most monstrous tyrants ever"?[7] Bellow's answer is both familiar and streetwise: "the hatred of one's own country," which he sees in retrospect as a "deep and perverse stupidity."[8] According to his son Gregory Bellow, Bellow's "political radicalism" in his student days of the 1930s and early 1940s included studying "politics, philosophy, and literature in search of an explanation for the human condition."[9] This intellectual agenda was intimately tied to his sense of vocation as a novelist, and when Bellow and Isaac Rosenfeld became part of the *Partisan Review* circle, it seems, according to his son, that, even though his father was aware of the political biases of the magazine, he saw his philosophical views about art and politics, and about their relation, as consistent with at least the intellectual version of the Old Left in that particular incarnation.[10] As Alan Berger points out, the link between "radical politics and modernist culture define the PR crowd."[11] It is only later when the Marxist pieties of the Old Left become the slogans of the New that Bellow, along with the PR group, came to see, post-Holocaust and post-1967, that the New Left had little interest in the history and genealogy of its own slogans.

Bellow thus sees, in the move from the Old Left of his background to its subsequent permutations in the New Left of 1960s America, a willed blindness to "the simple facts available to everybody," facts that, had anyone chosen to look at them unblinkingly, would reveal the ways in which people can so willingly be blinded by abstract notions of ideological truth.[12] Thus, Bellow sees Bloom's aggressive claims in *The Closing of the American Mind* about the depraved, hollow excesses of pop culture and their effect on American teenagers as part of the need "to show American society to itself nakedly" and not as the special pleading of a conservative party hack. For Bellow, the book is an orotund, even literary declamation of a truth by someone with the intellectual credibility, the "learning, confidence, and authority" to back it up (76).

Indeed, there is in *Ravelstein* an unstinting respect for and a palpable desire to protect Bloom's against-the-odds intellectual and social attainments as the character Ravelstein represents him from political oversimplification, attainments inseparable from what Bellow calls the "vital force" transmitted in his teaching. At one point, in describing the "foundations of [Ravelstein's] teacher's vocation," Chick is moved to say: "I am doing what I can with the facts. He lived by his ideas. His knowledge was real, and he could document it, chapter and verse" (53). That Ravelstein is indeed in command of something like the scriptural exactitude of "chapter and verse," that he knew Plato, Machiavelli, and Rousseau in the original languages and could cite them movingly, that he worked tirelessly, devotedly, and erotically "to make certain if he could that the greatness of humankind would not entirely evaporate in bourgeois well-being," all underwrite Chick's need in the novel to protect Ravelstein from the superficialities of political sloganeering, to eulogize him with a tribute to the great ideas and books by which he lived (53). As Chick puts it in the novel, "He had written a book—difficult but popular—a spirited, intelligent, warlike book, and it had sold" (4).[13] He defends Ravelstein's book, saying: "You have to be learned to capture modernity in its full complexity and to assess its human cost. . . . Universities were permissive, lax," incapable of teaching "politics as Aristotle or Plato understood the term, rooted in our nature" (9). Bellow has Chick say that the argument of Ravelstein's book, and thus of Bloom's, "was that while you could get an excellent technical training in the U.S., liberal education had shrunk to the vanishing point" (47). The book "was not at all wild," yet, as Bellow has Chick point out in defense of his friend, "all the dunces were united against him," consciously invoking the satires of Swift and Pope (47–48).

Of course, Bellow's own public scrapes with the burgeoning multicultural attitudes of the American cultural Left in the 1990s were not quiet ones, despite his characteristic public reticence. In 1988, James Atlas, Bellow's eventual biographer, did a profile of Bloom for the *New York Times Magazine* in the wake of the success of *The Closing of the American Mind*. The point of the piece was basically this: Who is this unknown, elite University of Chicago intellectual who wrote this scathing piece on American culture, read (or at least bought) by about a million people? Atlas's profile concerns itself mainly with the venerable high-mindedness of the Committee on Social Thought. But late in the article, following a reference to students at Stanford protesting, with Jesse Jackson's support, the university's Western Civilization program on the grounds of its racism, Bellow is quoted by Atlas parenthetically as asking, now infamously, "Who is the Tolstoy of the Zulus? The Proust of the Papuans? I'd be glad to read them."[14] This perhaps ill-conceived remark was given life again six years later in the *New Yorker* by longtime Bellow friend Alfred Kazin.

In a "Personal History" entitled "Jews," Kazin reflects on his own life as well as on other major figures of Jewish life, both literary and artistic, who were his acquaintances and friends. Bellow, no surprise, is among the latter category. In 1965, Kazin had written a tribute piece on Bellow in the *Atlantic* called "My Friend Saul Bellow," and in a letter to Kazin shortly after the article's appearance, a grateful Bellow modestly says that Kazin "may have been a little too generous."[15] But the 1994 *New Yorker* profile could hardly be called a "tribute." Kazin, who, in the 1980s was holding the line of old liberalism against the conservative positions of *Commentary* and the like, refers to Bellow as having "moved in the company of the conservative Big Thinkers at the University of Chicago" and that "he had been moving right."[16] The tone of the description here is far from the laudatory one of 1965, where Kazin calls Bellow "a scholar in the formidable University of Chicago style, full of the Great Books and jokes from the Greek plays."[17] A significant difference between the two assessments is that, in the 1965 piece, Kazin praises Bellow's Chicago affiliation with a genuine veneration of the academic study of the humanities. In the 1994 profile, however, Bellow becomes for Kazin an unfortunate dupe of a vast right-wing conspiracy, his University of Chicago connection no longer an intellectual credential but a lapse in political and ethical judgment. In this way, Kazin's remark reflects the intervention of "post-1968" cultural politics in the academic study of the humanities in an obvious and largely anodyne way. But then Kazin brings up the flippant witticism from the 1988 profile of Bloom by Atlas: "My heart sank when I heard that Bellow once said 'Who is the Tolstoy of the Zulus? The Proust of the Papuans? I'd be glad to read them.'"[18] One can imagine that hearts must have been sinking at *chez* Bellow, too, because, in an op-ed piece in the *New York Times* of March 10, 1994—curiously enough only days after the release of Kazin's *New Yorker* piece and two years after Bloom's death—Bellow is obviously seething about what he takes to be an attack on his integrity and possibly because of its unlikely source. Clearly, much more was at issue here for Bellow than the attributive accuracy of a perhaps injudicious witticism.

"Papuans and Zulus" begins indirectly, with an elegiac paragraph in the mode of ironic biblical prophecy. Bellow wishes for "a week's moratorium, dear Lord, from the idiocies that burn on every side and let the pure snows cool these overheated minds and dilute the toxins which have infected our judgments."[19] The phrase "toxins that have infected our judgments" refers nonspecifically to the cluster of positions of the emergent "new New Left" or "post-Left," the premises of which are familiar and, by now, sedimented in the micropolitics, not only of academe but also of public intellectual life. Bellow's frustration seems to refer to a cluster of positions recently outlined by Gabriel Noah Brahm as a "genealogy of *ressentiment*" and consisting in the following: an inverted sense of "American exceptionalism," where everything "American" is either racist, mammonistic, or "warmongering"; a celebratory "Third Worldism," where the empowered victims of American imperialism and capitalism possess a moral superiority whose capacity for "resistance" represents the potential for a "transformation of consciousness"; and an a priori consistency of belief impervious to revision, fact, or experience.[20] In "Papuans and Zulus," Bellow disclaims the remark, saying that "Nowhere in print, under my name, is there a single reference to Papuans or Zulus" and that the scandal is entirely . . . the result of a misunderstanding that occurred (they always do occur) during an interview."[21] However, the core of Bellow's outrage comes in this passage: "I had been quoted as saying that the Papuans had had no Proust and that the Zulus had not as yet produced a Tolstoy, and this was taken as an insult to Papuans and Zulus, and as a proof that I was at best insensitive and at worst an elitist, a chauvinist, a reactionary and a racist—in a word, a monster."[22] The problem here, for Bellow, is what he takes to be the simple-minded way he is labeled "an elitist, a chauvinist, a reactionary and a racist." He objects, that is, to the combination of the "celebratory 'Third Worldism'" and self-appointed moral superiority of his accusers, what he imagines as their impervious certitude of belief. It's not only that his integrity is attacked, nor that he is accused of abhorrent ethical lapses, though both reactions are at work here. Rather, what he takes to be a way of intellectual life is here abominated by "the official falsehood machine," a "petty thought-police campaign provoked by the inane magnification of 'discriminatory' remarks," a "kind of 'Stalinism.'" For Bellow, 1990s political correctness is a matter of what Brahm calls the *ressentiment* of post-1968 leftist politics in America, its self-justifying anger, which, as Bellow puts it, premises "the majority's admission of guilt for past and present injustices, and counts on the admiration of the repressed for the emotional power of the uninhibited and 'justly' angry."[23] For Bellow, while the "failure" of the post-1968 American Left is, in this editorial, an ad hominem failure—the failure of a faction of people whose pursuit of political self-interest includes hostile name-calling—the larger failure that emerges here for him are the attendant failures of reasonableness, judiciousness, and honest reckoning.

In this way, Bellow sees "politics," finally, as "not for the likes of us," who should "stick to fictions," as he tells friend and literary mentee, the novelist Martin Amis, in a letter of late 1990.[24] The advice speaks to the combination of high-modernist aesthetic indifference and politically ruffled feathers that continually converge in *Ravelstein*. The letter to Amis is occasioned by Salman Rushdie's later retracted "re-embrace" of Islam in an attempt to neutralize the fatwa pronounced on him. Bellow refers Amis to the mistaken belief that "the civilization of the West had once and for all triumphed over exotic fundamentalism."[25] Bellow sees "barbarism," very definitely *not* in the culture of "pre-literate peoples," whose cultures he studied as a University of Chicago graduate student in anthropology, but in 1990s leftist posturing against his quip about the achievements of two "Western" novelists. Indeed, Bellow is at pains in the *New York Times* editorial to point out his respectful acquaintance with cultural difference and its complexity.

If Bloom represents for Bellow a misunderstood modernist intellectual and aesthetic ideal in contrast to this kind of politicizing, then we should expect Bloom's own writing to offer a version of this ideal. *The Closing of the American Mind* is little more than popular provocation and was intended to be so. A more concise declaration of Bloom's intellectual position comes in his "Editor's Introduction" to Alexandre Kojeve's *Introduction to the Reading of Hegel,* originally from 1969. Kojeve, a Soviet émigré in France, was a lifelong friend of Leo Strauss and Bloom's teacher. He is also one of the most influential thinkers on the development of existential Marxism and poststructuralist thought in postwar France, linked often to names like Bataille, Lacan, and Foucault. There is, of course, an irony to this genealogical convergence, and it is an irony that should not be lost on those for whom, in the 1990s, concepts that had been rigorously interrogated by poststructuralism, concepts like "subject," "history," "agency," and class, were seen to reemerge unscathed in an ethically aggressive, often moralizing retrenchment of self-authorizing, freestanding "subjectivity," a subjectivity rooted, essentially, in the transparent agency of those touting a radical transformation of social consciousness.[26] While linking Bellow's thinking with poststructuralism does indeed make for strange intellectual bedfellows, the common concern here with an interrogation of unexamined subjectivism and redeemed moral confidence is significant for the way that Bellow sees Bloom's intellectual depth and importance.

In his "Editor's Introduction" to Kojeve's *Introduction to the Reading of Hegel,* Bloom somewhat tendentiously lays Kojeve's "special merit" in what Bloom calls "the contemplation of the fundamental alternatives" faced in the clashes of history and human reason.[27] This clash between reason and history is, for Kojeve, as Bloom sees it, reducible to the different positions of Hegel and Nietzsche. Hegel, as Bloom reads him through Kojeve, and in any standard analysis, represents comprehensive hindsight, the *après-coup* of philosophical analysis, the necessary after-the-fact of understanding and the potential basis of any "state grounded on the principles" of reason. But reason's dream of encompassing and comprehending all must acknowledge the chaotic, nomad impulses of its own motives. So, for Bloom, Kojeve "sees that the completion of the human task may very well coincide with the decay of humanity, the rebarbarization or even the reanimalization of man."[28] It is important to point out here that Bloom's reading of Kojeve is not in any way a simple-minded apology for a folk-Straussian version of Kojeve's "end-of-history" argument, where the unexamined celebration of liberal democracy, transcending state sovereignty and founded on the revolutionary principles of the "dignity of man," effaces the historicist, materialist version of evolving historical and cultural antagonism. Instead, Bloom sets up an opposition between reason and history, that is, between the ambitions of liberalism's sovereignty of human dignity and the inevitable forces (migration, insurrection, extremes of inequality, etc.) that destabilize it.

In doing so, Bloom raises the question "whether the citizen of the universal homogeneous state" isn't also "Nietzsche's Last Man, and whether Hegel's historicism does not by an inevitable dialectic force us to a more radical and somber historicism which rejects reason."[29] In other words, in Bloom's reading of Kojeve's "end of history," the antagonisms of what the Italian philosopher Giorgio Agamben calls "bare life" potentially erupt against social and intellectual complacency in ways that can't necessarily be incorporated by philosophical hindsight.[30] Indeed, as Bloom puts it here, the evolution of capitalism and liberal democracy might contain the very prescription for their own failure. In this way, Bloom gives Kojeve's Marxism full attention. In fact, Bloom is here surprisingly close to Benjamin's idea, from the "Theses on the Philosophy of History," that "historical materialism wishes to retain that image of the past which unexpectedly appears to man singled out by history at a moment of danger," the flash point of disruption where "danger affects both the content of the tradition and its receivers," so that, predictably, "in every era the attempt must be made anew to wrest tradition away from a conformism that is about to overpower it."[31] In other words, for both Benjamin and for Bloom, the idea of the past as a living present relativizes history in ways that redefine the significance of past and present, of each for the other, creating the space for radical forms of thought. Of course, for Benjamin, these radical forms of thought are theological, "messianic," while for Bloom, they open up the possibility for socially ordering "truths." But for both, and, indeed, for the elegiac motifs in *Ravelstein,* the opening up of history to thought and thought to history—the blowing up of history in the name of ideas—forms the basis of philosophical insight. Thus, while Bloom credits Kojeve as seeing in Hegel the proposition that reality is rational and hence provides its own homologous justification for rational discourse—that is, the ideal becomes the real at the "end of history"—the coalescence of rationality might also be the grounds for its own unraveling, resulting in the "decay of humanity" in the form of the "reanimalization" it unleashes.

Moreover, Bloom explicitly presents his reader with a picture of Kojeve as "above all a philosopher."[32] For Bloom, this means that Kojeve's "passion for clarity is more powerful than his passion for changing the world" and that he "despises those intellectuals who respond to the demands of the contemporary audience and give the appearance of philosophic seriousness without raising the kinds of questions that would bore that audience or be repugnant to it."[33] It is not insignificant that, in his review in the neoconservative journal the *National Interest,* of Frances Fukuyama's *The End of History,* a more-or-less Kojevean analysis of the possibility of a universalized, rational, liberal state, Bloom, while praising the Straussian Fukuyama for having "introduced practical men to the necessity of philosophy, now that ideology is dead or dying, for those who want to interpret our very new situation," also calls into question Fukuyama's reading of Kojeve.[34] Bloom asserts that "liberalism has won, but it may be decisively unsatisfactory," looking more and more like a victory for Nietzsche's "degraded Last Man."[35] In other words, Bloom, in 1989, after the success of his popular book, was not peddling neoconservative ideology. Rather, in this review of an influential book by a former student, he emphasizes the crucial social role played by the challenges and consolations of philosophy, which he sees as the most salient aspect of Kojeve's concept of the "end of history," one missed by Fukuyama. That is, rather than simply extolling the complacencies of liberal democracy, Kojeve, Bloom insists, thinks profoundly through Hegel and Marx as a "refutation of the claim that the end is a peak and of the possibility that reality can ever be rational."[36]

Thus, in Bloom's philosophical idealism, Kojeve should be a guide, not only for those antihistoricists looking toward "a reconsideration of Plato and Aristotle," but also for those historicists working with "that mixture of Marxism and Existentialism which characterizes contemporary radicalism."[37] Bloom's position here promotes philosophical engagement over politics, but with the ironic codicil of having the philosophical representative of his position form part of the left-leaning genealogy of his eventual detractors. And so, as Christopher Hitchens, with deft irony, put it in a review of *Ravelstein* in the *London Review of Books,* Bellow's Bloom is an intellectual whose "style [is] redeemed from being merely reactionary by its understanding of the ancients, and the understanding (to which it incidentally or accidentally assists us) that intellectuals never sound more foolish than when posing as the last civilised man."[38] Bellow would seem to agree with "incidentally" as the process whereby character unfolds in fiction; but even "accidently" serves Bellow's self-humbling elegiac purpose in the novel and scores a point against Bellow's critics on the Left, whose own posturing seems to him determined to sound the foolish notes of sanctimony at all costs, but most dismayingly at the cost of honest reckoning.

Thus, in *Ravelstein,* Abe Ravelstein—professor, provocateur, philosopher, and lover of wisdom—is Bellow's attempt to foreground an ethics of reading and enlightened observation against what he takes to be the simple, reactive political posturing of the post-1968 American Left. In the name of expansive, literate personhood, Ravelstein, as Chick presents him, is far from a simple human being. Though Bellow has Chick assert, "I am not interested in presenting his ideas," Bellow clearly finds those ideas, the ideas of the classical political philosopher Bloom, very congenial, especially those stemming from Plato's *Symposium* (14). This, of course, is no surprise. Bellow makes Ravelstein into Big Desire, all appetite and intellect and thus a seething, shining, shaking, stammering, looming, sartorially bedecked, slobbering, brilliant connoisseur of the Platonic paradox of erotic and intellectual passion. Ravelstein, Chick tells us:

> rated longing very highly. Looking for love, falling in love, you were pining for the other half you had lost, as Aristophanes had said. Only it wasn't Aristophanes at all, but Plato in a speech attributed to Aristophanes. . . . [I]f you were continually in his company, you had to go back to the *Symposium* repeatedly. To be human was to be severed, mutilated. Man is incomplete. . . . Without its longings your soul was a used inner tube maybe good for one summer at the beach, nothing more. Spirited men and women, the young above all, were devoted to the pursuit of love. By contrast the bourgeois was dominated by fears of violent death. (24–25)

Chick immediately qualifies this summary with a worry about its simplicity, but the Platonic allusion allows Bellow to make the connection between desire and intellect that characterizes the *paideia,* the education of souls to knowledge of the truth of their desire, which is the Straussian first principle that Bellow saw Bloom heroically upholding.

It also allows Bellow to cast the relationship between Ravelstein and Chick as lovers of wisdom," engaged in the shared enterprise of making knowledge, and thus introduces the theme of self-examination that dominates the middle of the novel, as Ravelstein declines toward death as a result of complications of HIV/AIDS. Bellow follows the Platonic turn here as a strategy of hoisting his critics on the cultural left with their own petard. Bellow, it has been alleged, "outed" Bloom, and the ethics of the outing colored the novel's reception.[39] But the Platonic themes locate Ravelstein's appetites in the deeply reasoned repertoire of the great-souled man, making him into a complex, heroic subject of desire and not a caricature or mere category of sexual orientation. This strategy also allows Bellow to discard as simplistic the "outside" of sexual orientation as a form of public identity and subsume it more generally under the classical ethical category of the proper disposition of desire. Ravelstein's excesses become, in this characterization, manifestations of passion in search of its Platonic other. Ravelstein's connoisseurship of expensive clothes and restaurants, the sojourns in Paris, the intoxicating success of his ranting book against popular culture, his deeply appreciative, deeply analytical relationships with his students, and his trenchantly intimate analyses of Chick, all amount to a "large-scale mental life" that manages the balancing act between indulgent desire and the discrimination of truth from self-deception (47, 115).

In a way, Bellow's critics fell into their own trap. Ravelstein's sexuality emerges here as an Eros that both transcends its object and yet still sees its own relation to those objects as fodder for "Catskill entertainments" (15). Bellow thus makes Ravelstein more enlightened and liberated than those on the academic left who would damn both of them as conservatively essentialist and revile Bloom for his seeming "hypocrisy" about his sexuality. In doing this, Bellow affirms Ravelstein's critique of modernity's weak solution to the problem of desire: "not love but a sexual attachment—a bourgeois solution, in bohemian dress" (120).

Bellow also presents Ravelstein's relationships with his students in a defensively positive light. The reason for being defensive is well enough known. The students of Leo Strauss, in the eyes of their critics, form both a cabal of initiates and a neoconservative political faction of sinister significance, especially in their role in the Bush administration and thus in the Iraq War. Moreover, as Anne Norton has argued in her book *Leo Strauss and the Politics of American Empire,* "Bloom, far more that Strauss, has shaped the Straussians who govern America."[40] According to Norton, *The Closing of the American Mind* "was meretricious, not merely speaking but pandering to the vulgar. Cavalier polemic had taken the place of scholarship," and Bloom's "turning from philosophy, his self-indulgence, his squandering of ability took literary form in it."[41]

In the novel, the character Gorman, Ravelstein's student, who is a stand-in for Paul Wolfowitz, President George W. Bush's secretary of defense, is said to have "a grasp of Great Politics" (60). Referring to the scene in the novel where Ravelstein proudly gets a phone call from Gorman with advance military information, Norton notes that "it says something about Bloom and something about Wolfowitz that most Straussians believe the incident to be a fictional gift from Bellow to Bloom, a moment of posthumous wish fulfillment."[42] But if this passage is the fulfillment of Bloom's wish to be important in educating conservative political leaders, those who understand "Big Politics," what would such wish fulfillment suggest about Bellow? Beyond simple respect and affection, it suggests that, for Bellow, the seemingly vulgar turning away from philosophy in *The Closing of the American Mind* should not be allowed to detract from the intellectual achievements and aesthetic vision that Bloom, through Ravelstein, represents. Bellow doesn't want his critics on the left, the ones who took what he thought to be a cheap opportunity to disparage him as racist for the "Proust of the Papuans" quip, to be allowed to cheapen either the elite intellectual world of Bloom or Bellow's own high-modernist principle of the relation of ideas and feeling. Moreover, Bloom represents in the novel, not only an endangered form of high-culture intellectualism and aestheticism and the access to difficult texts on which that world is built, but also its convergence with an endangered sense of cultural Jewishness. Bellow has Chick and Ravelstein talk about both the insider's perspective on high culture, but also the times and places where the alleged insiders, basking in their white male privilege, are still outsiders, Jews who, a generation before, had no access to worlds like the Committee on Social Thought or the salons of Hyde Park.

Yet, the novel *Ravelstein* is only partly about Ravelstein as Allan Bloom; it is also about Chick, and so about Bellow. The novel moves from the subject of biography, through the dying, great-souled being of Ravelstein, to Chick's near-death experience. As it does, the reader becomes aware of a subplot consisting of Chick's self-examination, which in turn consists of his own awareness of his projective relationship to Ravelstein, his Platonic other half. Here, the conceptual inflections of Chick's own ruminations on desire and death take on an aesthetic cast. But this self-reflexive aspect of the novel's last section is also, in a more covert way, a political response. As Chick puts it, "I permanently kept in mind the approach of death" (105).

The novel's elegiac mode turns the process of mourning a person and the intellectual comportment he represents—Athens and Jerusalem, ancients and moderns, the classics as living in the sometimes passionate, sometimes deadened lives of students and friends—into an appeal to see rightly the contribution made, to see that the work and its traditions continue. An ungenerous reading of Bellow's self-representation in this novel would be to see it as an appropriation of Bloom to mediate the endgame of his own literary legacy. If this is true, then it is trivially true. Less trivial, however, is the degree to which Bellow has, in this novel, articulated more clearly perhaps than anywhere else the metaphysics behind his aesthetics of fiction. The underlying notion of intense Platonic friendship that the novel gives us becomes a metonymy of a deep, atemporal conception of the whole of culture. In this conception, a single moment, if attended to in its complex qualities and relations, speaks suggestively of an interlineated univocity of being. It does so not only as an ideological gesture in the name of the Old Left's disdain for the New Left and its politically correct progeny, but also as an illocutionary act of faith in the name of this possibility of a shared tradition of ideas and textual methods. It speaks, that is, of a stratum of powerfully shared experience.

In this way, Bellow echoes Bloom's own complicated, Straussian evocation of the relation of historicism to texts and ideas in the introduction to Kojeve's notes on Hegel. Bellow is ahistoricist about the value of art and ideas, but he acknowledges, like Bloom, the radically historical moment of the revelation of an idea. Indeed, Bellow seems here to be reducing everything to a final moment, and the novel becomes a distillation of collective affect. Thus Chick speaks openly of the "overflow" of Ravelstein's persona and of the way that "the famous light of Paris was concentrated on his bald front" (31). This is more than admiration; it is a conception of a Platonically erotically interpersonal relation inseparable from both an aesthetics of fiction and an ethics of great ideas and books, one in which the qualities of character coalesce into a point of high cultural significance and do so on the model of "a magnetic imperative that was simply there" (96). This is Bellow's Bloom, but this, too, is Bellow's wish for his own character-centered fiction, with its famously keen, detached observations of a world of deep complexity.

Such high-minded theorizing, moreover, is consistent with the strong tones of Jewish identity and history in the book. Rosamund, Ravelstein's former graduate student and Chick's current wife, says astutely to Chick: "You've given lots of thought to all kinds of problems, except the most important one. You began with the Jewish question." And Chick replies: "Of course that's what this conversation is circling—what it means to the Jews that so many others, millions of others, willed their death. . . . As Ravelstein saw it I refused to do the unpleasant work of thinking it all through" (167). If this biographically inspired, elegiac novel can be considered a wrapping up of Bloom's life *through* fiction, then insofar as Bellow's life *in* fiction is wrapped up here as well, it is so by the belief that the apotheosis of Western morals is, finally, not solely Mosaic law or classical ethics, but is contained in Ravelstein's paraphrased remark that "we, as Jews, now knew what was possible" (174). "The Jews were historically witnesses to the absence of redemption," Chick quotes Ravelstein as saying in the manner of his teacher, Professor Davarr, the novel's stand-in for Leo Strauss (179). It is, after all, the smug confidence in achieved "redemption" that Bellow seems most to abhor in his critics on the left in the early 1990s, a stance not unsurprising given his explicit reembrace of Jewish identity in the late 1960s in the writing of *Mr. Sammler's Planet*.[43]

In this way, the encomium to Bloom becomes a trope for the impossibility of unqualified knowing, of moral confidence, and the question of the Jews looms as the central conundrum of the history of the cultural high life that Ravelstein embodies. The life of "the political history of this civilization" is the life of its failings for Bellow, and, though the novel defends his friend and himself from the ideological simplicities of their neo-Left detractors, Bellow is finally more interested, in *Ravelstein*, in exposing something of the history of that failure. One cannot forget that Germany, at the beginning of the atrocities against the Jews, was considered to be the height of culture. As the novel closes, Chick and Bellow can only console themselves with the "pleasure and astonishment" of "ideas in the form of feeling" (60, 252–53). Bloom was, for Bellow, a grand example of "ideas in the form of feeling," and so *Ravelstein*, Bellow's elegiac tribute to his friend, is also an elegy to an ideal of modernity's intellectual and aesthetic possibilities, his high-modernist "breather" in the face of the ideological "toxins which have infected our judgments."[44]

Notes

1. Saul Bellow, *Ravelstein* (New York: Viking, 2000), 50, hereafter cited parenthetically.

2. Saul Bellow, "Allan Bloom," in *It All Adds Up: From the Dim Past to the Uncertain Future* (New York: Viking, 1994), 277.

3. Ibid.

4. Saul Bellow, "A Half Life: An Autobiography in Ideas," in *Conversations with Saul Bellow*, ed. Gloria L. Cronin and Ben Siegel (Jackson: University Press of Mississippi, 2004), 261. This interview also appears in Bellow, *It All Adds Up*, 287–313.

5. Bellow, "A Half Life," 270.

6. Ibid.

7. Saul Bellow, *Letters*, ed. Benjamin Taylor (New York: Viking, 2010), 540.

8. Ibid.

9. Gregory Bellow and Alan Berger, "Blinded by Ideology: Saul Bellow, the *Partisan Review*, and the Impact of the Holocaust," *Saul Bellow Journal* 23, nos. 1–2 (Fall 2007 and Winter 2008): 9.

10. Ibid.

11. Ibid., 10.

12. Bellow, *Letters*, 540.

13. In a high-profile review of *The Closing of the American Mind* for the *New York Review of Books* ("Undemocratic Vistas," 34, no. 17, November 5, 1987), Martha Nussbaum tersely points out the book's popular intentions. She asks: "How good a philosopher, then, is Allan Bloom? The answer is, we cannot say, and we are given no reason to think him one at all. His book is long on rhetoric, painfully short on argument." Nussbaum, however, acknowledges that "if we approach Bloom's book expecting it to be a work of Socratic philosophy, answering the Socratic demand for definitions, explanations, and rational arguments, we may be mistaking its purpose," though that purpose upholds, she rightly points out, a "contemplative and quasi-religious" understanding of philosophy, one "removed from ethical and social concerns, and the preserve of a narrow elite." She suggests, instead, a democratically "noble wish for a country in which the souls of all citizens would flourish, each in its own setting, and find respect . . . as an antidote to Bloom's apocalypse."

14. James Atlas, "Chicago's Grumpy Guru," *New York Times Magazine*, January 3, 1988, 31.

15. Bellow, *Letters*, 250.

16. Alfred Kazin, "Jews" ["Personal History"], *New Yorker*, March 7, 1994, 67.

17. Alfred Kazin, "My Friend Saul Bellow," *Atlantic*, January 1965, 52.

18. Kazin, "Jews" ["Personal History"], 68.

19. Saul Bellow, "Papuans and Zulus," *New York Times*, March 10, 1994, A25.

20. Gabriel Noah Brahm Jr., "The Post-Left: An Archaeology and a Genealogy," *Democratiya* (Summer 2008): 108–9.

21. Bellow, "Papuans and Zulus," A25.

22. Ibid.

23. Ibid.

24. Bellow, *Letters*, 476.

25. Ibid.

26. See Fredric Jameson's "Transformation of the Image in Postmodernity," in *The Cultural Turn: Selected Writings on the Postmodern, 1983–98* (London: Verso, 1998), 93–135, esp. 94–96 and 103–5. For what remains an invaluable study in English of Kojeve's contribution of the existential roots of poststructuralism, see Mark Poster, *Existential Marxism in Postwar France: From Sartre to Althusser* (Princeton: Princeton University Press, 1975), esp. 8–18.

27. Allan Bloom, "Editor's Introduction," in Alexandre Kojeve, *Introduction to the Reading of Hegel: Lectures on the Phenomenology of Spirit,* ed. Bloom, trans. James H. Nichols (New York: Basic, 1969), vii–xii, xii.

28. Ibid., xii.

29. Ibid., xi.

30. Giorgio Agamben, *Homo Sacer: Sovereign Power and Bare Life* (1995), trans. Daniel Heller-Roazen (Stanford, Calif.: Stanford University Press, 1998).

31. Walter Benjamin, "Theses on the Philosophy of History," in *Illuminations: Essays and Reflections,* ed. Hannah Arendt, trans. Harry Zohn (New York: Schocken, 1969), 257–58.

32. Bloom, "Editor's Introduction," viii.

33. Ibid.

34. Allan Bloom, "Response to Fukuyama," *National Interest* (Summer 1989): 21.

35. Ibid.

36. Ibid., 20–21.

37. Bloom, "Editor's Introduction," viii.

38. Christopher Hitchens, "The Egg-Head's Egger-On; Review of *Ravelstein* by Saul Bellow," *London Review of Books*, April 27, 2000, 21–23.

39. James Atlas, *Bellow: A Biography* (New York: Random House, 2000), 596–97.

40. Anne Norton, *Leo Strauss and the Politics of American Empire* (New Haven and London: Yale University Press, 2004), 58.

41. Ibid.

42. Ibid., 58–59.

43. G. Bellow and Berger, "Blinded by Ideology," 16.

44. Bellow, "Papuans and Zulus," A25.

9

Our Father's Politics: Gregory, Adam, and Daniel Bellow

Gloria L. Cronin

What follows here are three invaluable anecdotal accounts on Saul Bellow's evolving cultural and political ideology as witnessed by his three sons, especially valuable because only inadequate biographical publications on Bellow exist. Given the gaps in age between the three brothers, Greg (b. 1944), Adam (b. 1957), and Daniel (b. 1964), these accounts offer progressive and overlapping chronological windows into some six decades of Saul Bellow's political evolution. They cover Gregory Bellow's perceptions of his father's early Trotskyite affiliations and seeming belief circa 1937 in the equality of women, his temporary disaffiliation with his ancestral Judaism, and his later reaffiliation as a nonobservant but culturally identified Jew. Following this is the account of his disaffiliation from the *Partisan Review* crowd and his renowned swing to the political right during the era of the civil rights and women's movements. All three sons recount their father's steady loss of youthful idealism, growing cynicism, misogyny, racial anxiety and fearfulness about inner-city violence. They also explode the dismissive label "neoconservative" as far too simplistic, and provide the first truly nuanced picture of a politically complex man whose primary concerns were always for the viability of civilization and high culture in America.

Already by the mid-1960s many were willing to call Saul Bellow "racist" and "misogynous." This was only intensified by his unfortunate public remarks and through his close collaboration with his culturally conservative Platonist friend Allan Bloom on Bloom's *The Closing of the American Mind* (1987). The label "neoconservative" inevitably followed. Critics noted his increasingly virulent anti-multiculturalism, and anti-activist politics, as well as his fixedness about traditional curricular matters and the university itself. While he tolerated a tiny few blacks and women as colleagues, the rest of the affirmative-action crowd need not bother knocking on the door of his faculty common room. In truth, Bellow felt the Democratic Party had betrayed him, and he found fellowship with the political Right only in matters of high culture and the arts. He was not a joiner.

Bellow truly believed in the historical achievement of European cultures, and that he, Isaac Rosenfeld, and Delmore Schwartz had paid the price in learning what the newcomers to the common room had not. Bellow's lingua franca and/or "stairway to the Stars," as Adam Bellow puts it, was his total mastery of the traditional European, British, and American literary and intellectual canons, not to mention the Eurocentric history of ideas. As Greg Bellow remarks, he was a typical Jewish snob of the generation that came of age with Hebrew, European languages, Yiddish, and English in a family that was cultured, had status, and did not represent the average North American immigrant family. They recount how in his later years Saul Bellow thought American politics was farcical, yet something we could afford to indulge ourselves in as a free country, and never put much trust in it. He rarely spoke out publicly on specific political issues, and on the rare occasions he did, he quickly regretted it. Israeli politics, however, were the exception to his general political contempt and aloofness. He remained vitally interested in the fate of Israel right up to the end. All three sons insist that he was almost never interested in specific political issues, and that ultimately he cared only for politics insofar as it affected the conditions for art and high culture in American intellectual life. That said, few in his family would deny his increasingly virulent sexism and racism. Ultimately, he was, as Daniel puts it, "an old-fashioned guy," refusing to take but a very few individual women and African Americans seriously, often angry, nearly always frightened for his safety, and always fuming about uppity women and African Americans seeking political empowerment. As Greg Bellow points out, he finally became his own virulently patriarchal father Abraham and even more patriarchal grandfather Berel Belo.

The following remarks were recorded by interviewer Professor Gloria L. Cronin in various recording sessions held in Orem, Utah, New York City, and Great Barrington, Massachusetts, between February and September 2011.

Gregory Bellow Biography

Dr. Gregory Bellow, born April 16, 1944, is the son of Saul Bellow and Anita Goshkin. By his eighth year, his parents' fifteen-year marriage was over. By then he had lived in Chicago, New York City, Upstate New York, Minneapolis, Paris, Salzburg, Rome, and Positano, Italy. He and Anita lived in Forest Hills, Queens, New York, during his elementary and high school years. Gregory had regular custodial visits with Saul, who continued to live and vacation around New York State. As Gregory left for college, Anita married a widower, Basil Busacca, a professor of comparative literature at Occidental College in Los Angeles, and she relocated to California. Gregory then began his undergraduate study majoring in psychology at the University of Chicago, where he completed a master's in social work in 1968. As the Vietnam War was raging, he secured a commission in the United States Public Health Service at a hospital in San Francisco followed by a postgraduate fellowship in child psychotherapy at Mt. Zion Hospital. In 1981, he completed a Ph.D., writing a theoretical dissertation entitled "The Psychological Functions of the Bi-Polar Self" at the Sanville Institute in Berkeley, California. He married his college classmate JoAnn Henikoff, also a social worker, in 1970, and they settled south of San Francisco, where they have remained for forty-five years, raising their two children and working at various clinics and in private practice. Greg and JoAnn are the parents of Juliet, an academic art historian, and Andrew, a researcher in the field of public health. They are the grandparents of Nora Schulman and Oliver and Lucy Bellow. Dr. Bellow is now retired and has recently published *Saul Bellow's Heart: A Son's Memoir* (2013).

Recording Session Orem, Utah, February 2011

The Politics of the Goshkin Family

My mother, Anita Goshkin, came from a family of committed socialists; YPSLs and Wobblies.[1] Anita got her left-wing political leanings via Russia from my maternal grandmother, who also insisted on education and upon independence for all her daughters. The household absolutely lived their socialism as the Goshkin kids chipped in to pay for each other's education, including Anita's (the youngest) tuition during the Depression.

My mother used to say, "What I like most is to help, to facilitate other people to do what they want to do." That attitude was the basis of her supporting Saul during the time he developed himself as a writer. She believed in him and in his talent from the outset. Over the course of her career, that attitude brought my mother to work at a Planned Parenthood clinic. She taught me about Margaret Sanger before I was ten. She spent the remainder of her career working for organizations she thought to be forms of socialized medicine: H.I.P. [Health Insurance Plan, New York], and Kaiser Hospital after she moved to L.A.

On the other hand, Saul's grandfather Berel Belo and his father, Abraham Belo, were both czarist anticommunists after the Russian Revolution. My grandfather Abraham had lived in St. Petersburg illegally, got caught, and was almost sent to Siberia. Yet he was opposed to the Russian Revolution and argued with Saul constantly about his socialist leanings.

Saul was always very knowledgeable about politics. The Humboldt Park neighborhood in Chicago was alive with political debates all through the 1930s. They were all immigrants, many of them out of Russia. For the first time, whole families could openly speak their minds about their government without fear of imprisonment. Saul had a boyhood friend named Rudy Lapp who was a Stalinist. Rudy had all sorts of stories about Saul and his politics. According to Rudy, Saul went to socialist lectures and debates, understood all of the subtleties of the viewpoints of all leftist factions, but joined no organized group.

Indirectly I was told the following story about Rudy, who had been assigned (by his Stalinist faction) to steal copies of the despised Leon Trotsky's *The History of the Russian Revolution* (1930), which were selling like hotcakes at Marshall & Fields. So he went down there and stole the books. Rudy was very angry that I'd been told this story and told me that Saul was a much better book thief than he.

Saul and Anita met commuting to the University of Chicago on the El in the summer of 1935. Anita immediately fell in with Saul's radical friends in Hyde Park. Saul was, by that time, in the deepest phase of his Trotskyite period, and when they started dating she too began going to Trotskyite circle meetings. She was usually the only woman present. Several members told me that the men were all interested in political theory, but that Anita was very down-to-earth and all about practical social action.

In 1938, Saul and my mother lived in the Goshkin home for nine months after they got married. The household was saturated with left-wing politics, and social issues were discussed and debated. Soon they were back in Hyde Park. Much later, when Saul was downplaying his radical past, he would say dismissively, "Ah, you know, we didn't have any money. We were all pals. We just lived together." But Anita gave me to believe that they lived in some sort of communal group after they moved to Hyde Park. Saul and Anita had a few friends killed who were in the Lincoln Brigade.[2] She would tear up whenever she thought of them. I was not yet born during the Moscow Show Trials that were going on during those years. Saul never said anything to me specifically about them, but years later he would just say, "Stalin was a murderer. Hitler was a murderer." He would continue to equate Stalin and Hitler unless he was talking specifically about the Holocaust.

It was difficult for me to separate radical political ideology from the rationalizations Saul offered for his chronic sexual infidelity. In later years when I inquired, many people told me that the free-love stuff was not ubiquitously done. But Saul and Isaac Rosenfeld convinced themselves that the Trotskyites believed in this and they both practiced it. My mother was for sexual freedom too. She talked the talk, but her few infidelities were in response to Saul's.

There is a map of Russia cut out of a wartime newspaper from the part that Anita's family came from, the Crimea. On the top Saul had printed "Long Live the Third International."[3] But my conclusion is that literature was Saul's life, not politics.

In 1961 when I went to the University of Chicago with Anita to interview to become an undergraduate, she told me a little about those years. She said, "I need to show you where I sold a hundred *Soap Boxes* [a socialist publication] an hour in the lobby of the social science building. Can you imagine that, Gregory?" I was sixteen at the time, and already a pretty self-defined socialist until I got to college and realized that compared to my mother I really wasn't very committed to it at all. But in high school I really thought of myself as a socialist. Anita never took a turn to the political right the way Saul did. In her career, her social attitudes, and her politics she stood up for the kind of idealism they once shared.

Politics in Our Household during My Childhood

I first became aware of some of the political climate in the family because the house was always full of magazines: the *New Leader, Commentary,* and

Partisan Review, all left-leaning publications. *Time* magazine was *verboten* because it was edited by the highly influential Republican Henry Luce.[4] In the early 1950s, Saul was friendly with Paulo Milano, a Dante scholar at Queens College who lived nearby. Paulo's son Andy was going to the Queens School, a school full of red-diaper babies that was run by Communists. Jackie Robinson and Roy Campanella's kids went there because they couldn't go to the schools in the upscale Queens neighborhoods they lived in. There was another black kid named Julius whose father was a postman, and at whose house I would stay for overnights. At this time Saul was still committed to Trotskyite ideals and that included permissive child rearing.

Saul had many political friends, including Mitzi and Herb McClosky, with whom he talked about politics for years and years. Herb and Max Kampelman (a boarder in our house) were involved with Hubert Humphrey, who was mayor of Minneapolis when we lived there in the late 1940s. Max had been a conscientious objector during World War II and had participated in the Minnesota survival studies.[5] Max and Herb remained advisors to Hubert Humphrey during his Washington years.

In 1952 I was eight, and we all lived in Queens, New York. My father was in and out of that apartment for a year or so before he finally left for good. During my childhood my relationship with my father was very personal, and he remained involved with me. When I grew up, Saul's politics shifted and we differed. But that never altered the fabric of our relationship. He remained very emotionally present for me.

But my mother's politics did not shift! In the early 1950s when we were at the movies, there was a newsreel announcement about President Truman integrating the military.[6] Anita stood up and applauded and hooted and hollered. She was the only person in the whole movie theater to make a sound, and everybody was looking at her. I was only about eight or nine, and I was just mortified with embarrassment.

Their political differences were apparent in 1959 when I graduated from junior high school. When they played the national anthem, my mother refused to stand up. There was Saul standing up with his hand on his heart and Anita sitting next to him in silent protest. He said, "What the heck's wrong with you?" Bear in mind, this was twenty years after his Trotskyite period. But he had long since abandoned such behavior.

As a child, I was used to having James Baldwin and Ralph Ellison in my home. Ralph, Fannie, Anita, Saul, and I would go out to Long Island fishing. By the 1960s I was in college during the upheaval of the civil rights movement. Before that I was already picketing at the Midtown Manhattan Woolworths in New York when I was sixteen or seventeen. I was going regularly to the Ethical Culture Society, participating in the political debates, and attending a high school class called "Problems of Democracy." I shared my mother's socialist politics and what I now consider to be my father's youthful views. I was thinking about going to college, and I was set on a career as a lawyer for the NAACP. I found a program at Cornell where you could get a B.A. and a law degree in five years. However, Anita insisted I get a general education first and then go to law school if I wished. "I veto this," she said. She was a tough cookie.

In the mid-1950s, Saul was also quite afraid that he would be called to Washington to testify before the McCarthy hearings. They knew many people who were being called to testify and were both afraid, though neither were ever registered communists. But I remember how palpable the anxiety was in the house during the McCarthy era. My parents were definitely Adlai Stevenson Democrats. Anita wrote a letter to Adlai Stevenson when he lost the elections telling him how sad she was. He sent back a postcard that Anita was sure he had really signed himself.

The political extremes of the late 1960s deeply affected Saul's positions on issues that remain at the core of public dialogue even today. You can see their outlines in *Mr. Sammler's Planet,* a dark book by any measure. Artur Sammler, Saul's narrator, is a frightened old Jew living in an urban nightmare. Being surrounded by blacks and danger were not abstractions for Saul and his friend Ed Shils living near the University of Chicago. A student was murdered on the street in Hyde Park during my last year of Social Work School. Everybody started wearing whistles around their necks and blew them when there was violence. Yet he, Ed, and I would walk down to a Chinese restaurant on the dangerous Sixty-Third Street after dark and we never had any trouble.

As for the Vietnam War, his argument was that the United States is a decent country with a benign government and that we should do what they say. He argued that people should not resist the draft. When I said, "This is an immoral war, I'm not going," he resisted me. He was definitely saying, "Look, this country has given me a pretty good shake in life and it's not oppressive, it doesn't throw people in jail for nothing. It doesn't torture people." I couldn't tell you for sure to this very day, whether he was for or against the Vietnam War. But he was definitely against me going to Canada, and he was definitely against me going to jail, which I (aged twenty-four) was pretty committed to doing were I forced to go into the Army. On the war he didn't change my mind, that's for damn sure.

Initially Saul was very supportive of the civil rights movement. He was all for the Freedom Rides. He was sympathetic about the three young men who were killed in Mississippi [Schwerner, Chainey, and Goodman]. I think he was all for the voting rights legislation. But Saul turned against the civil rights movement when African Americans started pushing, sometimes violently, for political power. He was not for black political empowerment and certainly not the form it took in Chicago. Saul really thought there was social anarchy in the city and in the country. He would just rail and rail and rail against blacks, and it became worse when prominent blacks made anti-Semitic remarks. Years later we were driving down the street in Chicago, and a black postal worker driving a huge truck cut us off, and Saul sarcastically said, "That's Black Power for you, Gregory." When Harold Washington became Chicago's first black mayor in 1983, Saul was just completely beside himself. According to him, blacks would now own the "city machine," which they would then turn to their own advantage just the way the first Mayor Daley had turned it to his.

At one point he had moved up to the North Side with his fourth wife, Alexandra. One day when I was visiting them he said to me, "I want you to come to the grocery store with me." So we walked through two blocks of white neighborhoods and then into four adjacent blocks of black neighborhoods, bought a few bags of groceries, and walked back. He said, "I just wanted you to get the picture—that we're surrounded by blacks. Chicago is a city that lives in fear." But Saul felt and reacted as if he were under siege. It played a large role in his moving to Boston, where he felt way safer. He and I used to walk up Commonwealth Avenue in Boston, and he'd say over and again, "Gregory, this is so much safer than Chicago." *The Dean's December* was essentially about a radicalized white kid. It's just ghastly, the stuff the young man described and condoned out of misguided radicalism. Those were Saul's own fears about social disintegration. He would have flipped if he had known that the park in front of his home in Hyde Park is now called Harold Washington Park.

On a visit to Vermont during the 1990s, I heard Saul say to his fifth wife, Janis, "Cancel my subscription to the *New York Times*. I've had enough of Tony Lewis" [a liberal editorial editor]. He also read the *Wall Street Journal,* so he must have liked that kind of argument better. On the other hand, several years earlier, Saul returned to Chicago after a visit to my family so he would arrive in time to vote for Paul Simon [a prolific writer and white Democrat]. After Saul died, Nathan Tarcov, the son of Anita and Saul's old friends Edith and Oscar Tarcov, told me that Saul and Allan Bloom (a mentor of Nathan's) felt as if the Democratic Party had deserted them rather than the other way around.

For many years Saul was riding on Allan Bloom's coattails and was beloved of the political Right. Saul loved Allan. He had loved Ed Shils, his previous mentor, too, but Ed tried too hard to twist his arm. I think Allan was a much subtler and more perceptive person who had a fuller, warmer relationship with Saul. As far as I'm concerned, *The Closing of the American Mind* (1987) was a joint project between Saul and Allan. Saul really believed in the accomplishments of Western civilization and what America had done with these ideas. He definitely was the defender of the dead white men under attack by the New Left. But there was an aristocratic flavor to Bloom's book that Saul tacitly acknowledged when we discussed it, a sense that there was a right way to read literature that was at odds with the views toward readers expressed most clearly in his essays. In them and in the novels, at least through *Herzog,* there is an unmistakable attack on the great thinkers, who are characterized as useless in helping a man to live every day in the modern world.

Saul's early Trotskyism represents the more optimistic and humane side of my father, a side I think got lost when his politics turned to the right. The personal side of his reversal of political sympathies and attitudes was to play itself out in his personal life and in our relationship during the rest of his life. Saul alienated many people, including me, with his racist or sexist remarks. And I did not accept what he said, beginning with the war in Vietnam. While our conflicts over the war passed after I was no longer in danger of having to serve, there were many, many times when he and I would go head to head about gender and race.

I was sympathetic to people who felt they needed a political voice. I'd say, "How can you say these terrible things about people?" We used to fight about whether people who felt themselves disenfranchised were entitled to a political voice and power. I did not win these arguments, nor did I lose them. When we argued I always felt as if I was trying to be his conscience, or remind him of what I thought his conscience ought to be, or used to be once upon a time. Each of us stood firm, and our relationship, which developed into a long cold war, was the major casualty. However, during the several decades this distance prevailed, there were thaws when the deep feeling between us came through over personal and emotional issues.

For Saul, racial matters were all about groups and power, and none of this affected his feelings about individual people. When he was married to Susan Glassman, they had this big fancy apartment in Chicago, and they hired a black woman named Gussie to take care of my baby brother, Daniel. Gussie was raising two kids of her own in the ghetto that was only a short bus ride away. Saul was always kind, gracious, respectful, and sympathetic to her, while Susan didn't treat Gussie particularly well at all. There were many domestics of all races and colors in the household over the years, especially at the end, of course, when he became so sick. There was even an Indian maid in Montreal when Saul was a kid, and he always remembered fondly how she used to mispronounce "tapioca." Saul loved Stanley Crouch and Ralph Ellison, even though he finally fell out with Ralph. With great aplomb, he once introduced me to the dignified black historian John Hope Franklin, whose office at the Committee on Social Thought was across the hall from his. But activist groups were a different matter. I don't remember ever saying to him, "But, Dad, you know, twenty years ago you were being excluded because you are a Jew," because he would have argued back vociferously. He felt blacks did not deserve entry because they had not paid the intellectual price of mastering Western thought and because they did not respect its traditions.

Frequently, it was over tea in the late afternoon that we would argue about politics. Saul always put his finger on the most essential point, and he was articulate no matter how angry he was. He never lost sight of the point, and he would whip people's asses in arguments because he didn't get carried away the way his opponents did. My success in arguing with him was that I was making moral points that he could not parry the way he did with logical counterarguments. He would just go on and on about all kinds of terrible social evils, and I would say, "I can't agree with you, Pop. I think these people deserve a place at the table, too."

But then he was seventy and I was forty—a living fossil of his political attitudes in the 1930s, 1940s, and 1950s. Anita and the radical history she represented were parts of his ancient past. I, as a living fossil, was a political thorn in his side who knew when and where to prick him with the thorn of his past. If you had to sum up his defense of the people that didn't deserve a place at the table, it was because he thought they were "uncivilized," "undereducated," on welfare, and not ready to participate in democracy.

As for the women's movement, there he was full of contradictions. In 1938, he was very proud to tell family members that his wife was an independent woman with a degree. Anita and others have made it very clear to me that at that time, Saul went out of his way to show that he and Anita were equals. But even though Saul was proud of her, his patriarchal father, Abraham, was horrified. My cousin Lesha Bellows Greengus (whose father Sam would not allow his wife to work outside of the home) exemplified the view toward women prevalent in the Bellow family. Abraham thought that expensive higher education for his bright granddaughters was a waste of money. "They should go to community college," he would argue. "Why are you paying hundreds of thousands of dollars to educate these girls?" Yet one became a doctor, one a lawyer, and one a designer of beautiful jewelry.

But after women in the 1960s began to clamor for equal power, he downplayed the equality he had touted in the early years of his marriage to my mother, and then he made Anita out as money-grubbing because she insisted on alimony. A few years after the divorce, Saul put a note in the alimony check he wrote to Anita saying, "Thank God for socialism in one country." The joke was that if Trotsky had prevailed and there was socialism everywhere, he wouldn't have to send her any money in a worker's paradise. But since Stalin won out, he had to send her a check. My mother got the joke immediately.

But after women began to put pressure on academia, he would just rail and rail about women, pushy women. He was against affirmative action, and when he was on the board of the MacArthur Foundation, he fought tooth and nail against awards to women or militant blacks. When Mary Ryan, a very well-thought-of feminist American historian and mother of my niece, won a prize for her scholarship he said, "Well, she was probably the best *female* candidate."

Despite the fact that he and his friends had fought so hard for a place at the academic table a generation earlier, he had no tolerance for the pressure blacks, women, and the young were putting on the academic hierarchies. He, Harold Rosenberg, Alfred Kazin, and dozens of his literary and critical peers had done their homework. They were brilliant and therefore deserved a place. But that did not extend to the next generation's strivings for recognition. For Saul it was all intermingled with his generational outrage at the thoughtless, radical youth and at family members whom he loved who had wronged him or their parents. *Mr. Sammler's Planet* is full of the most crippled women characters you could ever imagine. And they have the undying support of Artur Sammler—except when they assert their will. But the men in the novel are all snotty, rebellious, noncompliant, and selfish.

I believe that book pretty well describes Saul's true attitude toward women, and I think those attitudes played themselves out over the next thirty years of his life when Saul did a one-eighty in his personal attitudes toward independent women. Though the Goshkins took Saul and Anita in after they had impetuously eloped and had no place to live, he later complained that my grandmother ruled the roost and that she destroyed the men in the family. My Goshkin aunts were both professional women, librarians in fact. My aunt Catherine loved the theater. He complained chronically that the women on my Goshkin side were way too uppity and full of ridiculous cultural pretentions. My cousin from that side of the family, Beatrice Schenk De Regniers, wrote and edited children's books for a large publishing house. She won the Caldecott Medal and collaborated with Maurice Sendak. But Saul just pooh-poohed her, dismissing her as "such a romantic."

Now this didn't mean that he didn't respect women individually. He did. He chose Harriet Wasserman for his agent. My cousin Lesha Bellows Greengus was his executor, and frequently gave him financial advice. But as a group, particularly within academia, he was openly hostile toward them. When my daughter, Juliet, became a Ph.D. student, he absolutely refused to discuss intellectual things with her. He just pushed the idea to get married and have a kid before she was thirty. I think he just couldn't see beyond the fact that she was his granddaughter and didn't want to accept her as an intellectual. In Boston he lived in a building where there were copies of the Elgin Marbles on the walls. She walked in with him once and said, "Oh, Grandpa, you have the Elgin Marbles in your lobby." He thought that was cool, but he wouldn't talk to her about the artists, art, or the ideas that circulated in postwar Paris. Think about it—Matisse was still in Paris when he was there. She would have loved hearing about his friendships with Harold Rosenberg and Clement Greenburg, two of the twentieth century's most prominent critics of modern art. When she asked him, "Tell me about my grandmother Anita" (who had died when she was about twelve), all he could say was, "She was a good dancer." I mean, after fifteen years of marriage that's all he could find to say about his first wife to her granddaughter.

My cousin Lesha frequently observed Saul and Allan Bloom putting down liberated women. And I watched these sessions also, as Janis, Saul's fifth wife and a Ph.D. student of Bloom's, would just sit there and listen as Saul complained about liberated women. Saul basically ignored my wife for thirty-five years. Ten or fifteen years would go by, and he wouldn't see her and just barely asked after her when we spoke. This probably stemmed from an incident soon after our wedding when Saul was complaining about me to her. JoAnn confronted him and said, "You know I can't let you complain about my husband like that." On a visit to Vermont she also criticized how he was going about trying to force Daniel to study for his bar mitzvah. Daniel, who was twelve, was supposed to be studying the Torah. He either wasn't studying, or he wasn't studying in front of Saul. Saul got mad with JoAnn when, after asking her opinion on how he was acting toward Dan, she made a very mild comment that it might be better if he did it some other way. Basically, I just stopped taking my kids and my wife to visit him. He was no fan of either daughter-in-law and was not shy about voicing his objections to my brothers.

Many have asked me why Saul turned from being a Trotskyite to being a political conservative, if not a neoconservative. I think at a certain point he came to believe that the idealism of his early years and of the *Partisan Review* crowd and its socialist utopian beliefs were in error, and that they even turned out to have been destructive. This was partly because their idealism blinded them to the horrors of the Holocaust and to Stalin's atrocities. He thought the worldview of the *Partisan Review* crowd did not take into account either evil.

He truly feared the disintegration of society and for the future of mankind. In the 1960s, George Sarant, Isaac Rosenfeld's son, became a Maoist while enrolled at medical school in Hawaii. Saul was just furious at George for turning into such a Lefty. Saul really despised people who were trying to tear American civilization apart, including the nihilists and the Maoists. The conservatism seems to be his standing up against social anarchy. That is understandable enough, but it took a very nasty form. It was just his standing up for the general principles of solid education and a respect for the history of Western thought, positions with which I find myself sympathetic, that he was finally about. It was his solutions to what he took to be personal forms of anarchy that troubled me and plagued our relationship, including the patriarchal mentality in Saul and in Artur Sammler. As far as I'm concerned, *Mr. Sammler's Planet* is the sign of my father turning from the rebellious son into a patriarchal father. In personal terms, he literally became his own father, the controlling man with whom he had fought for decades. The father-son theme played itself out between us for thirty years. It began with legitimate differences over the Vietnam War, but over the decades I increasingly experienced it as generational. After having been raised by both parents to think for myself and to be independent, I was somehow then supposed to turn into the obedient son to the very authoritarian father Saul became.

As for his being allied with neoconservatism,[7] he would have said, "You're not getting the complexity. You can't just slap me into a literal conservative box." He did see great merit in some of the things conservatives were saying. I don't know exactly how much of it had to do with Israel, but I suspect a great deal. Eventually Saul broke with the "neocons" with the publication of *Ravelstein*. After years of Saul supporting many of their ideas in public, the neoconservatives thought he had joined them, and they thought that outing Allan Bloom was an act of betrayal. It was their error to think that Saul seeing "eye to eye" on certain issues made him a true believer of neoconservatism. I think his politics eventually had a lot to do with the disappointment he and Allan shared over the failed promises of the Great Society,[8] but it certainly did not extend to moralistic positions on personal behavior.

Saul also became very disillusioned with the social sciences, and he subsequently said some really snotty things about sociologists, political scientists, and the university itself. In the end, Saul just chucked over the whole business of academia and logical forms of thought and trusted his own instincts. But it took him a long time to get there. He really saw civilization trembling on the brink of chaos.

Saul was a very brilliant though complicated man whose personal solution to chaos was to return to the wisdom of the fathers. But I never saw how going back to personal forms of respecting patriarchal authority was going to solve any of the mess that he and I agreed the world was in. Brilliant or not, I need a better sage than Artur Sammler, a frightened, backward-looking Jewish man, upon which to base my life and social attitudes. I prefer the Jewish legend of the holy sparks—the idea that God is everywhere—that I learned about in college from David Bakan, who wrote about Freud and the Kabbala.[9] Within the notion that one of those sparks could be in the most unsuspected place, I find a leveling of humanity and a basis of concern for the welfare of others. I never discussed this notion directly with Saul, but it pervades decades of our political differences. I am sure that the father of my youth would be very enamored of such an egalitarian notion. Even the patriarch Saul Bellow became in his later years might have been pleased.

Adam Bellow

Adam Bellow was born February 19, 1957, to Saul Bellow and Alexandra Tschacbasov. He grew up in New York City and attended the Dalton School and Princeton University, where he majored in comparative literature. He also did graduate work at the University of Chicago, Columbia, and NYU. In 1988, he joined the Free Press (Macmillan) as an editor and has spent the last twenty-five years in book publishing. Adam Bellow is known as an editor of serious nonfiction books with a special emphasis on intellectual conservatives. In 1995, he became editorial director of the Free Press, and in 1999 he became an editor-at-large for Doubleday (Random House). In 2007, he moved to HarperCollins as VP/executive editor and is currently editorial director at Broadside Books. Bellow has also written or edited a number of books, including *In Praise of Nepotism* (2003) and *New Threats to Freedom* (2010). Adam is the father of Lily and Eden Bellow.

When I was born, Saul was in his late forties, and by the time I became old enough to have an adult conversation with him about politics or anything else he was nearly sixty—already very much in his "late phase." By then he always spoke of his youthful radicalism by dismissing it as a far-off folly. But as I've learned from reading the *Letters* and the Atlas biography, he was a much more radical young man than I had thought. I think he was attracted, like many young, bright Jewish kids, to Leon Trotsky. He was a very romantic figure then: a fighting intellectual with a seriousness about culture, someone who could write articles in the *Partisan Review* while being at the same time a hard man of action. This was pretty exciting for these young Jewish kids. Saul at that time was very susceptible to this romantic revolutionary image, and long after he outgrew it, he remained throughout his life very attached to his old Trotskyite friends from that period, people like Al Glotzer, the historian of the Third International, and Herb Passin from Columbia University.

I'm very proud of who my father was, and I gratefully acknowledge his influence. His main concern was with preserving the freedom of individuals and the variety and depth of human character, which he saw over the course of his lifetime being flattened out and standardized by modern mass society. This outlook, which is essentially literary, led him to astute political observations. But he arrived at them by an unconventional path. He was never really interested in conventional politics, at least not in a partisan way. He was a partisan of Truth and an inspiring exemplar of independence in thought and expression. He had lived too long and seen too much to invest great hopes in politics, which he considered a form of low comedy. Of course, this is exactly how a novelist *would* look at it.

I think you would find that he had more political conversations with my brothers because they were more politically left, Gregory and Daniel both. I think they argued with him more. But he and I didn't discuss politics per se, although I ended up being closer to him politically than the other two siblings. My overarching sense of him is that he was interested in individual freedom and the conditions that support culture and the arts—anything that supported an audience for his books, and that permitted him the freedom to write and express himself, which is something that he never took for granted.

Since I was born in 1957, the 1967 Six-Day War was really the dawn of my political consciousness. I was aware of the Kennedy assassination and Vietnam and the civil rights movement, but I was too young to have an independent view of these things, and I certainly never discussed them with my father. But I knew that he was very concerned about Israel, and I think maybe that was a way for me to feel connected to him. It wasn't a thing with a religious basis. Though he'd insisted that I have a bar mitzvah, he wasn't personally observant. But the fate of the Jews and the survival of Israel were very important to him. A few years later he went to Israel to cover the 1973 war and then produced *To Jerusalem and Back* (1976). It may have been the first thing of his that I read at the time it was published, so from this I developed a sense of my father as a writer who engaged with real-world issues, but in his own very idiosyncratic way. Some of the people he describes in the book I later met—John Auerbach, Dennis Silk. In any case, I patterned myself on him in regard to his views on Israel, and on politics in general. Not that it was always easy to figure out what those were. I was always aware that he was really, really good at not getting pinned down on anything. Let me repeat, he was really, really good at it. And he was never dogmatic about specific issues. I picked this up from him as well. It is the liberal reasonable part, the Talmudic part—the sense that there is probably another point of view.

I wasn't that interested in politics myself. But the distance between us as father and son was something that I felt I had to bridge by making myself someone with whom he could have a serious conversation. He argued politics with Gregory throughout the 1960s while all that was happening; he argued with Daniel in the 1980s to correct what he saw as his fashionable leftism. But politics wasn't my thing. I was interested in literature and books. When he would come to New York, we would first go to visit his agent, then have lunch, see a Marx Brothers movie, and end up at the Strand bookstore. This to me was heaven.

I was in college during a kind of politically fallow period of the Jimmy Carter years. We'd finished with the turbulence of the 1960s, Vietnam, and Watergate. Jimmy Carter was a genial Democrat, and then Ronald Reagan was elected in 1980. I did not vote for him, and the only thing that I remember thinking was, "Okay, it's their turn, you know." I think Saul's view of Reagan evolved as mine did. I'm also pretty sure he didn't vote for Reagan either. He probably considered Reagan to be sort of a third-rate actor, though he may have been more aware of Reagan's record as governor than I was. Ultimately it was Reagan's anticommunism that drew his approval. In my case, it was the Iran Contra uproar, El Salvador and the whole controversy about the Contras. I was twenty-two or twenty-three at the time, and I thought, "Why is it a good thing to have a Leninist revolutionary republic in Central America with Cuban military advisors all over it? Why do we want that? What do we do about it?" Well, I wasn't sure. But for the Democrats in Congress to harass and hobble Reagan's efforts to contain the Sandinista revolution was to me irresponsible. Hadn't they ever heard of the Monroe Doctrine? And that began to move me in a more politically conservative direction. Although for my father and I as Jews it was still very difficult to identify as Republicans, socially and culturally.

Saul's neoconservatism is curious and interesting because it is the Jewish third way—a Jewish political compromise. Later when I got into publishing, I met people like Irving Kristol and Norman Podhoretz. This was a small group of intellectual New York Jews with serious literary interests who had all started off on the left, and who had all moved to the right primarily because of issues to do with Israel and anticommunism. They remained somewhat liberal on social issues, at least initially, because they were urbanites and immigrants. They would never have been comfortable with the southern evangelical base of the modern Republican Party, or even with the Rockefeller Republican types, the patrician business establishment, or the Wall Street business class. Saul didn't like them either.

As for the 1960s and the civil rights and women's movements, Saul was personally upset by the outburst of irreverent disrespect for professors and for people with deep learning and caring—the tradition itself. For him it was only your mastery of the literary canon that allowed the WASP establishment within the university to tolerate your presence. It was his personal ladder to the stars, his passport of entry into the heritage of Western civilization, to a literary career, and to the entire world of letters. He understood its value. You know, there is a famous passage by W. E. B. Du Bois about being a black man who feels welcomed into the company of Shakespeare and Goethe and Dante, but not in the company of American society. It was this sentiment that Saul shared. He didn't care much for the WASP academic establishment, and he equally disliked the disrespectful young radicals and obstreperous feminists. By the 1980s, he was a proud reactionary. Earlier he was a little more careful because he didn't want to alienate everybody entirely. He really wanted to be left alone to write. But he also wanted to put provocative things in his novels about race and urban politics and not really be held accountable for them.

Then there were the years where he famously returned to Chicago to get away from things. He liked the distance it gave him from the eastern literary establishment, which he held in contempt long before it became fashionable on the right. But his grounds were purely intellectual—he thought the New York literary press were purveyors not of ideas but of intellectual fashions, just like the Garment District. He said to me once, "By the time a new idea reaches Chicago it's generally so threadbare that you can see right through it." He also said, "I worked my way through all of the major ideologies of the twentieth century, so you don't have to do it. You're exempt." And he meant everything, Freud and Marx as well.

But he did go through these phases. By the time I became an adult and was able to engage with him, he was pretty conservative in relation to the overall tendency of American elite culture and higher education. He thought the 1960s radicals were the privileged offspring of the richest, most powerful country in the history of the world. He thought the campus revolt and the antiwar movement was superficial and frivolous, just an excuse to break windows and get laid. I think he worried that it would undermine the serious attitude toward culture that he had embraced, and that his own authority as a writer rested on. It was very important to him that there be serious writers, serious readers, serious critics, and serious academics.

In the 1980s, I went to Chicago for a year as a graduate student in the Committee on Social Thought, where Saul was then still teaching. Allan Bloom recruited me. I had recently graduated from college, and I spent a year working at the *New York Daily News* as a copy boy, trying to become a writer. I was writing short stories, failing to finish short stories, and rewriting unfinished short stories. Then I went to Africa to visit a friend of mine who was in the Peace Corps. I came home and wrote an exuberant sort of travelogue about my trip. Saul paid me the highest possible compliment when he said, "It's real writing." I thought I had found my direction as a writer and decided to go back to school to learn more about history and politics. Bloom proposed to fix me up in that department, and he indoctrinated me into the thought of Leo Strauss. In that way I became a philosophical conservative before I became a political one.

Saul's deepest political concerns always revolved around Israel and the status of the Jews. In those years, the fate of Soviet Jewry was a very hot issue. There was much debate about the status of the Palestinian national movement. In those years, American Jews did not acknowledge so readily the existence of a Palestinian people with a distinct national identity. Also there was a war of ideas about the status and legitimacy of Israel. He unwisely gave an endorsement to a book written by someone named Joan Peters called *From Time Immemorial* (1984), which made a now-discredited argument that there is no such thing as a Palestinian people—that there was nobody in Israel when the Jews came. Later on it turned out that she was not much of a scholar, and he regretted going public with his endorsement. That's one of the things that was consistent in him—he understood that it was dangerous for him to opine too much about politics. During the 1980s and 1990s, when culture and politics merged, this worried him.

In the 1960s, Saul had gotten into trouble with his literary friends for accepting an invitation from Lyndon Johnson to go to the White House. He was very indignant about this, and I think he purposely withdrew from any public expression after that.

With regard to Saul's writing the introduction to Allan Bloom's *The Closing of the American Mind,* I don't think he ever regretted it. Not for a minute. It was his idea that Allan should write such a book in the first place, and he wrote much of it at Saul's kitchen table in Vermont, sitting up all night drinking coffee and chain-smoking cigarettes. Saul made everybody who came to the house read it, and he made Harriet Wasserman, his agent, represent it. Then, of course, it sold a million copies. Saul thought it was very funny that somebody in one of the reviews suggested that there *was* no Allan Bloom, that Saul Bellow had just invented him. I think Saul did become more vocal politically as a result of his friendship with Allan, and certainly more interested in political philosophy. They taught courses together in which they would read philosophical works as literature, or literary works as philosophy. I took some of these classes. They were really great. Allan was kind of like Milton Berle and even looked like him. He was the Milton Berle of political philosophy. Together they were very, very funny. Saul was always at his best when he found someone who could stimulate a conversation at a high level. He needed a pro like Allan. Allan's death was even harder for him in some ways than the deaths of his brothers. He was very attached to his brothers, of course, but with Bloom there was a special connection.

In the 1980s, Saul withdrew from the Committee for the Free World, a conservative organization founded in 1981, after they used his name on an advertisement about Soviet Jewry. There must have been some blowback from that because he was very sensitive about it. He felt he was a writer first and that his political opinions were private. But his views were about what you would expect from a neoconservative Jew of his generation. You get a lot of it beginning with *Sammler* and even more in *The Dean's December* (1982). During the period where he immersed himself in the racial politics of Chicago, he became darker and darker in mood. He took being an urban writer and a social realist very seriously. He did his homework firsthand, visiting the housing projects, the courts, the jails, big urban hospitals, and so forth. His problem with liberal academics and with the whole New York literary crowd was that he thought they were in denial. I recall very vividly the speech that he gave here in New York at the PEN Congress [a worldwide association of writers] in 1976, where he basically got up in front of a room full of writers from all over the world and insulted them. I mean really insulted them, calling them (in effect) political ninnies who should be minding their own business. He was like a bullfighter who was constantly concealing his sword behind his cape. But they knew that they'd been stuck. Then of course he got very inflamed when they attacked him in turn. I went to see him the next day at the hotel where he was staying, and we went to breakfast in the hotel dining room. I could have told him that would be a mistake. We entered the room and everybody was looking at him. He went directly up to Günter Grass, who had attacked him the day before. He was sitting at a table with Bill and Rose Styron. Saul went straight up to Grass and shook his finger in his face and said, "That was very bad what you did yesterday." You could see that he was hurt by what had happened. Then again, he'd asked for it, hadn't he? So these episodes would happen when he would let something out and there would be consequences.

I think he began fuming in the 1960s and he never stopped. He just fumed and fumed. It just built and built and built. I think Allan gave him an outlet for that. The curriculum debates and the cultural wars of the 1980s and 1990s also provided a legitimate focus for his anger and concern. So he could come out with statements like, "Who is the Tolstoy of the Zulus, the Proust of the Papuans?" Well—he liked alliteration. He caught hell for saying this—and it was relatively safe because he was talking about culture and literature. He would have been very reluctant to say anything publicly about, say, Harold Washington as the first black mayor of Chicago, but privately he would say all kinds of things. But again it wasn't about partisan politics. Politics was something that he considered to be a form of low comedy. Not unimportant, but theater that attracted idiots. In his opinion, politics attracted deformed specimens, people who conducted themselves with no shred of dignity, people who lied and deceived, who were hypocrites, and even corrupt. He was fascinated by monsters of egotism and vanity. For that reason he was fascinated by LBJ. Not because of his politics, but because he was larger than life. Saul told me once that he was thinking about writing a short story about LBJ in retirement. He never did it, of course. But he was impressed by the fact that Johnson had in retirement caused an office building to be constructed in Houston or someplace to house his enormous ego. He loved the exchange that LBJ was supposed to have had with a reporter who supposedly asked him a question like, "What do you have for breakfast?" Johnson replied, "What kind of a chicken-shit question is that to ask the leader of the most powerful nation in the world?" It is a wonderfully Jewish statement in its way. Saul liked it because it was witty. And he liked Johnson's bulbous nose and country twang and Elmer Gantry manner.

His social politics ultimately had to do with the cultural homogenization of America. He loved the immigrant rejection of WASP reticence and politeness, their individuality, their eccentricity of speech and dress and the way they made up names for themselves. He used to talk about a man who named himself after Lake Erie. In today's culture everybody dresses the same, talks the same. They are all plugged into their iPods, twittering, watching *American Idol*, all standardized, all products of the same mass education and mass culture. When Saul was a young man, America was a very different country of strong regional cultures and powerful accents. The different states were all like foreign countries. That was the America he grew up in. He liked the extreme variety and diversity of it all, and that's what he saw going out of modern life. But he was not a political man. He was a literary man. And as he aged he was increasingly aware that he was part of a generation that was passing.

I think the years in which I became close to him were the years in which he became most vocal in his conservative views. But he largely confined himself to issues of cultural freedom, education, the survival of the Jews and of the Jewish state, putting down the threat of communism both abroad and at home. He had lived through the Depression and World War II, and it's sobering to recall that he was born before the American intervention in World War I. What most affected him politically, however, was the era of the great fascist and communist dictators. I remember asking him in college what books I should read. I assumed he would recommend books by Conrad, Flaubert, and Turgenev. Instead he said I should read about the great figures of evil in the twentieth century, these massive biographies of Hitler, Stalin, Mao. He was fascinated with the dictators as human beings, with their banality, their mediocrity, their monstrousness, and by the fear and the terror that they inspired in people. He could not understand why people so easily forgot about all this. This is, I think, one of the curses of longevity. Just as today's baby boomers are sort of hung up on the 1960s. How could he forget?

He also engaged for a period in spiritual exercises. But these too were all in the service of his literary work. He just wanted to be left alone to pursue that. His politics were cultural in the sense that he began to fret extensively about distraction in the modern age. I attended the Jefferson lecture (1977) where he began by talking about Wordsworth's line, "The world is too much with us." He was still talking about it ten years later at the Nobel lecture. The big thing for him was contemporary distraction and its negative effects. He understood that it required the forces of collectivization and massification. He read a good deal about this, starting in the 1950s. He was also very interested in the works of Elias Canetti, who wrote about technology and the psychology of crowds. He came of age with the sociology of the 1950s and early 1960s, which focused on the bad cultural effects of mass society. His own social ideal was probably Greenwich Village in the 1940s. I don't think there was another period in his life when he was happier. Everybody was poor, and everybody was drunk or high on literature. They were all outrageous, outspoken, bohemian—and he was in his prime. His friends, mentors, brothers, and esteemed editors like Philip Rahv and Pat Covici were all still alive. New York was it as far as he was concerned.

I think he found Paris when he went there after the war too much like Chicago—dark, gloomy, stony, and shuttered. Scarcity in everything. Thrashed by war. He liked London and felt quite at home there, though he was well aware of their tradition of genteel anti-Semitism and keenly resented it. He was a very refined person, but I think he liked to act up when he was in that kind of excessively polite company. I went to London with him a couple of times. Paris, too—he took me on a walking tour of his old haunts and tried out his outdated French slang on the waiters at the Café Balzar. He liked London for its dignity and its lingering shreds of imperialism. But he was ambivalent about the British, and he was always unhappy with his English publishers. I think he felt that he was regarded as an upstart. He used to mock the sociologist Ed Shils for having put on an English accent. Ed had originally come from Oklahoma or some place, and he had turned himself into an Oxford man. But he also loved that about Ed, the power of the imagination to rework yourself. It was all an expression of some inner human power or spiritual capacity.

I never lived with my father growing up. I made brief visits to Chicago, and I traveled with him to foreign countries for a week here and there, but I actually spent more time with him in the country where he went to get away. He was quite a devoted gardener for a city kid. Always very proud of his tomatoes and his homemade blackberry jam, though he could never get it thick enough for my taste. You sort of drizzled it onto your English muffin and then picked the little seeds out of your teeth. For many years there was no TV, and the evening's entertainment consisted of reading aloud from Shakespeare by the fire. But being in the country didn't cut him off from world events. When the paper would come around lunchtime we'd pass the sections back and forth and we would talk about things. But it was always very Olympian. He didn't seem to have an opinion about specific political issues or even individual politicians.

As I've said, as a young man he was quite radical, but by the time I came along he had long since outgrown that youthful optimism about politics. He never invested hope in politics. He'd seen too much. He understood that American politics was fundamentally trivial and that that was a good thing because it was a luxury that we were able to afford. He once read me a passage from a book about Maxim Gorky, who after the revolution got up at a meeting of the Soviet writers guild and said, "Is it too much to ask that I should have my herring served to me on a clean plate?" To Saul, this was a great moment. Gorky was one of the literary heroes of the revolution, and he wasn't at all happy with the outcome. Gorky thought the civility of life had been sacrificed, just lost. Saul identified with this.

As for his travels in eastern Europe, there was never any sense of his wanting to revisit the Russian homeland. I don't think he ever went to see the death camps. He wanted to give the Holocaust a wide berth. I think it was very, very difficult for him. But the house was full of that holocaust literary and historical stuff. I remember I went to see him when I was about ten years old, when he was in one of his bachelor periods. He was living alone in Hyde Park. We had breakfast together, and then he went into his study to work, leaving me on my own. Looking for something to read I pulled a book off the shelf called *Babi Yar*. The title is taken from the name of a ravine in the Ukraine that was the site of the massacre of over 33,000 Jews in 1941. The book was written from the perspective of a young boy, so I was immediately absorbed by it. I got to the middle of the book and I'm going, "Oh my God, this is awful."

Ultimately he was more interested in people than in politics. He shared with Leo Strauss—another Jewish immigrant who ended up in Chicago—a certain sense of detachment from American society, but also a deep sense of gratitude and appreciation for it. At least here in America we're not going to be rounded up, he probably said to himself. He was never such a fool that he romanticized the Russian Revolution like so many others of his generation. I think he felt he had a narrow escape there. I don't think he was ever drawn to Russia. I think his grandfather Berel Belo had a lot of nostalgia for the old country, and maybe even Abraham, his father. Certainly his mother missed her family. But I don't think, given what Jewish life was like in czarist Russia, there were any grounds for nostalgia. Plus he knew perfectly well that Tolstoy himself would never have condescended to speak to him.

In many ways, people misunderstand him when they call him a conservative. For example, he seems to have had absolutely no issues about homosexuality. Obviously he knew all about that side of Allan's life and he didn't care. It made no difference between them and their friendship. His only objection to it was when it became a political movement and a part of the grievance industry. That he thought was narcissistic and silly. He just wanted people to be serious. He didn't really care what they believed—still less what they did in the bedroom. He was quite shocked when people accused him of outing Allan in *Ravelstein*, but that was because of the specific people who accused him. Everybody in Chicago knew that Allan was gay. It was not a secret, and Allan himself asked Saul to write about him after he was gone. I think Saul's critics were concerned that the Straussian enterprise,[10] Allan's legacy as a teacher, would be damaged by a charge that he was ashamed of his own sexuality. Or conversely that it was somehow an expression of the tortured soul of a closeted gay man.

Allan was, like Saul, someone who had fought his way through all the ideologies of the twentieth century. He also was a wonderful teacher, and he really liked young people. I was attracted to his radicalism and his humor. He was interested in the philosophical errors people made, and he wanted to straighten them out. Allan was a great Platonist and Rousseauean. So was Saul. And love was Allan's central theme. In contrast, Saul was very pragmatic about love and marriage. For him it was an arrangement, a bargain. He made the same bargain time and again. He would marry a woman to handle the practical side of things while he did his creative work. She was supposed to provide a stable and wholesome domestic environment. She would also perform secretarial duties. As payment for this (in his mind, anyway) he would give her a child. But then he would become restless and things would start to fall apart. Then he would move on. That's how it went. As he got older he became better and better at getting in and out of these situations. He discovered that his little boat would carry him safely to the next port and everything would be okay. And he always kept some options open. Not that he necessarily intended to exercise them, but it gave him comfort that they were there.

The problem with liberals in my view is that they think that human beings can be enlightened, and that we can have a society based on rational principles. I don't believe that. So I'm not disappointed or upset when people in the heartland of this country talk about the Rapture. That's fine with me, because it's the same as it was in the sixteenth century. Why should it be any different? Do you think standardized public education is going to change any of that?

I think Saul would have loved the Tea Party as an expression of stubborn adherence to the American creed of cantankerous individualism. He would have seen it as a rebellion against political and cultural conformity, and an assertion of our irreducible right as Americans to think and act with perfect freedom. It is an ethos that says, "Don't tell me what to do, what to think, how to act, what to say, or how to vote. And get the hell off my lawn!" He would have been especially gratified by their touching faith in books and the seriousness with which they turn to them for guidance, inspiration, and enlightenment.

One of the most interesting things Saul said to me back in the 1990s was, "There's going to be a big revolt against the media." He called it years before it happened. And I've thought about this a long time. I just published a book by a Canadian liberal journalist about the 9/11 truth movement and the broader conspiracist subculture in the United States. He and I had a long series of conversations and debates about it, and I finally prevailed upon him to accept that the media is responsible for this conspiracy stuff. Why? Because the liberal press denies the grain of truth in anything that the right wing believes, and in doing so they bring themselves into discredit so that the average American consumer of news understands this. I think Saul would say that they've turned off, and the reason they've turned off is that they know on a deep metaphysical level that what they see come across the TV and what they hear on the radio and what they read in the newspaper is a simulacrum of reality. It is not reality. That doesn't make it a lie, but it does make it a product of the imagination. And so they're free to discount it. It's just another narrative. And of course the postmodern academy has done its part in encouraging this. Saul expressed all of this. "People have an instinct for truth," he explained. "They always know when they are being lied to—even if they don't really know that they know." In my opinion it is this spiritual hunger for the truth that has led so many Americans to revolt against political correctness and against the liberal bias of Hollywood and mainstream news media.

Daniel Bellow

Daniel Bellow, the youngest son of Saul Bellow by his third wife, Susan Glassman, was born in Chicago in 1964. Educated first at the University of Chicago Laboratory School, he went on to Northfield Mount Hermon School and Wesleyan University, graduating from the College of Letters in 1987. He pursued a career in daily newspaper journalism, working at the *Berkshire Eagle* and the *Rutland Herald,* among others, first as a reporter, then as an editor and editorial writer. In 1996, he married Heather Hershman. They have two children, Stella and Benjamin. As the newspaper business collapsed all around him, he returned to his first passion: studio pottery. His work is sold in finer galleries in the Northeast and at Anthropologie stores from Los Angeles to London.

I grew up in Chicago in Hyde Park, at 5490 South Shore Drive. This was the apartment my parents bought when they thought they could afford it. It was a pretty safe address, although I do remember at age four, that spring of 1968, watching out the back west-facing window of the apartment and seeing the neighborhood burn only twelve blocks away, just past Ellis where the university neighborhood ended. Hyde Park was an island of white privilege in the seething ocean of poverty and hate that is the South Side of Chicago. It's only gotten worse on every side except for the East, where there's the lake. To the south there's South Shore. To the west there's Drexel and Cottage Grove, and to the north there's Woodlawn. Pop used to like this Chinese restaurant called Tai Sam Yan under the El tracks on Sixty-Third Street. We'd come out of the restaurant at night and it was sketchy, but Pop never acted scared.

In 1978 I was fourteen, and I moved to New York. It was the punk era and I was going to clubs, sneaking in, and hanging out with the dirt bags at the Central Park band shell. I had so much fun Saul and Susan had to send me away to prep school, to a place called Northfield Mount Hermon, a private boarding school that was founded by the Chicago evangelist D. L. Moody in the 1890s. Without the distraction of New York, I did really well in school. I made the dean's list and won the Joseph Allen Prize for excellence in studio art. I was the kid who went and hid out in the pottery studio rather than going up to Brattleboro to try and get served in the bars. It was the first time in my life where I'd really wanted something that I could only have by working really hard. Pop once famously said, "Well, at least you'll always have a pot to piss in." He was the great put-down artist of the twentieth century. Once he put you down, man, you were down. Like Groucho Marx. "It was an honor to be loused up by Humboldt, like being the subject of a three-nosed portrait by Picasso." He was brilliant that way. I wanted to be a ceramic artist. But my dad, with my brother Adam in a supporting role, just verbally beat the crap out of me until I agreed to go to Wesleyan, and then into newspaper work. I don't regret doing what I did. I saw a lot and I learned a lot.

We're a family of troublemakers. Adam makes trouble too. Watch him publishing those books while everybody gets pissed off and he's vilified in the press. He loves it. I'm filled with admiration for him. I like to make trouble too. To be a newspaper reporter, to expose wrongdoing, that's a job for a man. I helped a lot of people who were getting fucked over real bad, and you know, that's something to be proud of. The thing to know about my father is that he didn't give a damn about politics per se. All he cared about was literature and the truth of human relations. If politics could provide insight into this, it was interesting. I was brought up by my mother to despise Mayor Daley as a colossus of big-city corruption, liberalism, and bigotry. Pop regarded Daley as the ringmaster of the great circus of corruption. Of course the city is corrupt. It's Chicago.

I remember I would get upset over Ronald Reagan coming into office and taking the solar panels off the roof of the White House immediately, and approving the artificial sugar that causes brain tumors in rats for use in chewing gum. He'd say, "Come on, come on kid. You're a Chicagoan. Are you going to get upset about this? Of course this is the way it is." He was always trying to wise me up because I think he would have regarded it as humiliating if any son of his had been a sucker, or a patsy, or naïve. If you read his books, you can see how he understands people and their base desires, their ambitions and greed and foolishness. He tried to teach me how to see things as they are, not in contrast to what I thought they should be.

Our Father's Politics

In 1995, I was working at the *Brattleboro Reformer* and the paper was sold. The new company sent this little guy named Nick to fire everybody. Nick was the hatchet man, five foot two, big pot belly and a beard, like one of those dwarves from *The Hobbit*. He took me in the conference room and he said, "You're not really productive enough." I said, "Fuck you, Jack, I write two stories a day, sometimes three. I'm the best reporter at this paper. You just cut my pay by 15 percent, so stick around and watch what 85 percent of me looks like." So feeling very proud of myself, I went over to my father's, and I said I had met this dwarf hatchet man, and I told him to stick it right up his ass. I expected him to be proud of me for standing up to the Man, but he just shook his head and said, "Come on, Daniel. This guy's a clown. He's the guy that comes to town to fire everyone. You know he has nothing to do with you. You shouldn't even be moved by him. Just take a step back and look at it for the ridiculous farce that it is." "Well," I said, "I'm going to quit." He said, "Don't quit. Go and find yourself another job, but don't quit. You know you need money coming in." So there he was, the sensible father.

Well, that job just got worse and worse, and then I went and got married and went to Jackson Hole for my honeymoon. When it came time to go back to work, it had snowed three feet in the night, and I called up my editor and I said, "Look, there's three feet of snow here in Jackson Hole and I can't be back until Monday." And he said, "You're fired." I got fired on my honeymoon.

Somebody once said being a reporter is like being the horse in one of those horse tales for little girls. You go from one cruel master to another. Every once in a while somebody will take pity on you and give you a warm stable and some oats, but it never lasts. So that was my newspaper career. I don't think it did me any good to be Saul Bellow's son in that business either. The newsrooms are filled with these failed mediocrities who believe they have a novel in them somewhere if they could only stop drinking long enough to make it come out. They looked at me, the little prince, and said, "Let's send him to cover the Sewer Board, see how he does." It didn't matter that I was good, it didn't matter that I was fearless, and aggressive. And being an editor is a bore. You know, it's everybody else having all the fun, and you just sit in your chair and get fat. So I'm much happier doing what I'm doing.

Pop hated book reviewers. Every once in a while some famous guy's name would come up in conversation and Pop would make a face like he had swallowed a mouthful of pickle brine and he'd go, "That Stalinist!" It was the worst insult he could level against you.

In the 1930s he had a Trotskyite period, but as Mrs. Oppenheimer told the FBI man, "It was the 1930s. Every decent person was a socialist." We forget in our amnesia that capitalism had utterly failed. Nobody had a job. The whole structure had come crashing down on these boys on the West Side of Chicago. They saw capitalism in ruins everywhere. It was easy for some of them to close their eyes to Stalin's purges and believe the propaganda coming out of Russia. Pop always brought up Walter Duranty. Again and again, he'd say, "Don't be Walter Duranty. Be an honest reporter." Walter Duranty was a reporter for the *New York Times* who was a Stalinist stooge. He knew the truth about the gulags and the purges in the 1920s and 1930s and kept it from his readers. He won the Pulitzer Prize, which shows you what good the Pulitzer Prize is. The *Times* won't return it. They keep it there in their trophy room, which shows you what good the *Times* is. Pop told me he saw through Stalin as quick as he did Hitler, and he had nothing but contempt for those who didn't. Once he told me: "I never lined up with anyone. I always thought for myself."

By the time I was politically aware, the women's movement, the civil rights movement, the youth revolution, and the Vietnam War had already happened. When I was a kid I liked the hippies. They were for peace and love and justice, and who could argue with that? It was obvious to me that the war in Vietnam was utterly immoral. It was obvious to me that Martin Luther King was a hero, the bravest American that ever lived. But when I was a little kid, we didn't talk much about these things, because why bother talking to a ten-year-old about politics if you're Saul Bellow? The older I got the more interesting he became, and the more interested he was in me. He was not a very good daddy to a small boy, you know, but when I grew up and started to have ideas of my own, many of which he regarded as wrong, he undertook to correct them—from up on his high horse. I respected that. I mean he had seen Trotsky's body in the morgue in Mexico City. He'd been there. Not only did he know his shit, but he was fully entitled to his views. You can't argue with an apostate, right? It was an unassailable authority. You know, he had once been a true believer, not in a doctrinaire sense, but he did believe in the notion that the world could be a better place. And it was hard to argue with him when he said that certain social mores and graces are what allow civilization to continue, and civilization is something we all need.

He did think the 1960s were not good for civilization. I guess it all depended where you were standing in the 1960s, how you saw them. I mean, I've read *Slouching Towards Bethlehem,* which is a grownup's take on all the silliness and ignorance on the part of these people who thought they were changing the world. And I think he saw it that way, too. Certainly the scene at San Francisco State, which is repeated in *Mr. Sammler's Planet,* together with what I'm pretty sure are some stretchers, did not reflect well on the New Left. On the other hand, Pop loved Allen Ginsberg. He thought he was the fairy son of Whitman. Once when I was about twelve, I told him he was a square, and he took great exception. He appealed to Adam, and Adam said, "Squares lack soul." "Are you going to tell me I lack soul?" he said, fixing me with that bottomless stare. And I said, "No, no, that wouldn't be fair."

Once in the kitchen in the Vermont house, we were talking about Bernie Sanders, the "socialist" mayor of Burlington who is now a U.S. senator. I was a reporter for the *Reformer,* and I knew how Bernie would say one thing in Brattleboro and another in White River Junction, so I wasn't buying this straw man. Pop just went off on this tirade about the political Left, saying, "It's all nihilism, it's insincerity, it's hypocrisy." He wasn't completely wrong, either, but I said, "Did Abbie Hoffman just walk into the room behind me? I mean, who are you talking to? Don't you know me any better than that?" He stopped, and on the way out to the car, he apologized. Pop was the best. I'm so proud to be his son.

I always thought of him as a representative from a world that no longer existed. When he was born, there was still a czar of Russia, and he had kicked Grandpa Abraham Belo's ass out of Saint Petersburg. So Saul's early politics were shaped by the notion that the czar is a bad man and Russia is a state founded on injustice. So when Lenin showed up and said, "I must overthrow it," a lot of Jews said, "Knock yourself out." It took Jewish Americans of that generation a while to get over their identification of Lenin with Marx, and their vision of a world where everything is beautiful and peaceful, and where the dictatorship or the proletarian government eventually withers away into liberty, equality, and fraternity. Well, it wasn't working out that way, but the golden fleece of world socialism, the idea that there could be a better world, was a hard thing to give away, even in the face of mounting evidence that Lenin and Stalin were building a nightmare totalitarian regime that was more complete and thoroughgoing than anything the czar could have achieved. When Pop saw Stalin persecuting Osip Mandelstam[11] and putting him in prison to be worked to death in Siberia, he put two and two together. Not everybody could do that. Lots of people took Stalin's Moscow Show Trials at face value. But Pop saw they were a farce. So I grew up hearing that the government of the United States, with all its faults, is preferable to Stalinist dictatorship. I think that was his issue with the New Left—anyone who would equate the two was just not serious.

Once he said to me, "Show me where I've written something that makes me a reactionary." Again, I think he stood for the values of an older world, an America where people were actually educated so that they could have a real argument, where there was such a thing as high culture, and the American innovation was to make it available to anyone who wanted it. Somewhere in *The Adventures of Augie March* he talks about a universal eligibility to be noble. There were many cultural and political figures that he thought highly of, people who had had real experiences in the world, people with real souls. Pop believed that America, crass and materialistic as it was, could regenerate, could rediscover its soul through culture. American popular culture is often vulgar and stupid, and Pop thought it beneath contempt. I remember when I used to like the rock group Kiss (there's a damaging admission), and Pop just rolled his eyes. He never cared about anything but literature and high culture. People are mistaken if they think he cared who the president was. He thought Jimmy Carter was a weakling and *schmuck,* and that he was dangerous for America when Soviet Russia was run by Brezhnev, a real tough guy. He had seen Neville Chamberlain get rolled by Hitler. When Ronald Reagan got elected he was happy because he thought Reagan was a man of character and an anticommunist. I would say, "He deregulated the banks and let the thieves loose in the treasury," but Pop had lived through the Harding administration so he wasn't impressed. He thought Adlai Stevenson was a fool, easy pickings for Mayor Daley. Pop respected strength and savvy in a politician, and when a politician did not display those qualities, Pop considered that he was not fit for office.

When we were all at the dinner table with family, nobody stopped you from talking, but the conversation was at such a high level and went so fast that I just couldn't follow it. Every once in a while I would ask a dumb question and everyone would laugh. Then my father would explain to me very patiently who Kaiser Wilhelm was, and the conversation would resume several feet above my head. You had to run to keep up, and my legs were just too short. I had to study. He hated to hear me repeat propaganda. Almost to the point of physical violence he really hated it. He would say, "No son of mine is going to be ignorant about this. Read this book and don't talk to me until you're finished." So this is how I'm trying to raise my own children.

He took a very keen interest in my literary education and was handing me things like *David Copperfield* to read when I was ten. He just said, "Oh, you can read that." I said, "Pop, it's a huge book and it's got all these tiny letters in it." And he would say, "You can read it." There was nothing better than hearing Pop read out loud. He read me Jack London's *The Call of the Wild* when I was six years old. When Adam was a teenager, one summer he read us both the Dudley Fitts translation of *The Odyssey*. I've never had to reread it because I remember it all so well—the Cyclops, Polyphemus, smashing the guys' heads together. Adam and I after dinner would say, "Pop, what are we reading tonight? Pop, will you read to us?" He read me Joseph Conrad and Kipling too, all of it, *The Jungle Books, Kim,* the lot. He hated Hemingway. The whole first paragraph of *Augie March* is a declaration of war on Hemingway and his literary style and his emotional constipation. So I too hate Hemingway. I'm capable of admiring Hemingway's style because it's impossible to escape its influence. But Pop thought he was just a megalomaniacal pig and worse, an anti-Semite.

Pop was at his most conservative when he talked about the Jews, and anti-Semitism in all its colors, British, French, Russian, Arab. He was always talking about African Americans. All the time. Also the Holocaust, Zionism, and Black-Jewish relations in the cities. But he was never boring, like everybody who now writes for *Commentary*, and he wasn't always predictable. For instance, when Menachem Begin became prime minister of Israel, he remembered him as the pimply terrorist who blew up the King David Hotel.

I went to Morocco my senior year of high school, lived with a Moroccan family, and I brought back a full report. Pop received it without preconceptions, and he never tried to put any political grid on my experience. I wonder what he would have made of the Arab Spring. To see the Syrians who've lived all their lives under this awful dictatorship acting with such courage is a big, big deal.

When I went to see the film *El Norte*, in which the poor *campesinos* are monstrously oppressed and go to the North and get totally hosed by the capitalist system, I was about seventeen years old. I came back and I said to Pop, "How can you countenance this world where things are this way?" And he said, "Well, what do you want me to do about it? You know that Guatemala has a military dictatorship. What am I supposed to do?" He gave me that response a lot. "What do you want from me? You know, I didn't make this world." I said, "Yes, you did! You're a big important figure. You ought to be able to do something about this shit." He'd spread his hands in this "what can I do" gesture.

Back in the mid- to late 1990s I remember asking him about some political issue du jour. I forget now what it was. But he just said, "Ugh, I don't care about that." He just sort of shut me down as if to say, "That's not what you should be thinking about." He was too busy thinking of higher matters. I had lots of great professors in college, but he was the greatest of them all. I think Allan Bloom was a big political influence on Pop just because they got along like such a house on fire. And they agreed about so much already. Bloom was actually more learned in many of these things. Pop probably read Plato's *Republic* in college and never cracked it again until he met Allan. I think that Bloom's influence was just to deepen Pop's views and keep him company. Bloom was one of the most brilliant men you could ever meet. And such a forceful arguer. He argued and he spoke like he wrote, except he was always sucking his Marlboro down, you know, and going, "Arrr, arrr, arrr." That was the sound of his brain working and deciding what to say next. I would come in there with my half-assed ideas and would just be so utterly defeated in an argument with Allan Bloom. It happened again and again. Adam especially loved that when he was Allan's student.

My brother Adam and I agree on the most important things, those which we learned from our father. Adam expressed his view of the world to me very succinctly one day: "The world is run by gangs of bullies, and these gangs of bullies are in competition with each other. And the rest of us just have to live here."

Adam is doing a lot of writing about the Tea Party people. I think he is going to get fleas from lying down with dogs. I think that Adam believes that these are the people who have been Nixon's silent majority, who have been ignored by the government, which has mostly catered to minorities and labor constituencies.

These conservatives feel like they're being ignored and that the world is changing all around them. So they are confused and frightened and angry. Adam likes the fact that the constituency is speaking up and making an uproar. He thinks it's healthy and I agree, but that's where we part company. I think these are people whose parents were Wallace Democrats and whose grandparents were Klansmen. They don't like it that the United States is becoming so black, so Hispanic, so secular, so tolerant of what they regard as deviance. They're losing out and they're pissed off, so they're susceptible to manipulation by the Koch Brothers of the world, who don't give a damn about them or their concerns.

As for Saul's attitudes toward women, my cousin Lynn used to say, "Nothing scares a man of our fathers' generation like a woman with a college degree and a diaphragm." I think it's true, that he was just old-fashioned. I think he thought feminism was unsexing women, taking away the things about them which make them special. He was very shrewd in his judgments of individual women, well, some individual women, and their motivations in doing the things they did.

As for blacks, Pop had lived with Ralph Ellison. There is this story I tell my wife and children again and again and I never get tired of telling it. Saul and Ralph are at dinner at Gore Vidal's house. Gore Vidal is running America and its government up one wall and down the other. Finally Ellison says, "Gore, I don't know what your problem is. You're rich, you're white, you're pretty. I don't know what you have got to complain about." So in our house whenever somebody protests too much we say, "I don't know what his problem is. He's rich, he's white, he's pretty." Pop had enormous respect for Ellison and for Ellison's work. Too bad Ellison could only squeeze one book out of his head. But it's a hell of a book, and if Pop were here he'd tell you it's a hell of a book, and that Ellison was a hell of a guy. He also had this great friend named Stanley Crouch, who wrote "Notes of a Hanging Judge." Stanley's a tough critic and a marvelously expressive guy. Pop got a big kick out of him. Again, this is a generational thing. I love black people, have big sympathy with black people. I grew up in a different Chicago than Pop. My mother dated Richard Hunt. I kissed Myrna Everett in first grade. I'm a different person from my father. In his world, blacks and whites were segregated. And Chicago, don't kid yourself, was just as segregated as Mississippi. Chicago wasn't as loud about it, but black people kept to themselves, and Saul certainly didn't grow up with any black people. He didn't like multiculturalism, and he said it wasn't conducive to producing great writers. It probably isn't. Pop was all about the meritocracy. All he cared about was excellence. He thought Toni Morrison deserved that Nobel Prize she got. I read her books when I found them in his house. The books would be on their faces on the ottoman. He read them all.

Pop did mellow with age. Certainly toward me. But he never made it up with Greg. That argument only pretended to be about the Vietnam War. Really it was about Pop and Greg. Sometimes Pop's opinions had less to do with his political views and more to do with the person he was talking to. He was a great chain-yanker. He liked to dig a pit and cover it with branches so you'd come walking along, whistling away, and fall right in it. Then he would stand there at the edge and watch you as you sort of thrashed around. He liked that.

My view is that the government has a legitimate role in protecting the people from the depredations of corporations who will market aspartame and put it in every soda and every piece of gum that my kids eat. The government has been bribed, bought off, deceived. I think it's monstrous, a gross injustice, and I devoted twenty years of my life fighting these people as a journalist. The one regret I have is that I didn't do enough. Pop loved all this. He thought my ideals were a bunch of misty bullshit, but he liked to watch me make trouble. When I worked for the *Reformer*, he read my stories every day. If a couple of days went by and I didn't have a byline in the paper, he'd call me up and say, "Are you alright, is everything okay, you sick?" Once he said to me, "I've been watching you and you're very interesting. You don't join the organizations. You are not a joiner. You're a cat who walks by himself. You've staked out this place at the very margin of society and you just watch it. And you're making up your own mind. So I'm very proud of you." That was the greatest conversation we ever had. Boy, I miss him. I am sorry that I didn't have more time with him in the years that we really understood each other.

His wife Alexandra had the most influence on him politically. She grew up in communist Romania. Her parents were high officials. In 1957 she came to the United States to study mathematics at Yale. She is a pioneer in probability theory, my beloved ex-stepmother. Eventually she decided not to go back to Romania and Ceaușescu's government stripped her mother of high political office as minister of health. She became a nonperson. It wasn't easy to destroy someone like that who had hundreds of friends and people whose brain tumors she had cured, but they had their says, those hard old bastards. Florica Bagdasar was her name. She was a great, great doctor. But she was persecuted for thirty years for what Alexandra did. Alexandra taught us what it was to live under communism. She wasn't doctrinaire. All she had to do was tell stories of what happened when the Nazis came, and then the Soviets. I think she was a really big political influence on Pop and his thinking.

As for my mother's politics, one day there was a copy of *Time* magazine with Ronnie and Nancy on the cover. She turned it over on the table and said, "I can't stand to look at them. They just represent wealth and privilege without conscience." Now, I still think this is true, but I came to appreciate my father's view of the world, and I've largely adopted it as my own. I miss Pop, but he's always with me. When I was down in New York staying with Adam this summer, Adam said the cats had ruined his brand-new armchair by sharpening their claws on it. I'm allergic to his cats and I hate them, so I said, "You know, your ex-wife really stuck you with these cats. You know it's time for you to put them in the cat carrier and bring them up to Boston, leave them on her porch. Ring the doorbell and tell her, 'Here are your cats. It's time for you to have custody of them!'" And he said, "You know, I really should. You sounded just like Pop just now! For a minute it could have been him sitting here." I think we all feel like he never really left, even though he was such a pale shadow of his former self when he departed. But he was truly Pop when he was saying something particularly wicked. You grow up with it and you think it's normal, but I've never met anybody like him. I've met lots of cool, accomplished, and famous people. I've never met anyone who could touch him.

Notes

1. Young People's Socialist League; IWW, or Industrial Workers of the World international union, which at its peak in 1923 boasted a membership of three hundred thousand workers.

2. Abraham Lincoln Brigades often made up of Communist Party volunteers from the United States who were engaged as the International Brigades in the Spanish Civil War. After World War II during the "Red Scare" in the United States, these people were thought to be security risks.

3. Communist International, abbreviated as the Comintern, and also called the Third International 1919–1943, was organized in 1919 to fight and overthrow the international bourgeoisie.

4. Henry Luce (1898–1967) was married to the famous Clare Boothe Luce, both of them influential Republicans.

5. The now infamous Minnesota Starvation Experiment conducted at the University of Minnesota by nutritionist Ancel Keys concerning how few calories were necessary for survival.

6. Truman had actually struck down the segregation in the military.

7. In 1973, the neoconservatives were those who had criticized American liberals and the outcomes of the Great Society's welfare program.

8. President Lyndon B. Johnson's set of domestic programs presented in the U.S. Congress in the 1960s designed to eliminate poverty, and racial injustice through educational, medical, and urban problems.

9. The Jewish legend of the Holy Sparks from Lurianic Kabbalism; the Hassidic belief in the spiritual illumination inherent in all things.

10. Leo Strauss, 1889–1971, German Jewish classical political philosopher greatly revered by the Allan Bloom circle.

11. Osip Mandelstam, 1891–1938, Jewish Russian populist poet and essayist.

Saul Bellow's Politics: A Selected Annotated Bibliography, 1947–Present

Gloria L. Cronin

This bibliography is suggestive of the difficulty of finding exclusively political secondary material on Saul Bellow, mixed as it mostly is with articles dealing with a whole variety of metaphysical, moral, and aesthetic topics mostly of interest to literary scholars. Nevertheless, the articles here speak to Bellow's communist, Trotskyite, and then socialist politics, his transition away from the socialists of the *Partisan Review*, and his eventual political position as a famous and staunch neoconservative. An increasing number of articles written since the 1990s deal with his social class, as well as his academic, economic, ideological, cultural, political, gender, racial, and postcolonial perspectives. Much attention has also been given to his explorations of the politics of his male homosociality, the fate of the heterosexual pair, male friendship, women, gay sexuality, homophobia, the contemporary politics of sex, love and marriage, late capitalism, Israel, American Jews, the Holocaust, contemporary Jewishness, present-day Europe, and contemporary American urban life.

Abbreviations

AAM	*The Adventures of Augie March*
AAU	*It All Adds Up*
ATA	*Theft*
BC	*The Bellarosa Connection*
DD	*The Dean's December*

DM   Dangling Man
HRK   Henderson the Rain King
H   Herzog
HG   Humboldt's Gift
MDH   More Die of Heartbreak
MSP   Mr. Sammler's Planet
R   Ravelstein
SD   Seize the Day
TJB   To Jerusalem and Back
TV   The Victim

General Articles, Chapters, and Reviews

Adamowski, T. H. "The Devil in Disguise." *University of Toronto Quarterly* 65, no. 2 (1996): 452–65.

    Discusses Bellow as a young writer moving to New York and joining the midcentury socialist cultural critics associated with the *Partisan Review*. Discusses what people then thought of Bellow, the promise they saw, his representations of various theoretical positions, where distractions were most likely to occur, Bellow and Heidegger, and Bellow's politics.

Atlas, Marilyn Judith. "The Figurine in the China Cabinet: Saul Bellow and the Nobel Prize." *MidAmerica* 8 (1981): 36–49.

    Describes Bellow's mixed responses to winning the Nobel Prize in 1976. Comments on the judges' reasons for the award in terms of Bellow's ability to create character and critique contemporary culture. Summarizes Bellow's printed responses, Richard Stern's *New York Times* essay, and all of Bellow's previous awards. Documents Bellow's defensiveness after receiving the award and his refusal to become a cultural "functionary." Analyzes the content of Bellow's Nobel lecture in terms of his focus on the individual life, his identification with Conrad as a displaced person, and his artistic faith in character. Discusses the chief protagonists briefly and in chronological order in terms of their dimensions as "characters."

Bach, Gerhard. "Margin as Center: Bellow and the New Central Europe." In *Saul Bellow and the Struggle at the Center*, edited by Eugene Hollahan, 1–11. Georgia State Literary Studies 12. New York: AMS, 1996.

    Speaks of the current moment of silence in the immediate post–Cold

War years. Also addresses the self-silencing and melancholy of many intellectuals at the spectacle of materialist counterforces, which are replacing the ideological conflicts of former years and which represent a double defeat and a loss for words. Sketches the content of Bellow's public appearance at Rutgers University, Newark Campus, on 9 April 1992, at a conference entitled "Intellectuals and Social Change in Eastern and Central Europe." Describes this conference attended by Ralph Ellison, Czeslaw Milosz, Joseph Brodsky, Doris Lessing, Susan Sontag, and William Phelps, along with a large cadre of expatriate and expelled former Soviet writers. Reports the contents of Bellow's address, "Transcending National Boundaries," as establishing a compassionate distance in terms of the indictment of both the West for having abandoned higher values and the Eastern European governments for depriving their citizens of them. Reports that Bellow condemns both as spiritual deserts and calls the product of Western Enlightenment the "virtualization" of experience that decomposes social contexts and cultural bonds. Describes Bellow's reactions to the falling of the Berlin Wall and his general jeremiad urging writers everywhere to call upon their transhistorical spiritual powers to witness a set of guiding truths.

Baumgarten, Murray. "Urban Failures, Fictional Possibilities." *Jewish Book Annual* 41 (1983–1984): 6–23.

Asserts that the city has shaped Jews and that the key to understanding Bellow's Jewish protagonists is Chicago. Provides a detailed explication of Bellow's philosophical and cultural understanding of urban life. In celebrating the urban conditions, Bellow sees the city as the key to our individuality, imagination, and intellect. He then begins to see the failure of city life as more of a pathological condition than a key to maintaining civilization. When Bellow's protagonists enter the mainstream of American life as carriers of urban values, they find themselves confronting dying cities. What is possible for the West and the Jew, now that the city has lost its center?, Bellow asks. *The Dean's December* contains Bellow's vision of the Jew naked in the city before the onslaught of modern history.

Bilton, A. "The Colored City: Saul Bellow's Chicago and Images of Blackness." *Saul Bellow Journal* 16, no. 2–17, nos. 1–2 (2001): 104–28.

Argues that Bellow's writing witnesses the extent to which the environment and the physical represent that stubborn substratum that resists humankind's attempts to impose systems of order. Particularly, this site has its roots in the richly textured reminiscences of Bellow's old neighborhood and his adolescent struggles. Within this setting, the dualism between language and reality, as well as ideas and things, plays out in the urban street environment between the governing consulate and the marginalized other. In the classic colonial narrative, the black or alien other appears as a reflection of the fears and desires of the dominant gaze, thus signifying otherness as a source of both white anxiety and white fantasy. Such a paradigm is problematized in Jewish writing. Explores Bellow's engagement with the urban realities of Chicago and more—specifically with African American neighborhoods within it—as a nature of order and chaos. Then relates these categories to his own sense of identity and ethnicity. Chicago—both the colored jungle city and a monochrome prairie space—serves to illuminate and define the contradictions at the heart of Bellow's urban sensibility. Appearing under various guises, this conflict between civilization and savagery is obsessively formulated and reformulated in Bellow's fiction. Covers a variety of novels and shorter works.

Bloom, Alexander. "Saul Bellow and the 'Axial Lines' of Life." In *The New York Intellectuals and Their World*, edited by Bloom, 290–97. New York: Oxford University Press, 1986.

Discusses the axial lines of influence that provide Bellow's intellectual contexts. Details his connection with the *Partisan Review* intellectually and his personal associations in New York and Chicago. Provides an explanation of Bellow's artistic and intellectual coming-of-age throughout the several stages of his life. Asserts that the central themes of much of Bellow's fiction is so much more than the literary rehashing of the issues of the New York intellectual world, and maintains that these themes are intimately connected to his politics.

Bradbury, Malcolm. "Liberal and Existential Imaginations: The 1940s and 1950s." In *The Modern American Novel*, new ed., 169–75. New York: Viking, 1993.

Discusses Bellow in the context of the forces that shaped American social and literary history during the 1940s and 1950s. Suggests that the post-1940s novel, including Bellow's works, abandoned the large mythic themes of the early moderns, engaged in moral uncertainty and metaphysical complexity, was more alienated than its European counterparts, and was shaped in a dark, post-Holocaust era shaken by evil. Sees Bellow exploring the place of the individual as beneficiary or exile who suffers urban anonymity, behavioral indifference, and the totalitarian massing of social force. Also comments on the rich Jewish humanism and the heritage of European philosophical thought that shapes most of his heroes, who are also heirs of modernist romanticism. Comments on how each of the books published in these two decades reflects the decade in which it was written. Sees *Dangling Man* as a struggle between determinism and humanism, and *The Adventures of Augie March, Seize the Day*, and *Henderson the Rain King* as more ebullient and picaresque. Sees *Henderson* as exploring the notion of modern selfhood in the 1960s, and describes *Mr. Sammler's Planet* as a book about revolutionary consciousness, black power, florid romanticism, irrationalism, and hypercivilized Byzantine lunacy. *Humboldt's Gift* deals with two generations of writers, while *The Dean's December* is about a man trying to reconcile social observation with astrophysical knowledge.

Bradbury, Malcolm. "Saul Bellow's Intellectual Heroes." In *Saul Bellow at Seventy-Five: A Collection of Critical Essays*, 33–39. Studies & Texts in English 9. Tübingen: Narr, 1991.

Compares the prominence of Gyorgy Lukács to Bellow because Lukács was an exemplary European intellectual who fought against the "leaking away of life into nothingness" and set his face against the modern. Reviews Bellow's views of the modern and postmodern heroes in American fiction. Describes Bellow's protagonists as "heroes in space" who, like Lukács's, are distinctively flamboyant intellectuals burdened with the moral and philosophical duties of the thinking mind, and who are persistently in search of reality. Sees Bellow's writing over five decades as full of argumentative ideas and intellectual issues, as well as conflicts of the tricky, inchoate half century weighted down by the heavy inheritance of Romantic and modernist thought, which, in a new post-Marxist era, now comes to its close under the burden of its ideological and mental uncertainty. Compares Claudio Magris's account of the anguish of Lukács's trip down the Danube with Bellow's heroes also trying to find an answer to dissolution. Concludes that while rereading Bellow for his seventy-fifth birthday, he has set out on his own Danubian voyage with more than literary-critical interest, since he, too, is trying to write a novel about European intellectual existence in the world beyond Marx and Lukács. In his novel, he writes about a time when the great ideological preconceptions that guided much of the century have truly come apart, and when a vast mental reorganization is now due. Pays tribute to Bellow's "vital and glorious guidance" in this project.

Buelens, Gert. "American-Jewish Narrative and Multicultural Society—Then and Now." *Multiculturalism and the Canon of American Literature*, edited by Hans Bak, 228–39. European Contributions to American Studies 23. Amsterdam: Vincennes University Press, 1993.

Provides a history of American Jewish fiction, from its roots in eastern European culture of the nineteenth century to its immigrant experiences in America's cities. What follows is an endless dynamic of ethnic construction and deconstruction. Bellow's fiction provides a monadic narrative center incorporating the dual American-European stance of the protagonist in such a way as to suggest the possibility of an imaginary wholeness. Rather than having to engage too much in the fallen world, Bellow's protagonists are allowed to withdraw into a rarified existence as monads enjoying wholeness of their own imaginary making. Focuses largely on *Mr. Sammler's Planet*.

Chabot, C. Barry. "The Thirties and the Failure of the Future." *Writers for the Nation: American Literary Modernism*, ed. Chabot, 205–46. Tuscaloosa: University of Alabama Press, 1997.

Discusses the regional, agrarian, and proletarian impulses in the Depression era. Argues that there is a similarity in the literary work produced by leftist writers, which in some ways resembles that written by participants in the Harlem or New Negro Renaissance. Then describes the first existentialist novels of the 1930s, including *Dangling Man* and *The Adventures of Augie March*, as dispirited about the collapse of proletarian fiction, the Left, radical politics, and the status quo. Argues that these novels represent that early moment in Bellow's career in which he had set aside one vision of social life and not yet adapted another. As a result, terms such as "life," "death," and "freedom" possess little positive substance, despite the fact that Joseph and Augie try in vain to rub some saving vision from their too-smooth surfaces.

Christhilf, Mark M. "Death and Deliverance in Saul Bellow's Symbolic City." *Ball State University Forum* 18, no. 2 (1977): 9–23.

Argues that, with the exception of *Henderson the Rain King*, the cityscapes in the Bellow novel function as an inferno that threatens man's sanity and dignity at each turn. But Bellow's fictional city also has mythic, apocalyptic overtones. In the later works, the city, in terms of the physical imagery used to embody it, undergoes a transformation from a concrete narrative setting to a higher abstract place. Utilizing various novelistic forms and techniques, Bellow has dramatized the city as an extension of the evil potential within man, a theme he conveys throughout his works.

Christhilf, Mark M. "Saul Bellow and the American Intellectual Community." *Modern Age* 28, no. 1 (1984): 55–67.

Argues that a critique of the American intellectual community informs all of Bellow's work. Discusses his estrangement from this community. Discusses the middle and later novels in detail. Concludes with an estimate of Bellow's influence on this intellectual community, his politics and theirs.

Cronin, Gloria L. "Holy War against the Moderns: Saul Bellow's Antimodernist Critique of Contemporary American Society." *Studies in American Jewish Literature* 8, no. 1 (1989): 77–94.

Argues that Bellow's lifelong determination has been to deflect the main course of modernist thinking, which has dominated Western culture and American thought in the twentieth century. Traces throughout his interviews, essays, and fiction Bellow's consistent attempts to scorn absurdism, alienation ethics, historicist pessimism, the diminishment of the private self, and the belief in *Deus Abscondus*. Covers all of the novels up to *MDH*. Concludes that, as the great metaphysical comedian of contemporary letters, Bellow has quarreled powerfully with all the great nineteenth- and twentieth-century thinkers and waged a forty-year holy war in an attempt to rescue contemporary ideas of the Self from the cultural politics of contemporary America.

Dickstein, Morris. "For Art's Sake." *Partisan Review* 33, no. 4 (1966): 617–21.

Describes Bellow's address at a recent PEN meeting in which he indicts literary critics and teachers of literature. Finds Bellow's acrimony over the literary establishment somewhat ironic as well as worthy of serious attention. Criticizes the deficiencies of the speech and its tendency to dichotomize history as a Manichean struggle between artists and critics for possession of the Word, a struggle that Bellow seems to characterize as a contest between the forces of light and the forces of darkness.

Dresner, Samuel H. "The Jewish Bellow Reconsidered." *Midstream*, June/July 1996, 33–36.

Calls Bellow a man with an identity problem, given his long history of embracing and rejecting the label "Jewish" and all forms of parochiality in favor of "universal" writer. Argues, nevertheless, that by 1963 he is coming to terms with his Jewishness, and that by the time he has published *TJB* he is dealing very seriously with this issue. Suggests that on the twentieth anniversary of the publication of this seminal book on the ongoing crisis of Bellow's Jewish self-definition, it is fitting to point out its brilliant vignettes of famous and ordinary people, beautiful descriptions of land, and brilliant style. Suggests that in his later years Bellow has discovered not only the land of Israel and its energy, but that being a universal writer means that you must draw out of your own traditions with pride and understanding. Concludes that the goal for Bellow and other writers is to reinvent civilization, and not to see one's Jewishness as narrowness, but as a glory and a blessing for all.

Faraci, Mary. "Saul Bellow and Comparative Politics." *Saul Bellow Journal* 14, no. 1 (1996): 68–83.

Discusses how *DD*, set in the Ceauşescu years, is the first Western account of Eastern Europe to liberate reports of the region from the arrogance of ill-informed journalists, and to reflect on the sad state of language in their journalistic reports. Styled against such Western journalists, Dean Corde is capable of experimenting with language available to him, eschewing the use of stereotypes, and exploring new linguistic ways of talking about knowledge and freedom. Thus Corde manages to restore the missing emotions and values to the images that attracted Western reporters.

Fuchs, Daniel. "Literature and Politics: The Bellow/Grass Confrontation at the PEN Congress." In *Saul Bellow: A Mosaic*, 49–57. Twentieth-Century American Jewish Writers 3. New York: Lang, 1992.

Describes the Bellow/Grass confrontation at the PEN Congress of 1986. Outlines the political theme of the conference as "The Imagination of the Writer and the Imagination of the State." Describes Bellow on the alienation panel giving a pointed but casual talk discussing exile; the spiritual mansion of language in which we all live; the cultural history of alienation; American democracy; and the lack of culture, gods, and demons in American experience. Argues that his culminating point, shown so often in his fiction, is the substitution of the gratification of innumerable desires for all of these missing items. Hence, while we live in a country full of psychobabble, security, health, and justice, we also live in hells of spiritual alienation. Describes Günter Grass as not widely read enough. His [Grass's] view of Bellow's remarks was unjust, implying that Bellow had not taken into consideration the realities of political economy as class struggle and imperialism. Reports in great detail Bellow's sardonic response to Grass's rather crude remarks about the moribund nature of the capitalist state. Concludes that the heart of the Bellow/Grass confrontation is the vexed question of the relationship between truth and power, vision and action. Though the two writers can't be simplistically characterized by two opposite political poles, nevertheless artists need to respond to politics in order to defend themselves from it. Explicates both Bellow and Grass on these perspectives.

Furman, Andrew. "The Importance of Saul Bellow." *English Academy Review* [South Africa] 14 (1997): 59–72.

Argues against the theory-ridden climate of English departments today and their disdain of close reading, or neglect of the primary literary text. Argues that amid postmodern hoopla, we need to recoup the revelatory experiences and quality of good fiction. Explicates Bellow's 1990 lecture "The Distracted Public," centering on the question of whether the reading public's "mounting demand for thrill" can ever be "brought under control." Discusses at length Bellow's investment in ideas of soul, the humanistic enterprise, and moral and religious issues. Traces the redemptive thread that runs through Bellow's essentially modernist literary vision. Covers nearly all of the major works. Concludes that Bellow and our best literature drown out the deafening hum of our information age to express the heart's truths and essences.

Furman, Andrew. "Saul Bellow's Middle East Problem." *Saul Bellow Journal* 14, no. 1 (1996): 40–67. Reprinted in *Israel through the Jewish-American Imagination: A Survey of Jewish American Literature on Israel 1928–1995*, 59–81. SUNY Series on Modern Jewish Literature and Culture. Albany: State University of New York Press, 1997.

Considers it something of a puzzle that Bellow directs his moralizing energies toward the enigmatic Middle East, given Bellow's long-standing quarrel with being constantly labeled a Jewish writer, and also his early rejection of Meyer Levin and his Zionism. Points out, however, that the young Bellow who followed Trotsky and declared himself a Marxist is not the same writer who wrote *TJB*. Examines the contrary mood of the Jewish American community during the period of the 1967 Six-Day War, and presents Bellow's canny and slightly aloof stance in *MSP* and *TJB*. Suggests that the disparity between Sammler's perspective and Bellow's serves to illustrate the very real cost of Israeli might, particularly in the depiction of the violent Eisen. Also discusses Bellow's seeming confusion about the Middle East and his inability to penetrate beneath the surface of the Israeli condition. Considers that the book's strength lies in Bellow's bored voice and skepticism, and its weakness in the way Bellow's bookishness and erudition obscure his emotional investment in Israel. Concludes that it would be unfair, given the qualified affirmations of the novels, to ask Bellow to start fudging with regard to the Middle East.

Hall, James. "The Revolving Brush: Blackness in *Humboldt's Gift* and *The Bellarosa Connection*." *Saul Bellow Journal* 16, no. 2–17, nos. 1–2 (2001): 280–95.

Argues that Bellow's bigoted self, which makes him so uncomfortable each time it is revealed, is not a repressed form that somehow erupts through his comforting *bien penseés,* although, as his writing reveals, there are repressions enough. Bellow's racism, while it worries at his liberal heart and principles, permeates much of his writing. It is part of the ideological machine that legitimizes, even drives, his central persisting thesis. The differentiation between culture and the self, the social and the individual, mobilizes many of his novels and much contemporary American literary realism. Racial or ethnic imagery provides the leverage that forces that separation and is often central to the organization of these texts. Bellow sees Jewish life on the brink of the transcendent, fed as it is by Hasidic and Talmudic beliefs. The black life he depicts is constantly at risk of being sucked into catastrophe and the inferno. Blacks are at risk in a way Charlie Citrine never is. Middle-class blacks are also invisible to Bellow. Bellow's immigrants ultimately do what they can to erase all memory of that relationship, as is instanced by Bellow's suppression of black history. It is a withdrawal into a morally corrupted private sphere partly determined by Bellow's age and infirmity, but the greater part is forced by personal and class failure in the struggle for existence. The struggle takes on a moral timbre only when it is undertaken on behalf of others. Bellow sold out when his own group gained high ground and he did not take up the struggle for other oppressed groups. Concludes that Bellow clothes that betrayal in the moral integrity of the individuals in liberalism's defining sleight of hand.

Hogel, Rolf. "The 'International Theme' in the Novels of Saul Bellow." *Literatur in Wissenschaft and Unterricht* 23, no. 3 (1990): 233–47.

Examines *MDH* as a turning point in Bellow's depiction of Europe and France to the extent that it implies nothing less than a revival of the "international theme" developed so masterfully by Henry James. Traces the development of this theme through several of James's novels and then chronologically through the Bellow canon. Looks particularly at *MSP* and *MDH* as giving the theme of internationalism a Jamesian scope. Comments on how Bellow presents Europe as both geography and intellectual force affecting the thoughts and actions of modern people, including Americans. Concludes that James's and Bellow's treatments of this theme are consistent insofar as they present differences that invariably exist between Americans and Europeans and the strong fascination exerted on Americans by the politics of the Old World's culture, sophistication, and history.

Kramer, Hilton. "Saul Bellow, Our Contemporary." *Commentary*, June 1994, 37–41. Reprinted in *The Twilight of the Intellectuals: Culture and Politics in the Era of the Cold War*, edited by Kramer, 167–80. Chicago: Dee, 1999.

Describes how he and his generation eagerly received each one of Bellow's first few novels up to the publication of *Herzog*, a penultimate novel that he and his generation of Jewish intellectuals saw as defining their world. Then describes their perception of the courageous, sagacious, and prophetic qualities of *MSP*, which they saw as descriptive of the moral collapse of New York and of the emancipated Jewish middle-class fundamental to the Jewish intellectuals of his and Bellow's generation. Explains how he then drops out of the Bellow fan club with the publication of *HG* and registers his distrust of Bellow's fable of Delmore Schwartz's life. Describes *HG* as an extended exercise in self-exoneration, and complains that Bellow's subsequent books seemed bent on settling old scores and trying out metaphysical roles. From this autobiographical and historical perspective, he locates his assessment of *IAAU*, which he describes as containing things both "Herzogian" at their best and bogged down in a "moronic inferno" at their worst. Notes that from the Jefferson lectures through all of these pieces there is something unacknowledged—something offstage that sparks his indignation without ever being openly confronted or identified, something about the true sources of his anger. Writes of Bellow's early welcome by the *Partisan Review* and his later withering condescension toward them. Wonders about Bellow's scorn for the fallacies of Marxism and his suspicious silence on the subject at the time of his defection from the *Partisan Review*. Criticizes him for not being able to write the moral history of the Russian immigrants of his day, though recently it seems Bellow cannot stop talking about it in his 1990–1991 interviews—only one of the losses we are reminded of in *IAAU*. Also criticizes Bellow's fixation on degraded popular culture, the media's culpability, and its distractions because he seems to trivialize this malevolent phenomenon by reducing it to merely a major distraction for writers and intellectuals who are thereby deprived of an audience. Describes Bellow as ultimately inhabiting an invisible political place between the disabuses of a liberalism he clings to and the neoconservatism he both embraces and spurns—a space of intellectual refuge for a dwindling remnant of homeless liberals who identify their survival with a refusal of affiliation. Provides a detailed account of the attacks on Bellow as a racist and university intellectual, and criticizes Bellow's rather feeble responses. He accuses Bellow of remaining our contemporary in his copping out on such explosive topics as multiculturalism and political correctness.

Kumar, Vinoda. "Women in Bellow's Fiction: A Study." In *Saul Bellow: A Symposium on the Jewish Heritage*, edited by Vinoda and Shiv Kumar, 150–60. Warangal, India: Nachson, 1983.

Accuses Bellow of failing to make the leap into the consciousness of women characters in his unapologetically male-oriented and biblical notions of female inferiority. In fact, Bellow's heroes mar their otherwise admirable liberalism with their assumptions that women are nonintellectual, irrational, physical, animalistic, and Dionysian. Reviews other critics on the subject of Bellow and women. Traces Bellow's duality to his Jewish roots, *shtetl* origins, and personal experience. From a feminist perspective, the Bellow hero does not do well, a matter which derives from Bellow's ethnic base.

McConnell, Frank D. "Saul Bellow and the Terms of Our Contract." In *Four Postwar American Novelists: Bellow, Mailer, Barth, and Pynchon*, 1–57. Chicago: University of Chicago Press, 1977. Reprinted in *Saul Bellow*, edited by Harold Bloom, 101–14. Modern Critical Views. New York: Chelsea, 1986.

Attempts to place Bellow historically within a confusing postwar world where both realism and experimentalism have determined literary reputations. Bellow has benefited from the one fashion and suffered because of the other. Also discusses the central issues surrounding Jewish novelists and novels with reference to Bellow's historical position. Finally locates Bellow as an ideological novelist. A major article.

McGinty, Carolyn. "In These Words Are Life: Literature and Faith." In *Historicism and Faith: Proceedings of the Fellowship of Catholic Scholars*, edited by Paul Williams, 63–73. Scranton, Pa.: Northeast, 1980.

Argues, in the context of an essay focusing on the relationship between historicism and faith, that Bellow reminds us literature can no longer compete with miraculous wonders of technology. Points out that Bellow has reminded us to attempt to recover a sense of significant space, a region through which events must make their approach and be received on decent terms. Concludes that Bellow finds accounts of human existence given by modern intelligence unsatisfactory, and opts instead for the primacy of imagination and a listening to things rather than contemporary politics.

Phillips, William. "Intellectuals and Writers since the Thirties." *Partisan Review* 59, no. 4 (1992): 531–58.

A roundtable discussion moderated by William Phillips, editor of *Partisan Review*, with the following participants: Edith Kurzweil, William Phillips, Czeslaw Milosz, Ralph Ellison, Joseph Brodsky, and Saul Bellow. Its topic is a discussion about the differences between the United States and eastern and central Europe. Generally focuses on the leading role of writers and intellectuals in the liberation of Eastern Europe and the Soviet Union. Bellow's own remarks focus on the legacy of Enlightenment thinkers concerning social contract, civil war, tyranny, poverty, and internal chaos. He discusses the erosion of Enlightenment thinking in modern philosophy and the fate of spiritual matters. Concentrates mostly on eastern Europe. Makes careful distinctions between intellectuals and writers. Speaks on the triumph of popular culture in the East, the grip of technology, the shrinking sphere of the writer, aesthetic illiteracy, the failure of the universities, the attack on male privilege, the fate of art, the collective turning away from social contract, the shift from high art, and the ultimate power of the soul.

Pifer, Ellen. "Bellow's Career as a Writer: A Winner's Critique of Success," *Profils Américains* [Paris, France], ed. Claude Levy, no. 9 (1997): 19–30.

Delineates Bellow's eschewing of the paradoxical American obsession with money, American inability to escape the crushing weight of the everyday world, and the futility of numerous American evasions. From *HRK* to *HG*, *DD*, and *MDH*, Bellow's seekers cast off the creature comforts as they take up the quest for meaning, value, truth. Even in a novel as early as *TV* (1947), published when Bellow's own career was still being launched, the young writer examines the shadow side of America's faith in material success. Exploring this theme in his shorter works of fiction as well, Bellow abandons the expansive structure of the quest motif for more compressed methods and effects. In works as various as *SD* and *Mosby's Memoirs*, he exposes with particular clarity the paradoxical nature of human success: the tension between palpable profits and human loss, between the material demands of life and its spiritual requirements. Concludes that in most of Bellow's fictions we identify with the winner's hidden losses and the loser's secret gains.

Rice, Alan. "What Do We Say to Each Other When the Library Is Closed?," *Saul Bellow Journal* 16, no. 2–17, nos. 1–2 (2001): 3–25.

All contributors to this special issue of the *Saul Bellow Journal* address what Toni Morrison has called the "dark, abiding, signing Africanist presence." These presences are at the heart of many of Bellow's novels and short stories and often provide a key to their unraveling, even when they are apparently absent. Notes Bellow's haughty disdain within his own literary landscape of Chicago, and points to his depictions of Chicago as a city where white Americans are in danger from the disaffected black ghetto population. Notes Bellow's neoconservatism and comments on the racial views of Dean Corde, which closely parallel Bellow's view. Suggests that both are unable or unwilling to see a dynamic and workable culture created by the ghetto poor. Discusses how Bellow's depictions of the Africans and African Americans are elided and presented as stereotypes. Describes the outrageous stereotypes and a subtly racist depiction of the Haitian robber in *AT*. Using a frontier urban myth of black wildness, Bellow's fictions employ throwaway lines that suggest gaudily dressed, ghettoized victims interested only in libidinous pleasures. Deriving from minstrelsy and blackface mimicry, the black presence in these novels is reduced to a negative presence depicted by a voyeuristic gaze. Comments on *MSP* in particular, pointing out the cinematic visual mode employed in the fiction. The black male body stands for Sammler's repressed desires, and it participates in a white male libidinal voyeurism. His account of exoticized, eroticized blackness plays to a voyeuristic white readership. Summarizes the various approaches, based on whiteness studies, taken by the numerous contributors to this *Saul Bellow Journal* issue. Details post-1960s immigrant race relations with black Americans as a souring process. Discusses Bellow's assimilated positionality as he explicitly promotes an antimulticulturalist agenda in the 1980s. Argues that Bellow too often uses the lenses of the Eurocentric critic whose universalist agenda forecloses an imaginative and critical praxis that moves beyond familiar standards. Provides perspectives from a variety of writers and commentators on both sides of the racial divide and of the multicultural debate in order to locate Bellow in his moment and milieu. Concludes that, in all these essays, the black figure in American literature cannot be as easily dismissed as the black worker in postindustrial capitalism. Such figures are politically and socially central to Bellow's fiction, and their insistent voices and signaling presence continue long after the library is closed. They impact Bellow's fiction in a crucially determining way.

Shechner, Mark. "The Conversion of the Jews." In *The Conversion of the Jews and Other Essays*, edited by Shechner, 1–16. New Directions in American Studies. New York: St. Martins, 1990.

Discusses the predominance of American Jewish writers in the 1945–1960 movement. Examines the question of where the Jewish presence came from, what it consisted of, and why it flourished when it did. Argues that the rise of the Jewish novelist is attributable to Jewish reverence for the book and the life of the mind, and to a certain kind of brooding introspection. Examines the emergence of Bellow into this movement of spiritual confusion, turmoil, and conflict. Out of this movement has come a more brooding, introspective, studiously melancholy, occasionally neurotic, painfully self-conscious, and slyly Russian mood. Bellow's sultry interiority and technically advanced fictions made the human heart the battlefield of history. Bellow and many of these writers are Romantics in their egotistical, self-assertive, sometimes fanatical, and embarrassedly naked neediness. They are invested in the Romantic project of becoming rather than the classical ethos of being or contemporary political chaos.

Siegel, Ben. "Simply Not a Mandarin: Saul Bellow as Jew and Jewish Writer." In *Traditions, Voices, and Dreams: The American Novel since the 1960s*, edited by Melvin J. Friedman and Siegel, 62–88. Newark: University of Delaware Press, 1995.

Provides a detailed explication of how Bellow's complicated feelings about his Jewishness are frequently difficult to reconcile but are always challenging enough to merit close scrutiny. In his works, Bellow retraces repeatedly the Jewish familial and social elements that shaped his character and thought. Describes Bellow's rich impressions of his childhood in Montreal and later in Chicago, the intellectual culture out of which he and his Jewish family came, the legacy of Russian and Yiddish writings, twentieth-century American Jewish attitudes toward money, as well as the spirit of emancipation found in the *shtetl* and in the immigrant neighborhoods. Goes on to pursue these ideas in a close reading of several of the texts. Argues that despite the fact that Bellow was raised in a strictly orthodox environment and never practiced Judaism after his bar mitzvah, he nevertheless retraces repeatedly the Jewish familial and social elements that shaped his character and thought. Even his decision to become a writer resulted from his Jewish experience. Saul Bellow obviously likes being a Jew and likes being a writer, but he does not like being called a Jewish writer. Traces in biographical detail show Bellow's Jewish upbringing, his becoming a writer, the postwar significance of his fiction, his growing midwestern rather than Jewish identity, his Jewish heritage, and his prose style. Concludes that Bellow's *H* does embrace a Jewish belief in creation's essential goodness and life's ultimate worth, a viewpoint that should serve Jew and non-Jew alike.

Siegel, Ben. "Still Not Satisfied: Saul Bellow on Art and Artists in America." In *Saul Bellow and the Struggle at the Center*, edited by Eugene Hollahan, 203–30. Georgia State Literary Studies 12. New York: AMS, 1996.

For many years, Bellow has been unhappy with America's cultural condition. In his novels, he discusses the deflation of humanistic values and standards, as well as the country's particular disdain for writers. In *HG*, we see Bellow blaming the Philistines as well as the posturings and ambitions of poets and writers themselves. Among the culprits Bellow names are media intellectuals, the American university, and its humanities professors. The cumulative result is a sorry moral and cultural climate in which literature is consistently exploited. In this culture, art and narcissism equal amusement. Literary geography has also played a vital role, with Chicago and New York becoming glittering cities unconducive to the artist. This produces the phenomenon of the writer as shaman. The once truly questioning spirit of the writer has often been discarded for conventional emotions. Concludes that for Bellow writers might do well to once again start thinking about thought, Enlightenment ideals, Romanticism, the transcendent, and traditional humanism. But it is evident to him that they will have to do it without the help of critics.

Staples, Brent. "Mr. Bellow's Planet." In *"Parallel Time": Growing up in Black and White*, 191–242. New York: Pantheon, 1994. Excerpt reprinted as "Into the White Ivory Tower," *New York Times Magazine*, 6 February 1994, 24–26, 36, 44, 47, 54, 60.

"Into the White Ivory Tower" contains Staples's recollections of stalking Bellow on Dorchester Avenue for several months before he actually sighted him. Gives a vivid, unflattering portrait of Bellow's facial features, manner of walking, and habit of scanning the crowd ahead of him. "Parallel Time" contains Staples's anecdotal recollection of the first appearance of *Humboldt's Gift* in a Chicago bookstore; his acquaintance with the sociologist Edward Shils, who appears in the novel as Professor Richard Durnwald; Bellow's use of sexual body parts in characterization; the questionable depiction of the black pickpocket; and Ricardo Cantabile's references to blacks as "crazy buffaloes" and pork chops. Concludes with the comment that Bellow had taught him that to construct a book is to steal souls, to kidnap them into the pages, to stir in stories either from the papers or your life, and voilà!—you have a novel.

Sullivan, Victoria. "The Battle of the Sexes in Three Bellow Novels." In *Saul Bellow: A Collection of Critical Essays*, edited by Earl Rovit, 101–14. Twentieth Century Views. Englewood Cliffs, N.J.: Prentice, 1975.

Argues that Bellow is not a sexist if one considers his unflattering portraits of men. "The women in his novels are like the men, a sad, crazy, mixed-up lot. They tend to fall into two basic categories: the victims and the victimizers, the latter tending to be more colorful. If they appear less three-dimensional than the men, and if they are certainly less sensitive than Doris Lessing's heroines, this is the natural consequence of novels in which the protagonist tends to be a middle-aged Jewish male with a world view to match his ethnic bias." Concludes that Bellow's great talent is in chronicling the painful consequences of human behavior, ethnic identity, gender relations, and cultural frustration, male as well as female.

Books and Monographs

Bach, Gerhard, and Gloria Cronin, eds. *Small Planets: Saul Bellow and the Art of Short Fiction.* East Lansing: Michigan State University Press, 2000.

Cronin, Gloria L. *A Room of His Own: In Search of the Feminine in the Novels of Saul Bellow.* Judaic Traditions in Literature, Music & Art. Syracuse, N.Y.: Syracuse University Press, 2000.

Cronin, Gloria L., and Ben Siegel, eds. *Conversations with Saul Bellow.* Literary Conversation Series. Jackson: University Press of Mississippi, 1994.

Glenday, Michael K. *Saul Bellow and the Decline of Humanism.* New Directions in American Studies. Basingstoke, UK: Macmillan, 1990.

McCadden, Joseph F. *The Flight from Women in the Fiction of Saul Bellow.* Washington, D.C.: University Press of America, 1981.

Newman, Judie. *Saul Bellow and History.* New York: St. Martin's; London: Macmillan, 1984.

Interviews

Bellow, Saul. "An Interview with Myself." *New Review* 2, no. 18 (1975): 53–56.

Laments that in America there is no literary world and no literary public. The traditions of literary culture and the institutions are lacking. Discusses the phenomenon of writers being invited to the White House, asked to mingle with movie stars, and unable to discuss literature with government leaders. Believes modern industrial society dismisses art. Addresses the elements of distraction in American life and its avarice, as well as the fact that a good book might only find one hundred thousand readers, thanks often to failures in the university.

Boyers, Robert T. "Literature and Culture: An Interview with Saul Bellow." *Salmagundi* 30 (1975): 6–23. Reprinted in *Salmagundi Reader*, edited by Robert T. Boyers and Peggy Boyers, 366–83. Bloomington: Indiana University Press, 1983.

Discusses why writers, rather than churches, must hold the line of civilization against the threat of barbarism. Addresses whether or not supreme values can be generated anew, the current ideological and moral interregnum, skepticism, imitation, the modern need to be interesting, the New York intellectual community, the *Partisan Review*, Colombia University in the late 1940s, avant-garde magazines, the frenzy of the 1960s, pessimism and optimism as a racket, belief that the human species should continue, comedy, banality of evil, art, language, Freud, naturalism, self-destruction, John Barth, Hegel, and religion.

Brandon, Henry. "Writer versus Readers: Saul Bellow." *Sunday Times*, 18 September 1966, 24.

Describes Bellow's physical appearance, his deep resentment of the American government and intellectuals, university education, the debasement of literature, mass culture, anxiety about who will read *H*, and superficial knowledge. Discusses also Bellow's disappointments with his women readers, the amorphous state of people's souls, and the writer's task to speak to souls.

Dommergues, Pierre. "An Interview with Saul Bellow." *Delta* [Paris] 19 (1984): 1–27.

Discusses humanism in the twentieth century, surrealism, Andre Breton, European philosophical importations, the degradation of the Self, capitalism, the private life, the historical subject. The interview also touches on such topics as Rousseau, Hemingway, Proust, modern crisis, Eastern Europe, information chaos in the United States, human imagination, the idea of progress, communism, the glorification of rebellion, neoconservatism and neoliberalism, American courts, prisons and hospitals, love, death and pain, the city, and many other topics.

"A Half Life: An Autobiography in Ideas." *Bostonia*, November/December 1990, 37–47.

Discusses the sources of Bellow's ideas, epistemology, and metaphysics, the Jewish *Shul*, Hebrew study, reading the New Testament, being hospitalized at age eight, funny papers, death and children, moving to Chicago, becoming a confirmed reader, getting fit, his father and brothers, early memories, being Jewish, the Depression, reading the great Russian and French authors, the literary scene in Chicago, the WPA, the Holocaust, Isaac Rosenfeld and Delmore Schwartz, the failure of Stalinism, the merchant marine, Hiroshima, traveling in Europe after the war, writing *AAM*, his failure to take in and write about the Holocaust.

Henry, Jim Douglas. "Mystic Trade: The American Novelist Saul Bellow Talks to Jim Douglas Henry." *Listener*, 22 May 1969, 705–7.

Discusses his early ambition to be a writer, the influence of the city, his experiences in New York, American writers as mavericks, the Communist Party, Joyce, Jewish American writers, the devaluation of the individual, Tolstoy, bohemianism versus intellectuality, revolt and crisis, mass media, the influence of the public, and his invitation to the White House.

Miles, Jack. "Saul Bellow's Life Is an Open Book." *Los Angeles Times*, 30 March 1989, sec. 5, 1, 8–9.

The report of an interview with Bellow conducted in San Francisco in which Bellow describes the intimidation he felt as a young writer sensing his status as the son of Russian immigrants. Reports also on his literary use of the language of Chicago, his view of the demise of the Puritan and Protestant dominance in America in the 1960s, his comparison of his present views with the feelings and ideas he expressed in his 1967 *Paris Review* interview on various subjects, his 1930s communist sympathies, his loss of faith and interest in edifying fiction, and his conception of the role of today's writers to "reclaim the dignity and centrality of private life against technologically magnified aggressively projected public life."

Sanoff, Alvin. "'Matters Have Gotten Out of Hand' in a Violent Society." *U.S. News and World Report*, 28 June 1982, 49–50.

Discusses *DD*, the deaths of hundreds of millions in the twentieth century, horror, totalitarianism, his refusal to admit the defeat of the humane tradition, the failure of Great Society programs, the professionalization of the human sciences, the failures of experts, the isolation effects of cities, lawlessness, the great noise, startled modern souls, the TV culture, American liberalism, organized terror, the greatness of human beings, the 1960s, the loss of private inviolability, the necessity of the private sphere, scarred spaces, and the failure of American writers to serve humanity.

Steinem, Gloria. "Gloria Steinem Spends a Day in Chicago with Saul Bellow." *Glamour*, July 1965, 98, 122, 125, 128.

Discusses Bellow's grasp of Chicago's slums and Chicago's affluence, the landmarks in Chicago occupied by Bellow's characters, his belief that the literary world is ingrown and hardened, the failure of the New York literary culture, his personal elegance, his new wealth, his relationship with Richard Stern, the various public roles played by current American writers, Bellow's reviewers, the old immigrant neighborhood, the financial district, and his current writing project (three one-act plays). Also discusses his refusal to believe that America is a fraud and that all is blackness, bitterness, and hopelessness.

Essays, Articles, and Other Nonfiction

"Back to Jerusalem." *Jerusalem Report*, 2 January 1992, 27.

"Bellow on Himself and America." *Jerusalem Post Magazine*, 3 July 1975, 11–12; 10 July 1975, 12.

"Chicago: The City That Was, the City That Is." *Life*, October 1986, 21–23, 27. Reprinted in *It All Adds Up: From the Dim Past to the Uncertain Future: A Nonfiction Collection*, 240–45. New York: Viking, 1994

"Chicago and American Culture: One Writer's View." *Chicago*, May 1973, 82–89.

"Culture Now: Some Animadversions, Some Laughs." *Modern Occasions* 1, no. 2 (1971): 162–78. Reprinted in *The Norton Reader: An Anthology of Expository Prose*, 3rd ed., edited by Arthur M. Eastman. New York: Norton, 1973.

"The Day They Signed the Treaty." *Newsday*, 1 April 1979, 1, 4–5. Reprinted in *It All Adds Up: From the Dim Past to the Uncertain Future: A Nonfiction Collection*, 221–30. New York: Viking, 1994.

"The Distracted Public." In *It All Adds Up: From the Dim Past to the Uncertain Future: A Nonfiction Collection*, 153–69. New York: Viking, 1994. (The Romanes Lecture, Oxford University, 10 May 1990.)

"The Mass-Produced Insight." *Horizon*, January 1963, 111–13.

"My Paris." *New York Times Magazine*, pt. 2, "The Sophisticated Traveler," 13 March 1983, 36–37, 130–35.

"An Open Letter to General Jaruzelski." *New York Review of Books*, 27 June 1985, 8. Nobel laureates sign letter protesting imprisonment of Polish dissident leaders.

"Paris Falling." *New Republic*, 13 September 1943, 367.

"A Revolutionist's Testament." *New York Times Book Review*, 21 November 1943, 1, 53. Reprinted in *Arthur Koestler: A Collection of Critical Essays*, edited by Murray A. Sperber, 30–33. Twentieth Century Views. Englewood Cliffs, N.J.: Prentice, 1977.

"Saul Bellow on America and American Jewish Writers." *Congress Bi-Weekly*, pt. 1, 23 October 1970, 8–11; pt. 2, 4 December 1970, 13–16.

Major Nonfiction

It All Adds Up: From the Dim Past to the Uncertain Future: A Nonfiction Collection
    New York: Viking, 1994.
    London: Secker and Warburg, 1994.
    London: Penguin, 1995.

To Jerusalem and Back: A Personal Account

Published as "Reflections: A Strictly Personal Syllabus—I." *New Yorker*, 12 July 1976, 40–82; and "Reflections: A Strictly Personal Syllabus—II." *New Yorker*, 19 July 1976, 34–90.
    New York: Viking, 1976.
    London: Secker and Warburg, 1976.
    Large-print edition. Boston: Hall, 1977.
    New York: Avon, 1977.
    Large-print edition. London: Prior, 1978.
    Harmondsworth: Penguin, 1978, 1985, 1987.
    New York: Penguin, 1976, 1985.
    Penguin Twentieth-Century Classics. New York: Viking Penguin, 1998.
    Large-print series. Piscataway, N.Y.: Transaction, 2000.

Fiction

The Adventures of Augie March

Acocella, Joan. "Finding Augie March/Saul Bellow." In *Twenty-Eight Artists and Two Saints: Essays*, 381–92. New York: Pantheon, 2007. Reprint of "Finding Augie March: Saul Bellow's First Novels." *New Yorker*, 6 October 2003: 112–17.

    Celebrates the addition to the Library of America's series of *DM, TV,* and *AAM* on the fiftieth anniversary of the publication of *AAM*. Reviews the plots and settings of all three novels. Considers *AAM* embedded in historical circumstance as it responds to European modernists—the Wastelanders—as well as to the Jewish literary crowd and to the American intellectuals of the 1950s disengaging from the Soviet Union and busy reembracing their own country. Claims that nowadays the book enchants because of its comedy, generosity, density, and linguistic miracles. Concludes that as Augie drives across Normandy, the war dead beneath his wheels, he knows and can't stop hoping that there really is an America and hope in the future.

Shere, Jeremy. "'[G]Loving the Knuckles': Reading Bellow's *The Adventures of Augie March* as a Response to the Question of Postwar, American Jewish Culture." *Saul Bellow Journal* 20, no. 1 (2004): 87–101.

Claims that in order to understand *AAM*, we need to understand the intellectual and social context in which Bellow's vision as both a Jewish and American writer took place in the post–World War II moment. *AAM* reflects the ambivalence among Jewish intellectuals concerning assimilation into the American cultural mainstream and the prospects that a Jewish culture indigenous to America would be born as a result of this movement from margin of culture to its center. The Jewish American forces at work in this novel clash and compete, resulting in contention and something less integrated. Concludes that *AAM* represents one of the more fully realized products of postwar American Jewish culture and at the same time troubles the very notion of such a culture by highlighting the ambivalence at its heart. The cycle of change and assimilation for Jews is never complete. In the final pages of the novel, Augie is emblematic of the modern Jewish universal condition. Pays homage to Bellow, who for six decades shed light on man's foibles and posturing. Rereading Bellow's works evokes the humor and the laughter behind the magic of these pages.

The Bellarosa Connection

Berger, Alan. "Remembering and Forgetting: The Holocaust and Jewish-American Culture in Saul Bellow's *The Bellarosa Connection*." In *Small Planets: Saul Bellow and the Art of Short Fiction*, 315–28. East Lansing: Michigan State University Press, 2000.

Sees *BC* as an extended meditation on the appropriate role of post-Auschwitz memory. In fact, remembering the *Shoah* becomes the litmus test of Jewish authenticity for seeking to survive as a Jew after Auschwitz. European Judaism and American Jewish culture are juxtaposed, as are survivors and nonwitnesses, gratitude and indifference, remembering and forgetting. *BC* is a richly crafted tale with a super character portrait in which Bellow underscores the deleterious impact of American culture on the issue of memory. Traces Bellow's previous protagonists' attempts to confront the Holocaust. Describes the three models of "witnessing" that the novella provides, and shows Bellow himself coming full circle from ignorance to avoidance to acceptance. Details various characters and their remembering and forgetting. Describes the transitional understanding of Jewish history shared with Sorella. Concludes that in *BC*, Bellow notes that the roots of memory are in feelings and that remembering the past involves both man and God. What Bellow offers in place of a collective memorial ritual is a personal connection to a historical world event. Memory theory is like a body without a soul, and family connections are the life force of memory. Bellow reminds us that if we forget the victims, they die twice.

Sudrann, Jean. "Goings and Comings." *Yale Review* 79, no. 3 (1990): 414–20.

Connects a series of postcolonial narratives about the expatriate experiences of aliens, emigrants, immigrants, and world citizens, including those of the characters in *BC*. Suggests this book is mainly about the pitfalls that exist for the transplanted European by its focus on a second-generation American Jew from New Jersey who remembers everything but what he deliberately forgets, while the story furnishes us with the clues to the lost material. Demonstrates how Bellow seems to hold to the idea of a certain spaciousness, both literal and metaphoric, in this book, and shows how the American experience modifies the restrictions of life within the ghetto pale. Provides detailed character analyses. Concludes that Bellow has brilliantly woven together kinship, memory, and migration motifs in this novella. This book is also part of Bellow's continuing examination of himself as a Jewish writer and as a Jew in America.

Dangling Man

Ellis, R. J. "'High Standards for White Conduct': Race, Racism, and Class in *Dangling Man*." *Saul Bellow Journal* 16, no. 1 (1999): 3–30. Reprinted in *Saul Bellow Journal* 16, no. 2–17, nos. 1–2 (2001): 26–50.

Begins with Toni Morrison's *Playing in the Dark: Whiteness and the Literary Imagination* and suggests that most Bellow critics have not seen any need to establish this racial coordinate as they examined his works. Examines the Africanist presence and personae in *DM*, concluding that the presence of only two mentioned "negroes" taken together indicate a text in which not a single African American labeled as such utters a word. Furthermore, a hierarchy is set up in which white males are always positioned higher than African Americans, thus representing a social formation that defines an American as "new, white and male" (Morrison, 43). Reads *DM* through the national regimentation and centering of values that occurred after World War II and through Toni Morrison's theoretical paradigms in *Playing in the Dark: Whiteness and the Literary Imagination*. Focuses on the ways in which the narrator, Joseph, disconcertingly fails to define ethnic and racial issues and thus inevitably cannot explore how issues of race and ethnicity might relate to his constant concerns over class identity. Thus *DM* becomes a complex exploration of these relationships inside of an evasive critical white reading, one replicating Joseph's own evasiveness in a disturbing homology. Discusses Joseph's encounter with blackness, the social and sexual parameters that enmesh him, and the dyadic structures of desire that drive his imagination. Joseph's story makes clear strategic use of black characters to define and enhance the white characters. Provides a social history of segregated housing race riots and bombing campaigns in Chicagoan history. Points out the restrictive housing covenants that segregated white and black Chicagoans, as well as Joseph's falls in fortune that place him closer to his black ghetto neighbors. Invokes the parallels provided by *Invisible Man* since both *IM* and *DM* finally hinge on issues of self-knowledge. Joseph's ethnicity-free self-designation is what is at issue and makes him even more unreliable as a narrator. Evasiveness and slippage concerning racial and class identity causes his contempt for blackness and his stereotyping to increase. Expresses disappointment at Bellow's subdued treatment of Joseph and prepares the reader for the much more disturbing construction of race to be found in *HRK*. Joseph's final vulnerability causes him to deny that he is a Negro.

Newman, Judie. "Bellow's Ransom Tale: The Holocaust, the Victim, and the Double." *Saul Bellow Journal* 14, no. 1 (1996): 3–18.

Argues that the Holocaust provides the occasion and the major structural principle of *DM*, particularly in relation to its use of the "double" and the double plot. Suggests that Bellow's sense of having recovered from tuberculosis as a child has left him with a residual survivor guilt which he then expresses through Leventhal's guilt at having survived the Depression. Documents Bellow's explanation that until the fall of France he had completely misunderstood the war because of his orientation as a Trotskyite Marxist who did not believe that a worker's state would wage an imperialist war. Albee expresses the repressed side of Leventhal's own mind. Leventhal's repressed subconscious is mysteriously prompted into existence at the precise moment of the child Mickey's death. Describes the sea of faces in the crowd mentioned in the novel's epigraph as clearly reminiscent of the Holocaust victims, a pattern enacted in many of his other novels, as well as in such works as Morrison's *Beloved* and Erdrich's *Tracks,* where storytelling becomes a survival mechanism. Provides a sophisticated psychosocial explanation of the literary phenomenon of doubling via Otto Rank, Sigmund Freud, and drama theory.

Wilson, Edmund. "Doubts and Dreams: *Dangling Man* under a Glass Bell." *New Yorker,* 1 April 1944, 78, 81, 82. Reprinted as "Saul Bellow's *Dangling Man* and Anais Nin's *Under a Glass Bell.*" In *The Uncollected Edmund Wilson,* selected by Janet Groth and David Castronovo, 251–55. Athens: Ohio University Press, 1995.

Treats *DM* alongside *Under a Glass Bell.* Sees *DM* as an excellent account of the noncombatant in wartime and a remarkably honest piece of testimony on the psychology of a whole generation. Compares the novel to many others of its type that feature disillusioned communists and dangling heroes. Depicts the refusal of the hero to defend the status quo, his insistence on meeting the challenge of fascism, and his frustrated artistic and intellectual impulses.

The Dean's December

Aderman, Ralph M. "The Dean's Bucharest: Saul Bellow and Romania." *Journal of the American Romanian Academy of Arts and Science* 5 (1984): 41–48.

Confirms Bellow's gritty and detailed accounts of Bucharest from his own personal experience. An extremely detailed accounting of the veracity of Bellow's material facts and realistic, descriptive details of life in Bucharest. Commends and corroborates Bellow's treatment of personality types and their various social levels. Gives an extensive treatment of the psychological effects of intimidation and the omnipresence of spying, surveillance, and bugging, as well as regulations affecting sleeping accommodations. Describes the visa and passport restrictions, techniques of censorship, bribery, and various other despotisms. Concludes by tying all of these issues to the deals in *DD* and affirming the accuracy of Bellow's novelistic portrayal of Bucharest politics.

Chavkin, Allan. "The Feminism of *The Dean's December.*" *Studies in American Jewish Literature* 3 (1983): 113–27.

Suggests that critics of *DD* have ignored the feminist consciousness that informs the work, and argues that the book attempts to atone for previous prejudices. Distorted views because of a disturbed first-person narrator do not appear in *DD*. Bellow's feminism is a product of a radical political vision that defies traditional labeling and is neither liberal nor conservative. Corde and Bellow refuse to be tagged with labels that would vastly underestimate the severity of contemporary problems and limit human freedom—i.e., the "slum of the innermost being." While working out the theme concerning inequality between the races, he also subtly delineates subsidiary and complementary problems, such as inequality between the sexes.

Chupin, Helen. "Bellow's Changing Attitude to Couples: *The Dean's December*." *Etudes Anglaises* 36, no. 4 (1983): 455–60.

Reviews the theme of love and Bellow's attitudes toward female characters and marriage in earlier novels. Sees *DD* as a surprising departure from the failure of the relationships in the earlier novels. Concentrates primarily on Minna as an independent professional woman. Remarks also on the community of women in the novel. Concludes that Bellow now believes in the possibility of love and harmony between marriage partners.

Corner, Martin. "The Novel and Public Truth: Saul Bellow's *The Dean's December*." *Studies in American Fiction* 28, no. 1 (2000): 113–28.

Explores the idea that although Bellow's fiction recognizes the novel's historic investment in individual experience—his own work is centered on successful, powerful individualities—the public understanding of contemporary experience is an aspiration neither Bellow's characters nor their creator have ever abandoned. Wonders how the novel can move from private to subjective statement. Recounts the various critical responses to *DD* that accuse it of being solipsistic and univocal, and argues instead that Bellow tries to plot a route from individual consciousness to public truth by freeing both the central character and the novel itself from an inappropriate burden of totalizing explanation in order to have the novel engage with public reality. Through Corde, Bellow expresses an individual and public truth about the complicity of twentieth-century societies with a silent presumption for death. Whether it is Ceaușescu's 1970s Romania or Chicago, we are given entry to this world through the eyes of an individual, but what we see is the public truth of a society rooted and mired in its history, complicit in all its aspects with the pervasive realities of loss and death.

Hinchcliffe, Richard. "Striking A. Chorde: The Dean's Melancholy Vision of Blackness in Saul Bellow's *The Dean's December.*" *Saul Bellow Journal* 16, no. 2–17, nos. 1–2 (2001): 186–214.

Dean Corde's ocularcentrism sets him on a collision course with the principal defining themes of America in that the subject/object of his jeremiad, the predominantly black slums, is set in opposition to Americans as representative of Judeo-Christian Enlightenment culture and thus as quintessentially white. He represents the exclusivity of whiteness, something that is embedded deep in his beliefs and catalogues. He is busy mapping out the white view of society's problems without recognizing the presence of an antipodal culture. Corde's neocolonial gaze is built on illusive foundations of imperial power that confer on him invisibility and a panoptic, continuous history. He means well but fails to interrogate his own liberal principles. This is the source of his own self-doubt as a reliable narrator. Corde overprivileges the visual and can only see a grim and melancholy landscape in the manner of surveillance, tourism, or Western voyeurism, while the black man waits in the wings. His greatest indiscretion is the ocularcentricity of his gaze, revealing his white man's ideology. He is alienated from his subject, as revealed in his articles and in his courtroom depictions. Corde's metaphysical musings indicate his desire to transcend problems and difference. The universe, observed in black and white at Mt. Palomar, finally proves too great a reality for the white master narrative to comprehend. He can only apprehend partial realities. In terms of blackness, the focus on the whiteness of the stars represents another foreclosure on literary blackness synonymous with the exclusion of the African American in Corde's "world of death."

Kociatkiewicz, Juslyna Maria. "Aspects of Oppression and Decline of Freedom in Saul Bellow's *The Dean's December.*" *Anglica Wratislaviensia* (Wrocław, Poland) 31: (1996): 67–74.

Sees *DD* as a novel of two cities in which the question of personal and political freedom, as well as all issues of liberty, are weighed. Describes the inner workings of totalitarianism vis-à-vis *DD*, and then discusses the inner workings of democracy, which finally appear more dismal and sinister than those of Romania. Details deprivations within both systems and their failure to comprehend one another. At the bottom of both systems, in Bellow's view, lurk alienation, isolation, and decadence. Both exert pressure to give up the individual in favor of the universal and to reject its private aims, wishes, and needs. Ultimately Corde's solution is to temporarily admit defeat with the promise to compromise and come back to the world seeking a balance between oppressive and liberating political conditions.

Levine, Paul. "*The Dean's December:* Between the Observatory and the Crematorium." In *Saul Bellow at Seventy-Five: A Collection of Critical Essays*, 125–36. Studies & Texts in English 9. Tübingen: Narr, 1991.

Reviews the literature about the tragedy of Eastern Europe published in the West in the 1970s and 1980s, and discusses the readiness with which totalitarian regimes "air-brush" moral dissenters out of history. Goes on to discuss American and Western innocence versus the political experience of realpolitik in Eastern Europe with regard to book banning, banishment of the artist, and a future in which the literary critic has been replaced by the secret police in states under censorship. Discusses concepts such as "the culture of allusion" in which readers must read between the lines and the shifting of aesthetic policy in an increasingly one-dimensional culture. Sees *DD* as the continuing commentary of public issues, private concerns, how we collectively create a civil society, and how we individually face death. Claims that in Bellow's view, both East and West are in decline, the one endangered by dictatorial oppression, the other by anarchic violence, two forms of dehumanization producing morally unproductive obedience or indifference. Concludes that Bellow's *DD* demonstrates how the first order of morality is to disinter reality and represent it anew.

McGuinness, Martin J. "Invisible Man in Saul Bellow's *The Dean's December.*" *Saul Bellow Journal* 16, no. 2–17, nos. 1–2 (2001): 165–85.

In *DD*, the African American is still largely invisible, but then for Bellow so are so many other Americans. Invokes the nameless nomad of Ellison's *Invisible Man*, whose invisibility stems from the colonial processes of denial and division. Bellow's own experience with "othering" stemmed from being the son of Russian Jews. In *DD*, both exploiter and exploited lose their integrity when human power is abused. Chief among the factors that complicate the task of human authenticity is a phony language of euphemism. *DD* is Bellow poking fun at the self-conscious goodness of the Americans who pride themselves on being able to mouth the latest liberal race jargon, revealing a shallow approach to complex moral issues of race and gender. However, many of Corde's prejudices are related to African Americans whom he sees as stereotypes, although the liberal Mason Zaehner, who hates his own whiteness, can't see the wrong in his violent African American friend. Corde has tried to bring the rich negrophile economic issues to people's attention but fails. For him blacks are invisible spiritually and intellectually, known only for sexual prowess. Bellow views the latter obsession, and particularly the myth of the black stud, as decidedly unhealthy. This is a book about the devalued humans of all racial identifications.

Mutalik-Desai, A. A. "Innocence and Experience in Saul Bellow's *The Dean's December*." In *Indian Contribution to American Studies*, edited by B. P. Dalal, 87–94. Bombay: Somaiya, 1992.

Sees *DD* as a novel in which Bellow registers the terrible impact of technology and moral or intuitive human perception—on the human damage inflicted by the disturbing retreat of liberal humanism, and the gradual diminishment of the centuries-old American covenant and dream of innocence and idealism. It is a book about the inescapable sense of corruption, or the Fall. With Valeria, a generation's dreams may be dying. Concludes that in *DD*, Bellow brings us to the sobering realization that whether we live in a closed or a free society, evil, officially ignored and/or sanctioned, lurks just around the corner. Corde's final desire is to remain suspended, gazing into starlit darkness rather than returning to earth.

Neelakantan, G. "Beast in Chicago: Saul Bellow's Apocalypse in *The Dean's December*." *International Fiction Review* 30, nos. 1–2 (2003): 66–75.

Describes how Bellow differs from contemporary apocalyptic writers Malamud, Pynchon, Updike, and DeLillo. Locates Bellow's particular apocalypse and unique contribution to the apocalyptic representations of his time. Analyzes *DD* for its apocalyptic aesthetics and artistic vision while lauding the complex literary sensibility of its author. Points out the central contradiction in Bellow's critique of Blake and Nietzsche, describes Corde as a prophet desiring spiritual rejuvenation, and notes the Emersonian idealism that underlies the whole. Critiques Bellow's stereotypical treatment of the self-destructive behaviors of Chicago's African Americans and then describes Corde as typical of the post-1960s discouragement that spilled over into the 1980s and 1990s to produce America's shaken belief in Manifest Destiny. Concludes that *DD* is a neoconservative's meditation on the self-destructive proclivities of human beings that have almost paralyzed life in contemporary urban America.

Salomon, Willis. "Particularity and the Comic in Saul Bellow's *The Dean's December.*" *Saul Bellow Journal* 21, nos. 1–2 (2005–2006): 5–18.

Argues that it is through the intensity of Bellow's gaze at realist particularity that enables his fiction to engage ordinary life. At the same time notes that its ethico-political judgments are tendentious, its universalizing of ordinary life ultimately destabilizing of familiar points of reference. Uses *DD* to explore the particularity of Bellow's gaze and its treatment of physical and cultural history, large and small, as well as its response to the challenge of how to find universalizing fictional language for the mundane processes of physical and cultural death. Explains that this search involves detailing the Bellovian parade of irritations; delays and fiascos; functionaries; rumors; cryptic utterances both public and private, ordinary and scientific; plus all the fragmentation and decay of modern life. Concludes that *DD* is a unique kind of realist novel because it sidesteps the epistemological baggage of the modernist novel's subversion of the classical realist narrative's progression by staging action, not so much across time, but across the spaces of Chicago, Bucharest, black Chicago, white Chicago, the earth, and the heavens in such a way that space retains a finitude parallel to the finitude of a materialist conception of the psyche. Bellow's characters are real because he bases them on real people and because they are given speaking life in the closely quartered, even claustrophobic way that we encounter psychic otherness.

Wisse, Ruth. "Saul Bellow's Winter of Discontent." *Commentary*, April 1982, 71–73.

DD describes two cities, each of which is in the worst of times. Its strength is Bellow's ability to compass everything from the philosophical speculations on these times to the precise pattern of tapes across the face of a stroke victim (Valeria) hooked to a machine. To the normal abundance of the Bellow novel is added a political study in contrasts between communism and democracy. The coldest of Bellow's novels, *DD* is intentionally disturbing. However, Bellow himself shows too clearly through the thin disguise of Corde, and the claims made for the impact of the *Harper's Weekly* articles seem unrealistic and exaggerated.

Henderson the Rain King

Andreu-Beso, Jose Vicente. "Discourse and Gender in Saul Bellow's *Henderson the Rain King.*" *Saul Bellow Journal* 15, no. 1 (1997): 1–13.

Focuses principally on *HRK* and argues that female relatives such as wives, mistresses, mothers, and daughters develop tense relationships with the protagonist. On the other hand, men friends, colleagues, mentors, and family members are treated in a more egalitarian manner. Illustrates how, through structures of social class, status, race, and gender, Bellow illuminates the antihero's interrelations to illustrate male dominance. Hence women struggle to have a voice in the novel. Shows that Bellow's narrator does not reconcile with women through women or nature, but that he confides in males to solve his problems. Concludes that no matter how many situations the protagonist encounters, women will not be taken seriously as a solution.

Clarke, Joni Adamson. "A Negation Offering Possibility: *Henderson the Rain King* and the Paradox of Gender." *Saul Bellow Journal* 10, no. 1 (1991): 37–45.

Begins with the premise that gender relations are central to Bellow's texts, and particularly so in *HRK*. Sees Henderson establishing a clear pattern for later Bellovian heroes who always seem to tap into the creative power that is associated with the trickster figure, who mediates between humans and gods while behaving in the most antisocial manner imaginable. Describes how such trickster tales render formerly implicit limits or boundaries explicit and keep alive the possibility that they might be transcended. Within this paradigm, Henderson is tested in relation to his macho brutality and masculine need for control. Concludes that in *HRK*, Bellow acknowledges the inconsistency, paradox, and disorder in the world by merging both clown and culture hero, animal and divine, secular and sacred to create a bumbling trickster figure who ultimately rejects his own destructive, macho attitudes, thus negating normative assumptions of traditional gender patterning.

Gruesser, John Cullen. "First-Generation Postwar Writers: Ignoring Political Realities." In *White on Black: Contemporary Literature about Africa*, edited by Gruesser, 36–41. Urbana: University of Illinois Press, 1992.

In *HRK*, Bellow, like Graeme Greene, exploits Africanist discourse, but he does so not to create a work in the expatriate tradition, but rather one in the fantasy tradition. Just as Burroughs uses Africa as a fantasy world to illustrate the superior intellect and morality of the British nobility, so Bellow manufactures a fantastic Africa to make observations about the United

States in the 1950s. Henderson's Africa is a reflection of himself, and at no time is he a representative of his culture. The Africa that emerges is one full of alienation and death as well as binary oppositions and arrested development. It bears no resemblance to the rapidly changing continent on the eve of independence. In presenting Henderson as a buffoon rather than a morally superior character, Bellow resembles second-generation postwar authors who frequently portray whites and other outsiders in the continent as clownish, incompetent, or powerless. Bellow exhibits a consciousness of Africanist discourse, but he chooses to exploit it for novelistic purposes, either failing to see or deliberately overlooking its underlying violence. Either way he is somewhat schizophrenic about the white expatriate.

Hale, Thomas A. "Africa and the West: Close Encounters of a Literary Kind." *Comparative Literature Studies* 20, no. 3 (1983): 261–75.

Discusses images of Africa in confrontation with the West found in Western literatures. Treats *HRK* in the context of a discussion of the white man's search for salvation in Africa. Discusses also some possible African counterparts for Bellow.

Lamont, Daniel. "'A Dark and Empty Continent': The Representation of Africa in Saul Bellow's *Henderson the Rain King.*" *Saul Bellow Journal* 16, no. 2–17, nos. 1–2 (2001): 129–49.

Describes the colonial myth of Africa as a dark and empty continent, along with the genre of African adventure tales that emerged from the nineteenth century. Reads *HRK* through this lens and compares it to Conrad's *Heart of Darkness*. Both novels construct a colonial subject and discourse that functions to reinforce the power of the West, especially since aboriginal inhabitants function as primitive, untaught, and degenerate. However, Conrad critiques imperialism, unlike Bellow, who oversimplifies the relationship between colonizer and colonized, thus implicating himself in the colonial discourse. *HRK* is the inheritor of previous discourses about Africa and is therefore shaped by them. The tropes of barbarism, the primitive, and the savage are recurrent, as well as romanticization of the noble savage, all of which exhibit an egregious Eurocentrism. Furthermore, Bellow's imagining of his black other is self-reflexive. Africa is used as a source of contemplation about whiteness, civilization, and chaos. Henderson, like Marlowe, assumes a superior attitude toward native Africans. His Africa is shot through with Romantic primitivism. While Henderson is an antihero and a figure of paradox, unlike Marlowe, this does not redeem the novel from the colonialist paradigm. The question of race in this novel is inescapable. Concludes that, unfortunately, Bellow has added a new work to the colonial library.

Macintyre, Ben. "Who Is the Tolstoy of the Zulus?" *Times* (London), 19 March 1994, 18.

Discusses Bellow's response in the *New York Times* to charges of racism brought against him by Brent Staples. Describes Bellow's attack against such petty thought police and defends his remark to Alfred Kazin about there being "no Tolstoy among the Papuans or the Zulus." Describes Bellow's praise of Thomas Mofolo as a sort of retraction, and considers it humiliating for a literary master to be backed into such a corner for his merely anthropological observation about preliterate cultures. Hails Bellow's response to these charges as a hearty riposte written with great care, and criticizes Staples for failing to distinguish between Bellow and his characters. Suggests that Staples and his like with their vigilant political correctness ought to be equally careful, and then points out that Staples later retracted the word "mugged," which he had used in his comment about Bellow's response to his attack: "It's not every day you get mugged by a Nobel Laureate."

Muhlestein, Dan. "Wrestling with Angels: Male Friendship in *Henderson the Rain King*." *Saul Bellow Journal* 21, nos. 1–2 (2005–2006): 41–61.

Argues that the central issue in *HRK* is the establishment, maintenance, and decline of male friendships. Analyzes in considerable detail the bonds that connect Henderson to the other men in the novel. Suggests that these homosocial relationships connect men in socially powerful ways such as Henderson's male friends in Connecticut, his army buddies, Prince Itelo, King Dahfu, Romilayu, and the lion cub. Describes how these men relate to one another vis-à-vis the natural world and how they use women both as material signifiers of male desire and as an informal counterbalance to a latent but measurable impulse toward homoeroticism. Also explores how the colonial enterprise that authorizes the action in *HRK* simultaneously enables and undercuts important male friendships in the novel. Concludes that *HRK* is an odd blend of the colonial tradition and a parody and critique of this tradition. *HRK* is also a detailed exploration of the potent forces that encourage and undercut the colonial tradition, along with a celebration and a lament of the things which bind men to men—hence its dedication to his son Gregory.

Okeke-Ezigbo, Emeka. "The Frogs Incident in *Henderson the Rain King.*" *Notes on Contemporary Literature* 12, no. 1 (1982): 7–8.

Argues that the difference between how Henderson views the frogs and how the Arnewi view them sums up the opposition between the Euro-American and African worldviews.

Herzog

Cardon, Lauren. "Herzog as 'Survival Literature.'" *Saul Bellow Journal* 20, no. 2 (2004): 85–108.

Herzog's letters contain a subtext of reference to the Holocaust and the horrors of World War II. In this way, Bellow establishes a parallel between Herzog's experience of suffering and the condition of the modern world, still traumatized by the Holocaust. Herzog's struggle to overcome his suffering relays a message of strength, spirituality, and rediscovered identity; meanwhile, Bellow hints at a means of redemption for the post-Holocaust world as epitomized by the crowded cityscapes and Holocaust imagery depicted throughout *H*. His suffering reflects the postwar world. His survival and resistance of victimization send an optimistic message to a world recovering from war's horrors. Proves that even in the face of mass commercialization and city growth, the individual can still experience belonging with nature and God.

Lucko, Peter. "Herzog? Modelider Acceptance: Eine Erwiderung." *Zeitschrift fur Anglistik und Amerikanistik* [East Berlin] 17, no. 2 (1969): 189–95.

Lucko's article is a response to Dudley Flamm's article in the same journal issue. Arguing from a formalist Marxist position, Lucko criticizes Flamm's concept of *Herzog* as reductionist and apologetic about capitalism, pointing out that Herzog's experience is not only a subjective minority view of a society distant to him, but also a cybernetic model of alienation and passive acceptance within capitalistic American society at large.

Varvogli, Aliki. "'The Corrupting Disease of Being White': Notions of Selfhood in *Mr. Sammler's Planet* and *Herzog.*" *Saul Bellow Journal* 16, no. 2–17, nos. 1–2 (2001): 150–64.

Argues that both *MSP* and *H* employ discourses that center around disease, beneath which lies a racialized, specifically black, discourse. Argues that Bellow is not simply a racist writer, but rather one for whom the outside world can be experienced only through his own Holocaust experience. Hence racial blackness in the novel accentuates his introspective tendencies and causes him to be interested in little else. Sammler identifies with black aggressors as victims in a war. Considers the pickpocket's actions to be self-ironic and fails to empathize with him because of his own myopia. However, the pickpocket ironically becomes the vehicle that returns him to life. In *H,* Moses, too, suffers from the disease of the single self. The invisibility of racial blackness in literature does not always denote an absence. Moses carries within himself the power of blackness that threatens to engulf him. Jewishness and blackness carry connotations of disease. As a romantic novel, *H* is pitting the disease of his Jewish cerebral activity against the healing power of black sexuality. This interchange plays two stereotypes against each other. Given its proper historical and cultural dimensions, blackness may, after all, cure the disease of the single self.

Humboldt's Gift

Coleman, William B. "Rip Van Citrine: Failure of Love and Marriage vs. Sanctity of Male Relationships in *Humboldt's Gift.*" *Saul Bellow Journal* 8, no. 1 (1989): 12–23.

Rehearses Leslie Fiedler's thesis in *Love and Death in the American Novel* that it is the double resolve of the American hero to deprecate marriage and to define some nobler human communion between men. Applies this thesis to the love-failure pattern in *HG* by comparing the text to the story of Rip Van Winkle, an early archetype of the marriage and love failure story replete with the wife as shrew. Suggests that Rip perhaps doffs his comic role and appears in new guises, but he is still essentially the man on the run from his wife and the yoke of matrimony. Asks if perhaps Charlie Citrine is a Rip Van Winkle who disconcertingly suggests a general superiority of the love of man for man over the ignoble lust of man for woman. Also traces the death theme in *HG* back to Fiedler's thesis. Concludes by recommending a closer Fiedlerian reading not just of the novels, but of society as a whole and of American male attitudes toward heterosexual love and marriage. Suggests the possibility that American males, both writers and readers, still cling to their old-fashioned ideals through fiction in which their heroes, as they have for centuries, still associate love and marriage with tragedy.

Cronin, Gloria L. "The Quest for the Feminine Poetic in *Humboldt's Gift.*" In *Saul Bellow at Seventy-Five: A Collection of Critical Essays*, 93–112. Studies & Texts in English 9. Tübingen: Narr, 1991.

Argues that readings of Bellow as an antimodernist late Romantic who clings to notions of transcendence and a belief in the universality of the Western humanist self have dominated Bellow criticism since the 1960s, and that Bellow critics have largely ignored the many tasks of cultural criticism: gender critique, Marxist approaches, deconstructionist insights, and new-historicist approaches. Posits that Bellow, the social realist, would be the first to admit that all of his own writing is culturally marked by class, ethnicity, and gender. Discusses *HG* as Bellow's examination of American culture, and suggests that the novel focuses directly on the dilemma of Jewish American male writers whose poetic powers are all but blasted by their acculturation in a predominantly Protestant, "hypermasculine" capitalist American culture that has gendered the domain of the "poetic feminine" outside of normative masculinities. Shows how Bellow demonstrates through Charlie Citrine how this valuable "feminine" dimension of human experience can be reglimpsed by deconstructing his own peculiarly American brand of hypermasculinity.

It All Adds Up

Bawer, Bruce. "Chicago's Jeremiah Rails at Our Babylon." Review of *From the Dim Past to the Uncertain Future: A Nonfiction Collection. Wall Street Journal*, 1 April 1994, A7.

Refers to black *New York Times* columnist Brent Staples's memoir *Parallel Time* that accuses Bellow of racism. Agrees with others that Staples is too simplistic in confusing the author with his characters, but also agrees that for Bellow the charge is not completely invalid. Describes the pieces in this Bellow collection as "a truly eloquent critique of contemporary American society," but tainted with a tendency to think of America's past as all good and her present as all bad. Certainly there is much to fault in America's decline in morals and manners, but Bellow's denunciation of "the age of the information superhighway" implies that bigotry can never "be eliminated, only papered over."

More Die of Heartbreak

Davenport, Guy. "Urban Fiction Today." *Sewanee Review* 96 (1988): 698–99.

In the context of a discussion on writers and their depiction of cities, discusses *MDH* as a novel focusing directly on the relationship of city to money. Describes the ruination of Benn Crader through greed after a saintly lifetime of mystical communion with the plant kingdom. Offers a brief critique of the materialism of the Layamons and the many symbolic references to Chicago.

Michaels, Leonard. *Los Angeles Times: The Book Review*, 14 June 1987, 1, 12.

Calls the novel an anatomy of love in the postmodern age, "a loquacious, brilliant, entertaining book mixing long flights of ideas with comic scenes that say a lot about the entanglements of serious men and calculating, ditsy, depraved, disgusting and piteously needy women." Accuses Bellow of an almost merciless ability to see through the flesh to the spirit and leave little that is admirable behind. Notes ironically that Benn finally applies his ability to see in the harmless observation of lichens, while removed from the world of hapless encounters and sexual misery.

Mr. Sammler's Planet

Alter, Robert. "A Fever of Ethnicity." *Commentary*, June 1972, 68–73.

Comments briefly on *MSP* in the context of a broad discussion of the history of the American identity crisis issue and the two major alternatives of identity developed in the dissident movements of the late 1960s—submergence of individuality in the paramilitary collective or a flamboyant antinomianism among the proponents of the counterculture. Sees *MSP* as a compassionately sad comment on how the programmatic abandonment of modes of self leads to the unwitting imitation of lesser models.

Bennett, John R. "The Complex Fate of Being an Immigrant American: Bellow's *Mr. Sammler's Planet*." *Mei kuo yen chiu* [American Studies] [China] 10, no. 4 (1980): 77–93.

Invokes Henry James's treatments of the international theme and comments that being an American has turned out to be a far more complex fate in *MSP*. Points out that with the move of non-native-born American narrators to the literary center stage, America is under fictional surveillance from the margins. The Jamesian focus now becomes not the American abroad, but the outsider as American. *MSP* is that book in which Bellow is most directly concerned with the immigrant experience and more dedicated to capturing its complex rhythms and accents. Sammler's encounter is a collision course of national and racial myths as the archetypal wandering Jew meets the all-absorbing democratic melting pot of which the forefathers promised "life, liberty, and the pursuit of happiness." Defined by the sheer weight of his past collected experiences, Sammler views the decadence of his adopted land and thinks of Sodom and Gomorrah and the end of the world. America becomes the testing grounds where living history is confronted with his Old World values as an eternal outsider or symbolic alien. What elements of social satire reside in the book are transcended by Sammler's metaphysical awareness. Concludes that Sammler's holding fast to his own moral views in this tenuous world illustrates his willingness to grasp his own complex fate and become a pattern for a successful contemporary hero.

Budick, Emily. "The Black, the Israeli, and the American Jew in Saul Bellow's *Mr. Sammler's Planet.*" In *Blacks and Jews in Literary Conversation*, 149–60. New York: Cambridge University Press, 1998.

Paints the 1969 background in *MSP* as a moment of explosive black-Jewish race relations. Additionally, American Jewish identification with a Jewish homeland about to be annihilated by Arab insurgency means Jews were once again threatened with annihilation. The stunning victory for Israeli Jews causes American Jews much pride and reidentification; meanwhile, Bellow tries to think through his own situation as an American Jew by thinking through the situation of blacks. In this process, he differentiates himself from both Israeli Jews and American blacks. He resists the pride involved in identity politics and the rising multiculturalism of the universe. The black pickpocket represents American ethnicity gone wild. The racial implications of using a black man as morally and racially degenerate are serious, especially when coupled with Bellow's description of a New York gone mad as African. While Sammler is only a caricature of Bellow, the racism is, more accurately, Sammler's. Nevertheless, why does Bellow give voice to racist stereotypes? It is a book peopled by black-obsessed Jews and a racist protagonist. Both the black pickpocket and Eisen are examples of virility and potency. Bellow uses the pickpocket not only to construct American Jewish identity but also to portray the Israeli Jewish example that American Jews must resist. Underneath the plot, Bellow is asking if suffering produces morally superior human beings. The sheer act of survival with some degree of integrity intact must be granted its status. Sammler preserves tenuous ethical distinctions, and through him, Bellow is rejecting Enlightenment thought and its emphasis on individualism. Neither Eisen with his art nor the pickpocket with his penis provides a path for American Jewry to follow. However, it is the Israeli who is most to be feared. The passivity on the part of the American Jews in the face of the civil rights movement as embodied by Mr. Sammler is highly problematic when considered from the perspective of the African American reader who might construe Sammler as telling the embattled white community it was right all along.

Charlson, Joshua L. "Ethnicity, Power, and the Postmodern in Saul Bellow's *Mr. Sammler's Planet." Centennial Review* 41, no. 3 (1997): 529–36.

Focuses on the central encounter in *MSP* between Mr. Sammler and the nameless African American pickpocket. Attempts to draw a connection between the role of the pickpocket and the role of the Holocaust to establish not only their interdependency, but their centrality to the larger themes of the book. Argues that the ethnic body in this novel is a site over which power struggles take place, rather than an "Other" against whom Sammler must define himself. He is a double who allows Sammler to recognize the realities of oppression and victimization and his own implication in that network. The pickpocket is, therefore, a kind of postmodern agent whom both Sammler and Bellow resist but whose influence insinuates itself into the very structure of the novel, producing the inconsistencies that have so often bothered its critics. Concludes that the postmodern pickpocket appears in a narrative structure that circles and concludes with an openended, mysterious, and ultimately self-defeating position. The Holocaust is the event that shatters all the instruments of knowledge, ushers in this postmodern condition, and results in the breakdown of Bellow's careful realist aesthetic. The postmodern ethnic body, then, is the reminder of that racial difference continually arising from the repressed of the American collective unconscious.

Cronin, Gloria L. "Searching the Narrative Gap: Authorial Self-Irony and the Problematic Discussion of Western Misogyny in *Mr. Sammler's Planet*." In *Saul Bellow: A Mosaic*, 97–122. Twentieth-Century American Jewish Writers 3. New York: Lang, 1992.

Argues that, not surprisingly, Bellow uses some of his intellectual protagonists to interpret himself to himself. However, understanding this process hinges on how we view the constantly varying distance he projects between them and himself. Calls this the working space in which he critiques, interprets, and even deconstructs his own intellectual acculturation. Within this narrative gap lies the key to his self-irony and his culpability concerning gender issues, particularly since the distance between creature and creator is a sophisticated and shifting one that does not permit easy description. Proceeds to argue that *MSP* is Bellow's first really focused and searching psychosocial mapping of the phenomenon of misogyny, and that it is possible to read Mr. Sammler as Bellow's quintessential wounded misogynist, a "Western Civ" imago in whom converge the misanthropic and misogynistic Western intellectual traditions of Greek, Roman, Jewish, Christian, and modern literary cultures. Shows how in this novel Bellow delineates the shape of Sammler's misogyny through (1) indicating the host of intellectual mentors, (2) providing elaborate accounts of the intellectual age he spans, (3) describing his privileged, upper-class childhood upbringing, and (4) delineating his pathological fear of women. Concludes that, among other things, Sammler is a useful narrative device because he allows Bellow to take yet another kind of deconstructive measure of his own intellectual milieu, an exercise in which he uses the narrative gap between himself and Sammler to do self-irony, mea culpa, and a little deconstruction of the less admirable traditions of Western humanist culture. Or perhaps it is an exercise in character delineation that finally took on a life all its own. Concludes that perhaps we should simply celebrate the complex network of conflicting structures and multiple determinants, of which conscious intention is only one, that render this text so rich in its dimensions.

Crouch, Stanley. "Barbarous on Either Side: The New York Blues of *Mr. Sammler's Planet*." *Philosophy and Literature* 20, no. 1 (1996): 89–103. Reprinted as introduction to *Mr. Sammler's Planet*, vii–xxvii. Penguin Twentieth-Century Classics. London and New York: Penguin, 1996.

Treats *MSP* as Bellow's exposé of the vulgarity of our culture, its terrible children, bad politicians, and rampant sleaze across all classes, races, and religions as viewed by the European immigrant who is obsessed by understanding what makes or breaks a civilization and causes it to embrace ruthlessness and possible collapse. Describes the horrors and shallowness Bellow saw rising up from the sewers of our continental spirit as that which has gotten a more cavalier grip on our national passions. Notes that critics initially failed to see the deeper meanings of the book and dismissed Bellow as a racist fuddy-duddy instead of seeing him as a prophetic writer with a rich knowledge of world history. Bellow, like Balzac, gives the reader a thorough grounding in how the literary classes function in a time of corruption. Sees Sammler as a Père Goriot of the moment, the soul of his circle, and a force for heroic love and civilization.

Goffman, Ethan. "Between Guilt and Affluence: The Jewish Gaze and the Black Thief in *Mr. Sammler's Planet.*" *Contemporary Literature* 38, no. 4 (1997): 705–25.

The black thief in Bellow's *MSP* is perhaps the quintessential representation of Jewish American literature's view of blackness as dangerous, primitive, and very sexual. At the end of the 1960s, anxieties about social breakdown, especially in New York City, were acute as black anti-Semitism was rising. The black pickpocket Bellow writes about inflicts violence on a Jewish person. Concludes that in spite of this, Jewish perspective is not the perspective of the novel when it comes to the thief. It is that of the dominant society.

Grobman, Laurie. "African Americans in Roth's *Goodbye, Columbus*, Bellow's *Mr. Sammler's Planet* and Malamud's *The Natural.*" *Studies in American Jewish Literature* 14 (1995): 80–89.

Each of these novels portrays a multilayered relationship between a Jewish protagonist and the African American with whom they come in contact. Both members of the encounter are marginalized by the dominant culture, and both are involved in a relationship of mutual identification and mirroring indicative of the fragile Jewish American and African American relationship in our society. Describes Sammler and the pickpocket in *MSP* as parallels in alienation and oppression, and also begs the question of stereotypes. It is Sammler's repeated observations of the African American pickpocket viewed and filtered through his experiences as a Holocaust survivor that set in motion the events leading to his renewed and enlarged vision of the relationship of their mutual and historically constructed alienations. This victimizer is also a victim and is also human. But he is an emblem rather than a whole human being.

Kumar, P. Shiv. "Yahudim and Ostjude: Social Stratification in *Mr. Sammler's Planet.*" *Literary Half-Yearly* 21, no. 2 (1980): 53–67.

Examines the pattern of immigration into the United States that brought *Yahudim* and *Ostjude* into sociological conflict. Applies these observations to *MSP*, a novel that tries to vindicate the *Ostjude* ethic against the ethic of the WASP code. The novel projects this social stratification through Elya Gruner and his wife, Hilda.

Levy, Paul. "'Black Holes' versus 'Connections': Conflicting Visions of the Holocaust in Bellow's *Mr. Sammler's Planet.*" In *Reclaiming Memory: American Representations of the Holocaust*, edited by Pirjo Ahokas and Martime Chard Hutchinson, 131–48. Turku, Finland: University of Turku, 1997.

Argues that the issue of the Holocaust is an ever-present component in Bellow's fiction and comes to the fore in *MSP* and *BC*. Here Bellow explores not the tragedy but the various modes of response to it. In both novels, *Shoah* appears as the elusive center, the wide pool of darkness, around which the narrative keeps circling and scrutinizing in an effort to relate it to present history and experience. Here the Holocaust is presented as an abyss which no theory or discourse can circumscribe, and present too is the urgent need to draw from an event a historical and moral significance that may be salvaged through memory. However, after all the structures and strategies both books hold in common, they differ in perspective and tone. *MSP* centers on a survivor who tries to overcome his trauma and confront the American present. *BC* shifts attention from the survivor himself to an obtuse assimilated Jew who represents the American post-Holocaust generation. Seeks to explore the questions of what such changes reveal about the evolution of Bellow's post-Holocaust consciousness. Concludes that Bellow is sending a warning to the post-Holocaust generations that they should not be tempted to forget about remembering.

Oz, Amos. "Mr. Sammler and Hannah Arendt's Banality." In *Saul Bellow: A Mosaic*, 21–25. Twentieth-Century American Jewish Writers 3. New York: Lang, 1992.

Describes Margotte Arkin's rendition of Hannah Arendt's central idea of the banality of evil in *Eichman in Jerusalem,* and proceeds to discuss Sammler's perspective in *MSP*. Notes Ussher Arkin's impatience with this Jewish urge to grant Christian forgiveness to the Nazis, a tendency he calls Weimar Schmaltz. Goes on to expatiate on the concept of Weimar Schmaltz as dealt with in Claude Lanzmann's documentary *Shoah* and then returns to Mr. Sammler's view. Describes the sheer creativity of the Nazi bureaucratization of mass murder, and concludes that Mr. Sammler and Bellow himself seem to pick a fight not just with Margotte or Arendt but with Christ himself, who would "forgive them; for they know not what they do." For as Mr. Sammler says, "The truth of it is—that we all know, God, that we know, we know, we know."

Siegel, Ben. "Saul Bellow and Mr. Sammler: Absurd Seekers of High Qualities." In *Saul Bellow: A Collection of Critical Essays*, edited by Earl Rovit, 122–34. Twentieth Century Views. Englewood Cliffs, N.J.: Prentice, 1975.

Traces carefully the intellectual climate of the late 1950s and early 1960s that produced cries that the old novel was dead, that a generation of apocalyptic young novelists had arrived, and that postmodernism had triumphed. Shows *MSP* as an unpopular comment on the failure of this movement that was "more disheveled than revolutionary." The article illustrates the book's value as a social commentary of the times and as a protest against the failure of 1960s political radicalism to produce values, ideas, and a lifestyle that can stand the test of history. Points out how Bellow distinguishes in the novel between true radicalism and misused, phony radicalism.

Wirth-Nesher, Hana, and Andrea Cohen Malamut. "Jewish and Human Survival on Bellow's Planet." *Modern Fiction Studies* 25, no. 1 (1979): 59–74. Reprinted in *Saul Bellow: A Symposium on the Jewish Heritage*, edited by Vinoda and Shiv Kumar, 56–74. Warangal, India: Nachson, 1983.

Sees *MSP* as Bellow's best Jewish novel because it deals directly with the Holocaust, the state of Israel, and American Jewry's relation to both. The value system in the novel also is essentially Jewish with its unwavering belief in survival under any circumstances, as well as an emphasis on reason and human intellect. It is part of a long tradition of interpretation and commentary on scripture; a preference for good deeds and actions over contemplation; the concept of *mitzvoth*. All of these values constitute a rejection of despair.

Ravelstein

Apple, Sam. "Making Amends." *Jerusalem Report*, 31 July 2000, 46–47.

Considers *R* to be Bellow's great tribute to Bloom and making of amends for his sins of omission in his treatment of Jewish themes in his earlier work. It feels more like a character sketch than a book, and the plot takes a backseat to the details. Scattered throughout are discussions of Nazi atrocities, theories of nihilism, and direct emotional responses to the horror. It is also Bellow's novel of self-flagellation about assimilation and the relationship of this to the indelible Jewish stain that is both Ravelstein and Chick. Ravelstein appears in this book as a Greek aristocrat with a Jewish character who loves Jewish vaudeville and hates Nazis.

Bottum, J. "Bellow's Bloom: Love and Friendship in *Ravelstein.*" *Weekly Standard,* 8 May 2000, Books & Arts sec., 31–35.

Bellow, America's best living writer, is the chronicler of a certain kind of Jewish life that has almost disappeared and a life of the mind that has nearly closed. *R,* really an elegy, runs into four movements. The opening chapter paints a comic yet moving portrait of a visit to Paris by Ravelstein. Then comes Ravelstein's death, followed by Chick's dangerous infection, and finally we encounter the subject of Chick's portrait of Ravelstein. Bloom, however, is less the model than the reason for the book. Considers the book's treatment of Bloom's homosexuality important since it raises the question about what constitutes serious conservative thought, what the relation of that thought is to behavior, and what creates Eros—the drive, the love, the urgent passion—that makes a great teacher. On its face, the book is a mess, sadly disjointed, with cobbled transitions and signs of real tiredness. Paragraphs begin strong and sputter. Reiteration sets in early. These are minor problems, but Bellow forgets that, in the end, novels are not good devices for elegy. The novelistic elements create a cruel picture of Bloom. Ultimately, the novel is about the difference between the love of a wife and the friendship of a man. It is an elegy to male friendship, a poem to female love, and a declaration about what such love brings that friendship never can. Love lives, but friendship dies.

Canales, Gustavo Sánchez. "Life, Death and Aristophanes' Concept of Eros in Saul Bellow's *Ravelstein.*" *Saul Bellow Journal* 19, no. 2 (2003): 8–18.

In *R,* Bellow reveals some of Allan Bloom's deepest secrets and also enables himself to ponder the subjects of death and the need to be fully aware in our lives. Shows Ravelstein's highest spiritual feelings toward life and friendship. Ultimately Ravelstein's legacy to Bellow was to give him a subject and another chance to mediate on death and Eros. Discusses Bellow's use of the metaphor of the relationship between Agathon and Aristophanes, as well as Plato's discussions of Eros, Philia, Absolute Beauty, and the incompleteness of being.

Kramer, Larry. "Empty Except for Insult." *Lambda Book Report,* July/August 2000: 14–15.

R presents many problems for the gay reader, not only because it is peculiar, but because it is not good enough. Bellow writes his portrait of Bloom with bold, violent, unsympathetic strokes. It is an unpleasant book. The writing is oddly clumsy, sloppy, sparse, and repetitious. The novel raises questions about Bellow's homophobia. Bellow has written of an Abe without homosexuality and without AIDS. Stated briefly up front, these two monumental facts are left dangling throughout the entire book, which is mostly filled with details about Chick's heterosexual life. Sadly, Chick's near-death from food poisoning is meant to equal Abe's death through AIDS. Rosamund is the heroine caregiver, not Nikki. When you look beneath all the blankets, all that is there are two once-admired emperors who have unwittingly shown us they have no souls.

Stephens, Bret. "A Posthumous Portrait." *Wall Street Journal,* 14 April 2000, eastern ed., W11.

A reminiscence about Bloom's teaching reputation at the University of Chicago. Argues that the characters and setting of the novel are correct, right down to the colony of parrots that made their nest in the campus neighborhood. Wonders if Bloom, had he lived, would have appreciated his "outing" and his depiction as a spendthrift and slob, his cultivation of groupies, and his unseemly interest in their sex lives. However, at the end of the portrait the reader is aware that Bloom is concerned for the complete care of his students' souls and is completely committed in friendship. Bellow's portrait of Bloom brilliantly captures his humor and brilliance.

Wilson, Jonathan. "Bloom's Day." *New York Times Book Review,* 23 April 2000, 6.

R is Bellow writing in his gold-standard prose as an antidote to mindlessness, captured in a lively, lovely, and haunting novel that caresses Allan Bloom's life. *R* is alive to irony and relishes it. Bellow, a lifelong intellectual and bandit-trickster, presents a novel with selective imagination and the burnished sentences of an accomplished writer. It is a novel that celebrates a much-maligned item—American male friendship—and especially its Jewish version. However, it is a relationship with fractured ambiguities of differing sexual preferences and variations in age and philosophy. Chick ultimately resists his "younger brother in need of reality instructor" role with Ravelstein. *R* is Bellow's most Jewish novel, and as such it is a cause for celebration. This is a deep, rich, and unnervingly entertaining novel. *R* is proof of Chekhov's theory that great art can never be depressing.

Seize the Day

Bordewyk, Gordon. "Saul Bellow's Death of a Salesman." *Saul Bellow Newsletter* 1, no. 1 (1981): 18–21.

Argues that Bellow relies heavily on Miller's plays for the themes and characters of *SD*. Traces similarities in names, occupational fortunes, problems with insurance companies, similar postwar backdrops, alienation of the middle-class, family breakdown, a strong pastoral nostalgia, urban misery, and other shared material between the two playwrights.

Budick, Emily Miller. "Yizkor for Six Million: Mourning the Death of Civilization in Saul Bellow's *Seize the Day*." In *New Essays on "Seize the Day,"* edited by Michael P. Kramer, 93–109. Cambridge: Cambridge University Press, 1998.

Argues that *SD* is a novel in which Judaism itself is laid to rest. At the center of the text lies a dark and despairing consciousness of life in the modern world as a fact of the Nazi Holocaust. *SD* is largely about the Holocaust, but the novel treats it in an oblique and understated way. It works like counterscripture in which Bellow provides a new post-Holocaust testament, replacing both the Old and the New Testaments. It is a *yizkor* for the 6 million and for the death of civilization. The final scene in the funeral parlor is not only for the world's lost Jews but for the world itself. The *kaddish* is also for the loss of the father of Christianity, Judaism itself. Here Bellow provides a full measure of contempt for European and American culture. Hence *SD* unfolds as something of an allegory of prewar and postwar Europe. However, its notions of the real soul and the pretender soul also suggest that Emersonian Romantic American models of self are not immune to the diseases of European and Jewish culture. Bellow takes the Jews' complicity in their own victimization a step further. He critiques the religious impulse in Judaism, Christianity, and Emersonianism to imagine souls in the first place, since such imagining is dangerous to humanity. What Bellow calls for is the unwriting of all scriptures, the eradication of the world as we know it, the dismantling of the Western theological and philosophical tradition, and the self-restraint not to indulge in their rewriting. Tommy's final scene in the funeral home is Bellow's de-creation of the world through the de-creation of the self—a veritable great flood preparatory to the development of an entirely new world. Hence atonement is now an undefined moment in the future, a private and personal day of reckoning unbound by Christianity, Judaism, or humanism.

Chametzky, Jules. "Death and the Post-Modern Hero/Schlemiel: An Essay on *Seize the Day*." In *New Essays on "Seize the Day,"* edited by Michael P. Kramer, 111–23. Cambridge: Cambridge University Press, 1998.

Argues that *SD* is a brilliantly written account of the World War II explosion of violence and madness that abruptly ends modernity and ushers in the contingency and flux of postmodernity. Claims that this is a death-haunted, Holocaust-inflected book in which the "normal" is *der Tod*. Here Bellow seems to exist in some kind of liminal state between options and realities making demands on him. Among other things, it is also a story about the end of patriarchy, as well as about other belief systems. Here fathers are no fathers and sons no sons. Details how Bellow and his peers lived through the dashed hopes of socialism, Stalin's betrayals and brutalities, the Ukraine Massacres, the Purge Trials, Trotsky's assassination, the killing of the Jewish writers and intellectuals, the Depression, the Spanish Civil War, fascism, World War II, the atomic bomb, the Holocaust, and the Hungarian Uprising. Concludes that all of this violence affirms to Tommy Wilhelm that there is only the death of the Self, a culture in tatters, and an ungraspable future. Tommy has no choice but to weep and live on one day after another.

Weber, Donald. "Manners and Morals, Civility and Barbarism: The Cultural Contexts of *Seize the Day*." In *New Essays on "Seize the Day,"* edited by Michael P. Kramer, 43–70. Cambridge: Cambridge University Press, 1998.

Examines *SD* for evidence of Bellow's preoccupation with the costs for the human soul of achieving civilization. Sees *SD* as one of Bellow's major discussions of "civility" in the novel's staging of contrasting styles of behavior, moral and economic, within the psychosocial dynamics of the father-son relationship. Sees *SD* as a reverse immigrant novel showing the intrafamilial costs of new American economic striving and the loss of "Old System" eastern European emotional styles. Argues that Bellow is fiercely attached to the immigrant generation and that spiritually he is descended from the baffled and heroic Jewish fathers with their "Jewish opera." Uses the "Old System" as a cultural and familial context for *SD* by examining the emotional losses and dilemmas of Isaac Braun. Also uses Irving Howe's *A Margin of Hope: An Intellectual Biography* (1984) and Isaac Rosenfeld's *Passage from Home* (1946) to provide further context for *SD*'s complex examination of the immigrant past, its fathers, the palpable sense of loss and cultural estrangement, and its filial rupture.

Wirth-Nesher, Hana. "'Who's He When He's at Home?': Saul Bellow's Translations." In *New Essays on "Seize the Day,"* edited by Michael P. Kramer, 25–41. Cambridge: Cambridge University Press, 1998.

Explains how other languages and language texts, especially Bellow's own translations from Yiddish, shape the context of *SD*. Describes each of Bellow's three major acts of translation and how they create a dynamic that then takes place in the imaginary fictional space. Notes that all three were performed by Bellow in the decade between 1953 and 1963, thus framing the period in which *SD* was written. Provides a detailed account of how Bellow construes himself as cultural mediator in his translations of "Gimpel the Fool" and the *Great Jewish Short Stories* by removing the Yiddish and Hebrew liturgy and language for an American audience. Describes how, for Bellow, Singer serves as a point of departure, an origin and sign of the authentic past now annihilated, abandoned, and assimilated. Hence the Bellow/Singer intertextual dynamic is instructive with regard to the rewriting of Jewish literary memory. Provides an exhaustive treatment of the intertextual Hebrew and Yiddish sources that permeate *SD*. Demonstrates how Bellow has crossed the boundary to the past and reshaped the representation of that past to achieve both continuity and discontinuity. In this way he simultaneously creates the survival of the Yiddish text in Jewish literature and accommodates for it in American literature. Concludes that this leaves open the question of who Bellow is when he is at home.

A Theft

Feeney, Mark. "What Made Frederic Seize the Ring?" *Boston Globe*, 5 February 1989, 86, 88.

Calls *AT* a book with ugly moral undercurrents of racism because its political picture of the city as a dark, threatening ethnic jungle is presented with neither subtlety nor differentiation. Complains that the book chugs along in ungainly fashion toward no particular destination. Concludes that this is that rarest of volumes in the Bellow canon: an unmemorable book.

To Jerusalem and Back

Budick, Emily Miller. "The Place of Israel in American Writing: Reflections on Saul Bellow's *To Jerusalem and Back.*" *South Central Review: The Journal of the South Central Modern Language Association* 8, no. 1 (1991): 59–70.

Considers *TJB* the straightforward test case of Bellow's Jewishness. Describes his utter realism concerning the world's attitude toward Jews and the Jewish state, as well as his decidedly non–Jewish American attitudes. Argues that *TJB* reveals aspects of a larger American tradition of thinking about Israel that resists the idea of Israel as a material place. Notes this tradition of resistance to a literal Israel in Melville's *Clarel* and Twain's *Innocents Abroad*, pilgrimages that precede Bellow in the American tradition. Points out that unlike Twain and Melville, Saul Bellow comes to Israel as a friend and a Jew, and yet he conveys attitudes toward Jerusalem that virtually reproduce the salient feature of Twain's and Melville's texts. Comments on Bellow's anti-Zionist prejudice, his mocking Twain-like attitudes toward Hasidism, and the world of his Jewish childhood. Notes Bellow's humor and irritation with the literal and sacred historicity. Concludes that *TJB* is an important contribution to America's literature of Holy Land pilgrimages. By reading it within the tradition of recycling nineteenth-century resistance to a literal Israel into the twentieth-century pilgrimage, Bellow enacts the very problem his predecessors in the tradition would warn against: imposing someone else's destiny on one's self. Bellow can accede to Jerusalem only by going back to America.

Duchovnay, Gerald. "The Urgency of Survival." *CEA Critic* 43, no. 1 (1980): 20–24.

Sees *TJB* as an awakening or a reassessment by Bellow of his attitude toward Israel and his own Jewishness. Recounts Bellow's comments on such categorizations as Jewish American writer. Sees the major theme of the book as survival. Describes Bellow's mixed feelings on his return to America. Portrays him as a man trying to retain a footing on a tottering world.

Halio, Jay. "Saul Bellow and Philip Roth Visit Jerusalem." *Saul Bellow Journal* 16, no. 1 (1999): 49–56.

Notes Bellow's and Roth's mutual concern with Arab-Israeli relations, the poor prospects for peace between them, and the quality of Israeli life under siege conditions. Bellow punctuates his discourse on these matters by frequent reference to the views of others such as Sartre, Harkabi, Kolech, and Alsop, as well as many other notables. Argues that Bellow does not provide a piece of conventional travel literature; instead he seizes the opportunity to contemplate and comment on people, events, and most of all, related writings by others mentioned above. Thus we come away from his books enriched by the ways his views have been tested, informed, and altered. By contrast, Roth has given us no meditation of his own as such.

The Victim

Crownshaw, Richard. "Blacking Out Holocaust Memory in Saul Bellow's *The Victim*." *Saul Bellow Journal* 16, no. 2–17, nos. 1–2 (2001): 215–52.
    Albee's employment of the figure of Caliban as a racist metaphor is the reification of modern racism. Furthermore, his casting of Jews as immigrants outside of American culture erodes racist and anti-Semitic discourse. The governing dynamic of Bellow's narrative seems to be a deflection of anti-Semitic identification of blackness and serves to exacerbate the desire of those outside traditional and predominant definitions of Americanness to occupy the centers of cultural power and exercise the powerful discourses that emanate thence. Other characters also participate in this anti-Semitism. *TV* is an illustration of postwar scientific rationalization of racist politics and racist anti-immigration policies. Eventually desire for assimilation conflicts with remembering the Holocaust, producing, in *TV*, Bellow's anxious configurations of post-Holocaust self-hatred and his projections of blackness onto others. Leventhal is traumatized by his survival. In *TV*, the excavation of anti-Semitism, and more particularly the Holocaust and its remembrance, will also drag a coterminous and concomitant black history to the literary surface. Embedded in Bellow's Caliban is a literary history of the configuration of blackness. It is the anxious return of Holocaust memory that raises issues of blackness. Witnessing blackness in *TV* registers the failure of a collective memory to, in effect, rewitness the Holocaust. The figure of Caliban is the paradigmatic locus of translation and metaphoricization of relations along the European American/Native American frontier. Bellow admits the grounds on which the articulation of blacks, Jews, slavery, and the Holocaust can take place in America itself. Finally traumatic effectivity, though, in Bellow's America of 1947, with the Holocaust too recent an

event, prevents his fuller articulation of the black-Jewish Atlantic displacing in *TV* anything other than the traces of such a matrix.

Nilsen, Helge N. "Anti-Semitism and Persecution Complex: A Comment on Saul Bellow's *The Victim*." *English Studies* 60, no. 2 (1979): 183–91.

TV treats the problem of anti-Semitism as being sustained by Jew and Gentile alike. It can only be created by two willing parties. Leventhal is the eternal Jew, accepting moral responsibility for a world he has not created. Traces in detail the paranoia and ghetto psychology of the Jew and the hostility and prejudices of the displaced WASP. These twin responses deny the common humanity of all people, as evidenced by the recurring images of faceless throngs of people throughout the novel. Though Leventhal is able to deal with Allbee in the last scene of the novel, new stresses would probably induce the old traumas.

Doctoral Dissertations

Browne, Phiefer L. "Men and Women, Africa and Civilization: A Study of the African Novels of Haggard, Greene, and Bellow." Rutgers University, 1979.

Cagan, Anita P. "Sons and Misogynists: A Study of the Protagonists in Saul Bellow's Novels." New York University, 1983.

Connor, J. D. "The Language of Men: Identity and Existentialism in the American Postwar." Johns Hopkins University, 2000.

Gaboune, Aicha. "Aspects of 'Mass' Culture in Selected Work by Henry James and Saul Bellow." University of Alberta, 1990.

Geddes, Gregory Edmund. "Literature and Labor: Harvey Swados and the Twentieth-Century American Left." State University of New York at Binghamton, 2006.

Grace, Nancy McCampbell. "The Feminized Male Character in Twentieth-Century Fiction: Studies in Joyce, Hemingway, Kerouac, and Bellow." Ohio State University, 1987.

Hoberek, Andrew Paul. "White-Collar Culture: Work, Organization, and American Fiction, 1943–1959." University of Chicago, 1998.

Kanyandekwe, Daniel. "Dreaming of Africa: American Writers and Africa in the Twentieth Century." State University of New York at Buffalo, 1996.

King, Cynthia Lynn. "Examining Proper Communicative Conduct in the

Discursive Construction of Racialized Others: An Analysis of Perspectives in the Case of Saul Bellow and Brent Staples." University of Washington, 2004.

Mama, Raque. "Images of Africa and Africans in Western Literature." University of Michigan, 1990.

Shastri, N. R. "The Dialectic of Identity: A Study of the Bellow Hero." Osmania University, 1981.

Tewarie, Bhoendradatt. "A Comparative Study of Ethnicity in the Novels of Saul Bellow and V. S. Naipaul." Pennsylvania State University, 1983.

Contributors

Victoria Aarons is the O. R. & Eva Mitchell Distinguished Professor of Literature and Department Chair at Trinity University in San Antonio, Texas. She is the author of *A Measure of Memory: Storytelling and Identity in American Jewish Fiction* and *What Happened to Abraham? Reinventing the Covenant in American Jewish Fiction*.

Michael Austin is provost and vice president of academic affairs at Newman University. His publications include *New Testaments: Cognition, Closure, and the Figural Logic of Sequel, 1660–1740*; *Useful Fictions: Evolution, Anxiety, and the Origins of Literature*; and *Reading the World: Ideas that Matter*.

Gloria L. Cronin is professor of English at Brigham Young University. She is coeditor of the *Saul Bellow Journal* and serves as executive director of the International Saul Bellow Society. Her publications include *Encyclopedia of Jewish American Literature* (with Alan Berger); *Conversations with Saul Bellow* (with Ben Siegel); and *Jewish American and Holocaust Literature: Representation in the Postmodern World* (with Alan Berger).

Andrew Gordon is professor emeritus of English, University of Florida, and author of *An American Dreamer: A Psychoanalytic Study of the Fiction of Norman Mailer*; and *Empire of Dreams: The Science Fiction and Fantasy Films of Steven Spielberg*; coauthor, with Hernan Vera, of *Screen Saviors: Hollywood Fictions of Whiteness*; and coeditor, with Peter L. Rudnytsky, of *Psychoanalyses/Feminisms*.

Daniel K. Muhlestein is assistant professor of English at Brigham Young University. His previous publications on Bellow include several entries in *Encyclopedia of Jewish-American Literature* and articles in the *Saul Bellow Journal*.

Judie Newman is professor of American studies at the University of Nottingham. Her publications include *Saul Bellow and History*; *John Updike*; *Nadine Gordimer*; *Dred: A Tale of the Great Dismal Swamp*; *The Ballistic Bard: Postcolonial Fictions*; *Alison Lurie*; *Fictions of America: Narratives of Global Empire*; *Public Art, Memorials, and Atlantic Slavery*; and *Utopia and Terror in Contemporary American Fiction* (forthcoming).

Willis Salomon is associate professor of English at Trinity University in San Antonio, Texas. He has written on the early modern English lyric poem, the psychoanalytic study of lyric poetry, the modernist aesthetics of American jazz, and comedy in Saul Bellow's fiction.

Ben Siegel was professor of English and foreign languages at Pomona College. He has written and edited sixteen books, including *The Controversial Sholem Asch*; *Daughters of Valor: Contemporary Jewish American Women Writers*; *Playful and Serious: Philip Roth as a Comic Writer*; and several volumes of conversations with such notable authors as Robert Penn Warren and Saul Bellow. He passed away on January 7, 2010.

Carol R. Smith is Senior Fellow and director of American Studies at the University of Winchester, U.K.; and director of the Cultural Studies Research Center at King Alfred's College, Winchester. She is the author of *Gender, Ethnicity, and Sexuality in Contemporary American Film* (with Jude Davies) and numerous articles on identity and American culture.

Lee Trepanier is professor of political science at Saginaw Valley State University. His publications include *Political Symbols in Russian History*; *LDS in USA: Mormonism and the Making of American Culture* (with Lynita K. Newswander); *Citizens Without States* (with Khalil Habib); and *Eric Voegelin and the Continental Tradition* (with Steven F. McGuire).

Index

Adams, Henry, 30
Adventures of Augie March, The (Bellow), 14, 19, 22–23, 45, 153
affect, 168
African Americans: Bellow's views on, 192, 194, 217, 219; depicted in Bellow's fiction (*see* Blackness)
Agamben, Giorgio, 176
alienation, 1–2
American Africanism, 68
"American exceptionalism," 170, 173
American hero: in postwar Jewish writing, 35–36
American identity: Blackness used to define, 105–23 (*see also* Blackness); in the works of Bellow, 101–5
American language: Jewish writing as "corruption" of, 37–38
Amis, Martin, 174
anti-Semitism: Bellow's early career and, 29–31; depicted in *Mr. Sammler's Planet,* 148; depicted in *The Victim,* 137–41, 148; gentile resentments of Jewish writers, 36–41
Arendt, Hannah, 144–45, 146–47
Atlas, James, 29, 30–31, 158, 172

Bagdasar, Florica, 221

Bakhtin, Mikhail, 82–83, 92, 93–94
Baldwin, James, 190
banality of evil, 144–45
Barshevsky, Yetta, 9
Beacon (journal), 12
Begin, Menachem, 217
Bell, Pearl, 31, 33–34
Bellow, Adam: biography of, 199; birth of, 3; political beliefs of, 201, 210, 218–19; on Saul Bellow's politics, 199–211
Bellow, Daniel: biography of, 211; birth of, 3; experiences as a journalist, 213, 220; on Saul Bellow's politics, 211–21
Bellow, Gregory: biography of, 187; birth of, 3; on the Goshkin family's politics, 187–89; on *Mr. Sammler's Planet,* 154–55, 163, 191, 196, 198; on Saul Bellow's politics, 170, 189–99
Bellow, Juliet, 196
Bellow, Naomi, 4
Bellow, Saul: Adam Bellow on politics of, 199–211; on African Americans, 192, 194, 217, 219; on anti-Semitism and gentile resentments, 29–31, 39, 40–41; on Arendt, 145, 146–47; on the civil rights

Bellow, Saul *(cont.)*
  movement, 119, 192, 202;
  concern for Israel, 200, 203; as a
  conservative/neoconservative, 185–
  86, 197–98, 201–2, 203; Daniel
  Bellow on politics of, 211–21; early
  life and career, 2–4; friendship
  with Bloom, 193, 204, 218;
  Gregory Bellow on politics of, 170,
  189–99; the Holocaust and (*see*
  Holocaust; post-Holocaust world);
  the immigrant tradition and,
  32–36, 40–41; Jewish identity and,
  41–45; on "Jewish-writer" label, 39,
  46–52; Kazin's characterizations
  of, 45, 172–73; marriage to Anita
  Goshkin, 2, 188–89; philosophical
  concerns of, 1–2; on politics and
  the writer, 153–54; pragmatism
  on love and marriage, 209; on
  radicalism of 1960s, 202, 203, 215;
  sexual infidelity of, 189; on "small-
  public" and "great-public" writers,
  50; on spiritual freedom, 104–5;
  Trotskyism and (*see* Trotskyism);
  Vietnam War and, 154, 191–92;
  views on multiculturalism, 172,
  173–74; views on New Left, 158,
  170–74; on women and the women's
  movement, 119, 195–97, 202, 219
Belo, Abraham, 188, 195
Belo, Berel, 188, 209
Benjamin, Walter, 176
Berger, Alan, 131, 170
biography: intersection with elegy in
  Ravelstein, 167–68, 180–82
Blackness: deployment in Bellow's
  fiction, 105–7; Enlightenment ideals
  and, 104–5; in *Henderson the Rain
  King,* 110–18; in "Looking for Mr.
  Green," 107–10; in *Mr. Sammler's
  Planet,* 118–23; suppression in
  Humboldt's Gift, 101–4

Bloom, Allan: Bellow's defense of in
  Ravelstein, 167, 169, 171, 178–80;
  Bellow's friendship with, 193, 204,
  218; philosophical ideas of, 175–77;
  as a teacher, 209
Bostonia (magazine), 169–70
Bradbury, M. S., 81
Brahm, Gabriel Noah, 173
bricoleur, 96
*Brief and True Report of the New
  Found Land of Virginia, A*
  (Harriot), 94
Burnham, James, 13, 14

Canetti, Elias, 207
Cantine, Holley R., 17
capitalism, 15–18
Capote, Truman, 37
carnivalesque, 82–89, 95–98
carnival laughter, 82–83
carnival spectacle, 83–84, 85
Carter, Jimmy, 216
characters: analysis of Bellow's female
  characters, 57–64; meaning in
  Bellow's fiction, 167–68
civil rights movement, 119, 192, 202
Closing of the American Mind, The
  (Bloom), 167, 171, 179, 193, 204
colonial library narratives: definition
  and examples, 69–70; heteroglossia
  in *Henderson the Rain King* and,
  93–98; identified in *Henderson
  the Rain King,* 71–81; Lamont's
  analysis of *Henderson the Rain
  King* and *Heart of Darkness,*
  70–71; subversion in *Henderson the
  Rain King,* 81–93
Committee for the Free World, 204
Communist Manifesto, The (Marx and
  Engels), 10
Conrad, Joseph, 70
conservatism, 185–86, 197–98, 203
Cronin, Gloria, 155

Crouch, Stanley, 118–19, 219
cultural homogenization, 206

Dahlberg, Edward, 34
Daily Northwestern, 12
Dangling Man (Bellow), 13, 44, 133–34
"Dark and Empty Continent, A" (Lamont), 69, 70–71
Dean's December, The (Bellow), 192
death: Bellow's fear of, 2
"Death of the Jewish Novel, The" (Lelchuk), 42–43
Depression, the, 15
De Regniers, Beatrice Schenk, 196
Derrida, Jacques, 59, 96
Dickstein, Morris, 155, 164
Didion, Joan, 38
domestic-foreign dichotomy, 63
Du Bois, W. E. B., 202
Duranty, Walter, 214

Eichmann in Jerusalem (Arendt), 144–45
elective assimilation, 104, 105
elective migration, 103
elegy: intersection with biography in *Ravelstein*, 167–68, 180–82
"11.30 A.M. the Gambler" (Bellow), 16–17
"Eli, the Fanatic" (Roth), 135
Elkin, Stanley, 33
Ellison, Ralph, 190, 219
End of History, The (Fukuyama), 177
Enlightenment ideals, 104–5
ethnic labels, 48–49

Farrell, J. T., 12
fascism: "The Hell It Can't" as a critique of, 12–13
Faust, Irvin, 33
female characters: in Bellow's fiction, 57–64

feminism. *See* women and the women's movement
Fiedler, Leslie, 33, 36
Freedman, Janis, 4
Friedrich, Marianne, 108
From Time Immemorial (Peters), 203
Fuchs, Daniel, 31, 156, 163
Fukuyama, Frances, 177

German question, 11
Gilroy, Paul, 103–4
Ginsberg, Allen, 34, 215
Glassman, Susan, 3, 194
Glotzer, Albert, 9, 200
Gold, Herbert, 33
Goldman, L. H., 49
Goodman, Paul, 34
Gorky, Maxim, 208
Goshkin, Anita, 2, 187–89, 190
Gould, Nathan, 11
Grass, Günter, 205
Great Depression, 15
"great personhood," 169
"great-public" writers, 50
Greenblatt, Stephen, 94
Greengus, Lesha Bellows, 195, 196
grotesque realism, 89–93, 95–98
Gubar, Susan, 121

Harriot, Thomas, 94
Harris, Mark, 42, 156
Harris, Sydney J., 12
Hayakawa, S. I., 157, 158
Heart of Darkness (Conrad), 69–71
"hedonists," 34
Hegel, Georg Wilhelm Friedrich, 175–77
"Hell It Can't, The" (Bellow), 12–13
Hemingway, Ernest, 29, 217
Henderson the Rain King (Bellow): colonial library narratives in, 71–81; critical perspectives on the use of race in, 68–71, 110–18; functions

Henderson the Rain King (cont.)
  of heteroglossia in, 93–98;
  subversive use of comedy and the
  carnivalesque in, 81–93
Herskovits, Melville J., 2, 95
Herzog (Bellow), 29, 193
heteroglossia, 93–94
Hitchens, Christopher, 177
Holocaust: avoidance of in *Dangling Man*, 133–34; Bellow on
  his difficulties addressing,
  130–32, 136; Bellow on moral
  and philosophical problems posed
  by, 145–48; in Bellow's fiction,
  132–37; postwar Jewish writing
  and, 129–30, 134–35. *See also*
  post-Holocaust world
homosexuality, 209
Howe, Irving, 32, 131
Humboldt Park, 188
Humboldt's Gift (Bellow), 40, 42, 101–4

Idea of Africa, The (Mudimbe), 69
I Married a Communist (Roth), 170
immigrant tradition, 32–36, 40–41
"In the Days of Mr. Roosevelt"
  (Bellow), 16
Introduction to the Reading of Hegel
  (Kojeve), 175
Introduction to the Reading of Hegel,
  "Editor's Introduction" (Bloom),
  175–77
"Invisible Bullets: Renaissance
  Authority and Its Subversion"
  (Greenblatt), 94
Israel, 200, 203
It All Adds Up (Bellow), 169
It Can't Happen Here (Lewis), 12, 13

James, Henry, 30
Jewish identity: Bellow and, 41–45; of
  Bellow's characters, 2; Blackness
  used to define, 103–23 (*see also*
  Blackness); immigrant tradition
  and, 32–36; postwar Jewish writing
  and, 30–32; in *Ravelstein*, 181–82
"Jewish Literary Establishment," 37
"Jewish-writer" label, 39, 46–52
Jewish writing. *See* postwar Jewish
  writing
"Jews" (Kazin), 172–73
Johnson, Lyndon, 205–6

Kampelman, Max, 190
Kazin, Alfred, 45, 172–73
Kiernan, Robert F., 81
Kojeve, Alexandre, 175–77
Koler, Hannah, 159, 160
Kremer, S. Lillian, 132–33

Labor Action (journal), 14
Lamont, Daniel, 69, 70–71
language: Jewish writing as
  "corruption" of, 37–38
Lapp, Rudy, 188
"Leaving the Yellow House" (Bellow),
  57–64
Lelchuk, Alan, 38, 42–43
*Leo Strauss and the Politics of
  American Empire* (Norton), 179
Lewis, Sinclair, 12
liberal humanism, 104–5
liberalism. *See* New Left; Old Left
Lindqvist, Sven, 70
Lippit, Noriko M., 57, 58
London Review of Books, 177
"Looking for Mr. Green" (Bellow),
  107–10
love and marriage, 209

Macdonald, Dwight, 15
Mailer, Norman, 33, 34, 37
Making It (Podhoretz), 31
Malamud, Bernard: gentile
  resentments and, 37, 38, 39;
  immigrant tradition and, 33, 34, 35

Mandelstam, Osip, 216
Markos, Donald W., 118
marriage, 209
material nonachievers, 34–36
McCadden, Joseph, 155
McCarthy hearings, 191
McClosky, Herb, 190
Mencken, H. L., 38
merchant marine, 14
"Mexican General, The" (Bellow), 18–22
Milano, Paulo, 190
Miller, Ruth, 155–56
modern civilization: in Bellow's writing, 1–2
Morrison, Toni, 68, 109, 219
"Mosby's Memoirs" (Bellow), 23–24
"Mr. Katz, Mr. Cohen, and Cosmology" (Bellow), 17–18
Mr. Sammler's Planet (Bellow), 198; anti-Semitism depicted in, 148; Gregory Bellow on, 154–55, 163, 191, 196; post-Holocaust world depicted in, 134, 136–37, 141–49; as a response to 1960s radicalism, 154–64; San Francisco State incident fictionalized in, 161–64; use of Blackness in, 118–23
Mudimbe, V. Y., 69
multiculturalism, 172, 173–74

National Interest, 177
Nemerov, Howard, 150
neoconservatism, 198, 201–2
New Left, 158, 170–74
Newman, Charles, 57–58
Newman, Judie, 110–11
New York City: as post-Holocaust landscape, 138–41
New Yorker, 172
New York Times, 50, 192
New York Times Book Review, 42–43
New York Times Magazine, 172

Nietzsche, Friedrich, 175–77
"9 A.M. Without Work" (Bellow), 16
"noble savage," 74–75
nonachievers, 34–36
Northwestern University, 11
Norton, Anne, 179, 180
Nuñez, José Manuel, 18
Nussbaum, Martha, 183n13

Odets, Clifford, 35
Old Left, 170–71
Orwell, George, 163
Ozick, Cynthia, 50, 51

paideia, 178
"Papuans and Zulus" (Bellow), 173–74
Paris Review, 42
"parochial" literature, 49, 51
Partisan Review, 9–10, 14–15, 170
Passin, Herb, 11, 19, 200
Patzcuaro, 18, 19
Pawnbroker, The (Wallant), 134–35
Peretz, Isaac Leib, 35
Peters, Joan, 203
"Pets on the North Shore" (Bellow), 12
Phillips, William, 131
Plato, 178
Playing in the Dark: Whiteness and the Literary Imagination (Morrison), 68
Podhoretz, Norman, 31–32
political correctness, 168
politics and the writer, 153–54
Porter, Katherine Ann, 37–38
post-Holocaust world: Bellow's fictional exploration of, 132–33, 135–37; Bellow's vision of America in, 148–49; in *Mr. Sammler's Planet*, 134, 136–37, 141–49; question of how to live in, 134, 149–50; in *The Victim*, 134, 136, 137–41
postwar Jewish writing: Bellow's fiction in milieu of, 30–32; gentile

postwar Jewish writing *(cont.)*
  resentments and, 36–41; the Holocaust and, 129–30, 134–35; the immigrant tradition and, 32–36
presence-absence binary, 64

Quiroga, Vasco de, 20

Rabelais and His World (Bakhtin), 82–83
race. *See* African Americans; Blackness
radicalism (1960s): Bellow's views on, 202, 203, 215; *Mr. Sammler's Planet* as a response to, 154–64
Rahv, Philip, 10, 131
Ravelstein (Bellow): Bellow's stance toward the Left as context for, 170–74; defense of Bloom in, 169, 171, 178–80; intersection of biography and elegy in, 167–68, 180–82; Jewish identity and history in, 181–82
Reagan, Ronald, 201, 216
ressentiment, 173, 174
Retort (journal), 17
Rhea, Thomas, 133, 150
Rice, Alan, 98n1
Rooke, Constance, 58
Rosa De Xochimilco (film), 18–19
Rosenfeld, Isaac, 11, 186, 189
Roth, Henry, 31
Roth, Philip, 33, 37, 39, 47, 135, 170
Russell, Marian, 120
Ryan, Mary, 195

Salas, Floyd: clash with Bellow, 159–61; fictionalized in *Mr. Sammler's Planet*, 163–64
Salinger, J. D., 36
Sanders, Bernie, 215
San Francisco Chronicle, 160
San Francisco State College incident: described, 158–61; fictionalized in *Mr. Sammler's Planet*, 161–64; protests as backdrop to, 157–58
Sarant, George, 197
Sartre, Jean-Paul, 153
Saul Bellow, Drumlin Woodchuck (Harris), 42
Scholem, Gershom, 42
Schwartz, Delmore, 31, 131, 186
Seide, Michael, 33
Seize the Day (Bellow), 36
sexual infidelity, 189
Shachtman, Max, 13–14, 22, 23
Shaw, Irwin, 36
Shechner, Mark, 32–33, 155, 156
Shils, Edward, 9, 158–59, 193, 207
Simon, Paul, 193
Singer, Isaac Bashevis, 37
"small-public" writers, 50
Smith, Carol R., 68–69
Soapbox (magazine), 11
spirituality and spiritual freedom, 1–2, 104–5
Stevenson, Adlai, 190, 216
Strauss, Leo, 179, 208
"subjectivity," 175
Symposium (Plato), 178

Tarcov, Nathan, 193
Tate, Allen, 30
Tea Party, 210
Teller, Judd, 34, 35–36, 38–39
Theft, A (Bellow), 57
"Theses on the Philosophy of History" (Benjamin), 176
"Third Camp," 23
"Third Worldism," 173
"This Is the Way We Go to School" (Bellow), 11
Time (magazine), 190
To Jerusalem and Back (Bellow), 200
"trace," 59
Trilling, Diane, 43–44
Trilling, Lionel, 43, 131

Index

Trotsky, Leon, 10, 11, 13, 18–22, 199
Trotskyism: Bellow's early writings and, 12–13, 15–22; Bellow's later views on, 23–24; development of Bellow's early enthusiasm for, 9–12
Tschacbasov, Alexandra, 3
Tulcea, Alexandra, 3, 220–21
"Two Morning Monologues" (Bellow), 16–17

University of Chicago, 11, 158–59

Value, Price and Profit (Marx and Engels), 10
Veblen, Thorstein, 33
Victim, The (Bellow): anti-Semitism depicted in, 137–41; Bellow on writing of, 44; Bellow's postwar remorse and, 13; post-Holocaust world depicted in, 134, 136, 137–41
Vidal, Gore, 38, 219

Vietnam War, 154, 191–92
Voorhis Act, 15

Wallant, Edward Lewis, 134–35
Wall Street Journal, 193
war: Trotskyite position and Bellow's early views on, 13–15
Washington, Harold, 192
Wasserman, Harriet, 196
Weidman, Jerome, 33
"white man's burden," 75–76
Wilson, Edmund, 30, 31, 133–34
Wolfe, Thomas, 29
women and the women's movement: Bellow's views on, 119, 195–97, 202, 219; portrayal of women in Bellow's fiction, 57–64
Workers' Party, 14
Works Progress Administration Writers' Project, 3
Wouk, Herman, 36
"Writers, Intellectuals, Politics: Mainly Reminiscence" (Bellow), 153

POLITICAL COMPANIONS
TO GREAT AMERICAN AUTHORS

SERIES EDITOR
Patrick J. Deneen, University of Notre Dame

BOOKS IN THE SERIES

A Political Companion to Saul Bellow
Edited by Gloria L. Cronin and Lee Trepanier

A Political Companion to Walker Percy
Edited by Peter Augustine Lawler and Brian A. Smith

A Political Companion to Ralph Waldo Emerson
Edited by Alan M. Levine and Daniel S. Malachuk

A Political Companion to Walt Whitman
Edited by John E. Seery

A Political Companion to Henry Adams
Edited by Natalie Fuehrer Taylor

A Political Companion to Henry David Thoreau
Edited by Jack Turner

A Political Companion to John Steinbeck
Edited by Cyrus Ernesto Zirakzadeh and Simon Stow

www.ingramcontent.com/pod-product-compliance
Lightning Source LLC
Chambersburg PA
CBHW020640230426
43665CB00008B/248